Scarne's Magic Tricks

John Scarne

DOVER PUBLICATIONS, IN[C]
Mineola, New York

Bibliographical Note

This Dover edition, first published in 2003, is a slightly altered republication of the edition published by Crown Publishers, Inc., New York, in 1951. The Contents have been reset and the original Publisher's Note has been omitted.

Library of Congress Cataloging-in-Publication Data

Scarne, John.
    Scarne's magic tricks / John Scarne.
        p. cm.
    Originally published: New York : Crown Publishers, c1951.
    ISBN 0-486-42779-X (pbk.)
    1. Magic tricks. I. Title.

GV1547 .S24 2003
793.8—dc21

2002034891

Manufactured in the United States of America
Dover Publications, Inc., 31 East 2nd Street, Mineola, N.Y. 11501

CONTENTS

FOREWORD

Ever since my work for the War Department and my appearances before millions of G.I.'s during World War II, I have received innumerable requests for a book on general magic without the use of sleight of hand.

I discussed the idea with laymen and magicians alike, receiving from all the opinion that such a book has long been needed. Particularly enthusiastic was my good friend Dr. Ben Braude, prominent New York dentist and clever amateur magician. At this time I want to thank Dr. Braude for the assistance he gave me in the writing of this book, particularly for his tireless "research" in reminding me of tricks which I had long since forgotten, and for letting me use many of his original "dodges."

I also wish to thank U. F. Grant, the clever professional magician, for his contributions.

In accordance with the policy followed in my other books, I assembled the greatest variety of magic effects ever collected for a book of this type. Then came the long process of eliminating the manipulative moves found in the majority of the tricks and replacing them with subtleties and subterfuge. In preparing this book I adhered to several cardinal principles, which I should like to enumerate for you.

First, every trick selected had to be practical, and if a manipulative move was required, a means of eliminating the difficult move and substituting an easy one had to be discovered.

Second, I wished to present the greatest variety of tricks possible, using only common articles that are easily obtainable.

Third, any special apparatus required for a trick must be simple enough to be made by the average person (and any materials needed for the production of the apparatus must be easily obtainable).

Fourth, the tricks must be suitable for every conceivable situation. There are tricks in this book that can be performed on a large stage; others are for platform work; many can be done on a night club floor; and still others are suitable for presentation in the parlor. In addition, many of the effects are designed for close-up performance: at the dinner table, in a cocktail lounge, or for demonstrations before a few friends.

Fifth, the tricks selected must make use of the large variety of common objects found in most homes or restaurants. In addition, apparent feats of mind reading, hypnotism, fortune-telling, spiritualism, and psychological experiments have been included.

Further, remembering that many good effects have been ruined by poor presentation, I then sat down and wrote little stories—patter, to the magician—to accompany many of the tricks. The patter serves to make the trick more interesting to the spectators, and at the same time affords a logical reason for those subtleties which have replaced sleight of hand.

In order to eliminate the sleight of hand found in most tricks, I had to devise many new principles and aids to the performer, such as:

New dodges and devices.

New ruses to help performer apply psychology to aid deception.

New means of misdirection (the art of diverting the spectator's attention away from the secret).

New simple moves that appear to be clever sleight of hand.

New gimmicks (that unseen apparatus that makes the trick work).

In learning to do these tricks, the reader must bear in mind that although no manipulative skill is necessary, they must be studied carefully before being performed in public. In learning a trick the scientific approach should be employed. Pick out a trick that you like particularly. Study it for a day or so, learning the patter and presentation, and perform the effect without an audience until you no longer have to think about each step. Then try the trick on one of your closest friends and get his reaction to it, for very frequently a spectator will see a flaw in the presentation that may have eluded the performer. After correcting any flaws, perform the trick for your friends until you have mastered it completely. You are then able to perform for a stranger without embarrassment.

Next, select another trick and repeat the procedure. Do this until you have learned several tricks. Blend the tricks into a routine, so that each naturally follows the preceding one, and you will have added that professional touch to your performance.

A few words of caution and we will be able to go on to the description of the tricks themselves. For your first tricks don't select any that require elaborate preparation or full stage presentation. Select a more simplified effect, one that requires little or no preparation, that can be performed for a small audience—there are many such tricks in this book—and gradually work your way up to the more complicated ones.

Learn to use patter with your tricks to make your performance more entertaining to your audience. It is not expected that you will memorize the patter in this book; use it only as a guide in preparing your own.

When performing, be natural. You can attain this objective by not memorizing your patter—outline what you wish to say, and then enlarge on it, naturally, as you go along.

Do not perform all the tricks you know for the same audience at one time. Present just a few tricks, well performed, and retire. Assort your tricks intelligently. Plan a varied routine of dissimilar effects, no two of which use the same principle. Don't let appreciation or applause induce you to perform as an encore a trick you haven't perfected or one similar to a trick you've already done. Leave the audience wanting more.

Never reveal how a trick is done. A good trick is like a precious diamond, and must be closely guarded. When you have astounded your audience with a trick, you may be met with the question, "How did you do it?" Don't tell! If you do, your standing as a performer will drop.

After completing a trick, you will frequently be asked to "Do it again." Never repeat a trick for the same audience at the same performance, for this can easily lead to exposing the secret. The value of a trick lies in its mystification. If you repeat a trick you are no longer entertaining your audience, for most people will not be mystified by the second performance. On the contrary, they will be attempting to figure out how the trick is done, and the psychology of deception present in the original performance will be missing. Also, it isn't very comforting for a performer, who has just completely awed his audience, to repeat a trick and to have some smart alec learn the secret and reveal it to the rest of the audience. I say again: *never repeat a trick for the same audience at one performance.*

Remember that as a magician you must always "be onstage." Even when sitting with your friends, you must constantly be alert to the possibility of creating a minor miracle in your surroundings, or of preparing some object in your vicinity for use in a trick.

Once you have started to do magic, people expect you to be able to perform tricks with all sorts of material. Learn effects that employ different items found about the house—and you might take a look at some of my other books for this purpose.

Remember that there is a code of ethics among magicians. Just as you would not appreciate it if another magician were to reveal how your tricks were done, don't tell how another magician performs his effects. Should you see someone else performing a trick, afford him the same courtesy and consideration you expect from others.

But that's enough of my chatter; let's get on with the tricks.

JOHN SCARNE

Fairview, N. J.
August, 1951

1. *The Talking Mirror*

EFFECT: The performer has a mirror on the back of which there are several spots of different colors. Upon one of the spots a coin is placed while the performer's back is turned. The coin is removed and the performer, by looking into the mirror, divines the color that was covered.

PREPARATION: Obtain a small, cheap, circular or rectangular mirror, similar to those in a woman's handbag or vanity case. Remove all the trimmings from the mirror, and paint the reverse side white. Over this cement or glue a thin piece of glass of the same size and shape as the mirror. On this glass make four or five small dots, each a different color. Use luminous paint, which can be obtained in any art shop.

PRESENTATION: Hand this prepared mirror to a spectator, and tell him that you have been successful in experiments of divination, by looking into a mirror. You may mention Cogliostro, and the story of the mirror in which Marie Antoinette saw her future unfolded. Tell the spectator to place the mirror on the table, back side up. Tell him that you will turn your back so that you cannot see, and ask him to cover any of the spots with a coin. Keep on pattering and concentrating for a few moments. Then tell the spectator to remove the coin. Turn around and take the mirror off the table. Go to a darkened portion of the room, explaining that the vision can be best seen in subdued light. Turn your back for a moment and place the mirror, back side up, under the side of your coat so as to obtain even more darkness. When the coin covers one of the spots for a few moments, its luminosity dims, so that when you observe it in the dark, it is shadowed. This determines the spot that was covered. Raise the mirror slowly, and gaze into its reflecting side with deep concentration. Turn around and announce the correct color.

2. *Coin Through Handkerchief*

EFFECT: The performer makes a borrowed, marked coin penetrate the center of a handkerchief without damaging the handkerchief.

PRESENTATION AND METHOD: Hold a borrowed, marked coin (preferably a large one) vertically, between the thumb and first finger of the left hand. Drape a handkerchief over the coin so that its center touches the coin. With the thumb and first two fingers of the left hand, grasp the bottom

9

edge of the coin through the handkerchief (Fig. 1) and turn over both coin and top point of handkerchief toward yourself. Then hold the coin in this position under the handkerchief with the left thumb. Lift up that side of the handkerchief which is facing the audience and bring it back as far as possible to show that the coin is still under it (Fig. 2). When the spectators are fully satisfied, snap forward the wrist of the left hand so that the lifted side of the handkerchief returns abruptly to its original position (Fig. 3). However, if the proper snap is used, at the same time the portion of the handkerchief facing the performer will also fall toward the spectators. Yet it appears as though the handkerchief has merely returned to its original position.

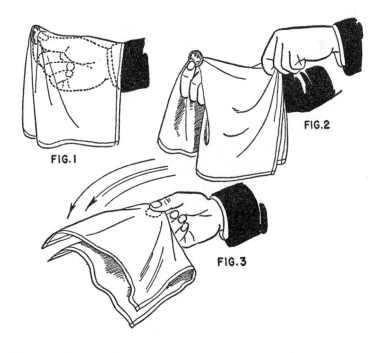

FIG. I

FIG.2

FIG.3

Now revolve the coin several times so that it seems to be twisted thoroughly within the handkerchief. Slowly, as a little pressure on the edge of the coin is exerted by the fingers of the left hand, the coin is seen to rise through the handkerchief. Hand it to a spectator for examination and identification, and then show that the handkerchief is unharmed in any way.

3. Smoking Sleeve

EFFECT: Performer blows smoke down one of his sleeves and the smoke comes out of the other sleeve.

PRESENTATION AND METHOD: This little trick, to be performed by a smoker, is both mystifying and humorous. Obtain a piece of rubber tubing, long enough to reach comfortably from wrist to wrist through the sleeves and under the back of your coat. The tubing should be soft, pliable and long enough to allow for completely natural movement of the hands. The ends of the tubing must be taped to the inside of the wrist in such manner that they cannot be seen no matter how you move your hands. The tube openings should face the palms of the hands.

You are now ready. Fill your mouth with the smoke of your cigarette. Lift your right hand and blow the smoke through the tube. To the audience this looks as though you are blowing the smoke down your sleeve. At the same time, hold your left arm up. The smoke you blow through the tube will appear to come out of the other sleeve. This is usually good for laughs as well as mystification.

4. Predicto

EFFECT: The performer predicts the sum of a series of numbers, none of which he could possibly have known previous to the performance.

PREPARATION: This effect requires a secret assistant in the audience. Usually "stooges" are frowned upon by most magicians, but this effect is so strong that it becomes one of the exceptions.

PRESENTATION: Take a slip of paper out of your pocket and tell the audience that you are about to make a prediction. Write down a four-digit number, for instance, 9569. Fold the paper, hand it to a spectator, and tell him to place it in his pocket for future verification. Now ask another spectator for the year in which he was born. Let us say he says 1889. Write this on top of a large slate, or a piece of cardboard, so that the audience may see what you are doing. Ask another spectator for a year which he thinks has been most important in his lifetime. Say 1903. Write this immediately below the first number. Now ask a third spectator to mention any year which has been important historically, such as 1914. Write that down also.

Now say to the audience, "As you have seen, the numbers I have listed, one under another, have been very fairly chosen and there is no possible way in which I could have known what years would be named. To make it even more difficult, I am going to add a fourth figure, written by someone in the audience. Will you, sir [address your secret assistant], kindly add a fourth four-digit number to the other three. Then add the four numbers and announce the total." As you thus address your assistant, hand him the slate, or board, upon which the other numbers are written. Tell him to read aloud the sum he has arrived at. Now ask the spectator, to whom you had given the folded paper, to read the predicted sum, and the audience will be immensely surprised to find that the sums match.

EXPLANATION: Your secret assistant must have knowledge of and remember the predicted sum. When he is handed the slate, or board, upon which the three dates are written, all he must do is add a fourth number which would give the required sum of 9569.
Example below may clarify this:

1st line	1889	Date of Birth
2nd line	1903	Important Personal Event
3rd line	1914	Important Historical Date
4th line	(3863)	Assistant's Number
TOTAL	9569	

5. *Ring on the String*

EFFECT: Under seemingly impossible conditions, a solid ring is placed on the center of a string without apparently touching the string or threading either of its ends through the ring.

PRESENTATION: Take a piece of string, about two and a half to three feet long, and stretch it out full length on a table covered with a table cloth. Make a loop in the center of the string, and secure this loop by placing a safety pin through both sides of it and pinning it to the table cloth (Fig. 1). Take a borrowed ring, place it next to the loop and ask the spectator whether he thinks it is possible to place the ring on the loop without touching, or using, either end of the string. The spectator should of course say no. And then you tell him that by means of magic you are able to perform this remarkable feat.

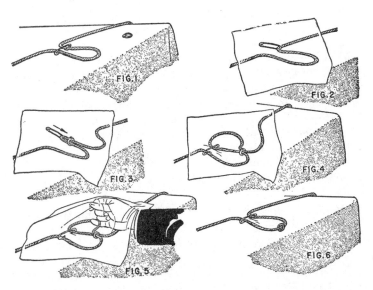

Borrow his handkerchief and place it over the loop and ring, telling him that it is necessary to hide the magic "secret" process. Also tell him to watch both ends of the string carefully to make sure that they are not used in the experiment. Place your hands under the handkerchief and proceed to do the following. Open the safety pin and withdraw it from the table cloth; now close it again, leaving only one side of the loop in the pin (Fig. 2). Take the ring and thread it over the safety pin and string, forming a second loop (Fig. 3). Open the safety pin again, pin it through the table cloth and enclose the other side of the original loop, as in Fig. 1 (Fig. 4). Place your little finger through the new loop (Fig. 5) formed by the ring. Take hold of the handkerchief with the other fingers and casually but quickly move it way over to the right of the string, as if getting rid of the handkerchief. Make sure that you hold the ring with the other hand to retain the loop. This action will cause your little finger to pull the right end of the string through the ring. This will not be noticed, as the movement of the handkerchief to the right covers the entire action, and that end of the string looks as if it has not been disturbed. The ring is now looped on the string, as in Fig. 6.

Note: It is not necessary to work with a table cloth. This is just added misdirection. However, always remember to hold the left end of the string down to the table with the other hand when you move the handkerchief.

6. The Magical Shirt

EFFECT: Though the performer's hands are securely tied together, nevertheless he removes his own shirt from under his buttoned vest and coat.
PREPARATION: In order for the trick to work, the shirt must be put on as follows. Throw the shirt over your shoulders like a cloak. Bring the collar around your neck in normal fashion and button it. Also button the top one or two buttons of the shirt. Place the cuffs of the shirt around the wrists and button them. Put a tie on, then put your vest and coat on over the shirt and button them. For all purposes you are apparently well dressed. This is a swell party stunt, and takes only a few minutes to get set.

PRESENTATION: Announce to your audience that you are going to demonstrate a feat, impossible according to the laws of science. You will prove that you are able to pass a solid through a solid. Hand one of the spectators a piece of strong rope, long enough to tie your wrists together strongly and firmly. Tell the spectator to do this in any way he wishes, but to make sure that it is impossible for you (the performer) to loosen your hands in any way.

When the spectators are thoroughly satisfied that your wrists are so tied, go into another room, closet, or behind a screen, so that the audience is unable to see you. You will find that though your wrists are thoroughly tied together, you are still able to manipulate the fingers of your hands so that you can do the following. Loosen your tie (do not untie it) and take it off, bringing it over your head. Unbutton your collar and the remaining front buttons. Unbutton your cuffs, by means of your teeth. This may sound difficult, but it is quite easy when you try it. By taking a firm grip on the back of the collar of the shirt, you are

able now to pull the shirt completely off. Replace the tie around your neck. Put the shirt over your arms, and appear so before the audience. They may examine your tied wrists as much as they wish, but they will be completely baffled.

7. *Chalk Penetration*

EFFECT: The performer makes a chalk mark on the table top. He shows that his hands are empty. Then he places his left hand under the table and with his right hand he rubs out (erases) the chalk mark on the table top. The left hand is now brought above the table, and the chalk mark is seen in the center of the palm of this hand.

PREPARATION: Prepare in advance by covering the fingernail of the third finger on the left hand with chalk. Rub as much as possible on the nail so as to cover the complete nail (illustration). Have a piece of chalk handy. You are now ready to perform the trick.

CHALK MARK

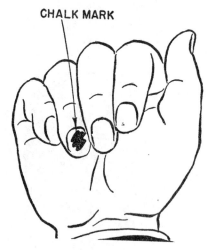

PRESENTATION: Show both hands, palm up. Take the chalk with your right hand and place your left hand under the table. When your left hand goes under the table, you merely close the hand into a tight fist so that the fingernail of the third finger goes next to the palm. This leaves a chalk mark in the palm of the left hand. While your left hand is still under the table, with your right hand make a chalk mark on the table similar to the mark on your left hand. A little experimenting will show you the type of mark to make on the table top. Erase this mark by rubbing with your right hand, stating you are rubbing it through the table top. After a bit of erasing, show the palm of your left hand, proving that the chalk did penetrate the table top.

You will discover that there is enough chalk on the fingernail so that you can repeat the trick about five or six times. This repetition is what makes the trick so mystifying, as after you work the trick a couple of times, the spectators will want to examine the under side of the table. Then they will want you to work it through another table or a board or a book. You may work it through anything, as long as the item is large enough to cover up the fact that you are always closing your left hand into a fist. If a pointed piece of chalk is used, you may make the letter X penetrate the table, or even the initial of a spectator's name. If you want to use a bit of patter with the above trick, the following will be found suitable.

"Let me show you a piece of Spirit Chalk that was picked up in England and mailed over to me. This Spirit Chalk has the same properties as a real live spirit. That is, it can pass through solid walls or doors, without leaving a trace behind. You will notice I have only a short piece left, and I only use this in front of real special friends and celebrities. Once this is gone, chances are I will never get any more.

"For example, I will place my examined left hand under this table, and with the right hand I'll rub a bit of chalk on the table top, merely rub it, thus, and it penetrates the solid table top—and here it is reposing right in the center of my left hand. Don't ask me how it is done, as I do not know myself. I merely follow the instructions sent me with the chalk.

"I will do it again, as I see you are all very interested. But before I repeat it, please examine the under side of the table. Now, for the third time I will use any other solid surface you suggest. And, last, I will show you that it will penetrate a solid door. I will place my left hand behind this door and rub the chalk right here and rub it through, and as you can see the chalk is now in the palm of the left hand. And as the saying goes, 'Seeing is believing.'"

8. *The Magic Calendar*

EFFECT: The spectator marks out several days of the week on a calendar page. The performer, without knowing the dates on which these days fall, is able to give the sum total of the dates.

PRESENTATION: Tear off from a calendar one of the monthly sheets, and hand it to a spectator. (For simplification, make sure that there are five Wednesdays in this month.) Tell him to mark off a day on each line of the calendar, representing one day of each week. He may, if he wishes, mark off duplicate days, such as two or three Mondays, etc. When he has done this, ask him how many Sundays he has marked off, how many Mondays, etc., down the line. When he has finished giving you this information, you immediately announce the result of the addition of the marked-off dates.

EXPLANATION: Let us suppose you gave the spectator the following calendar page. You must note that the total of the five dates falling on

AUGUST						
SUN	MON	TUE	WED	THU	FRI	SAT
			1 ⁰	2	3	4
5 ³	6	7	8	9	10	11
12	13	14 ⁻¹	15	16	17	18
19	20	21 ⁻¹	22	23	24	25
26	27	28	29	30 ⁻¹	31	

Wednesday is 75. Remember this total. Also remember the formula:

Sunday	—	3
Monday	—	2
Tuesday	—	1
Wednesday		0
Thursday	+	1
Friday	+	2
Saturday	+	3

As you can see, this is not too difficult to remember. When you ask the spectator how many Sundays he marked out, if he says one, mentally note — 3. If he says no Mondays, you repeat — 3. If he says one Tuesday, add — 1 to — 3, result, — 4. If he says two Thursdays, add 1 + 1 (2) to — 4, result, — 2. Continue this until you have exhausted all the days in the week. You will arrive, by the addition and subtraction of the key numbers, at a final result. Add this final result, or subtract, as the case may be, to or from 75 and you will get the result of the addition of the marked-out dates. For example, taking the dates as marked out in the illustration:

One Sunday — 3
No Mondays — 3 + 0 = — 3
No Friday or Saturday — 3 + 0 + 0 = — 3 (Total Key)
Two Tuesdays — 3 — 2 = — 5
One Wednesday — 5 + 0 = — 5
One Thursday — 5 + 1 = — 4
75 — 4 = 71   Total of Dates = 71

9. Name, Please!

EFFECT: The performer predicts the result of the addition of several numbers, as yet unknown to him. In addition, when the digits of the result are translated into letters, according to a code previously set up, they will spell out the name of the spectator who added the numbers.

PREPARATION: Find out the first name of a spectator in the audience. Try to get one with five letters, though any number will do. Let us assume the name is Peter. Make up a table, as follows (Fig. 1). Write this table on the second page of a pad. Leave the first page blank. You will find, when you translate the name Peter, substituting the digits in the table for the letters, that you get the number 65058. Put a 2 in front of this number, and memorize it, as this will be the result you will predict. By putting a 2 in front of the first figure, you have a six-digit figure, 265058. You now require a key number for the trick to work successfully. This is obtained by adding 2 to your original number of 65058. This gives you a key number of 65060. Remember your key number. You are now ready to proceed.

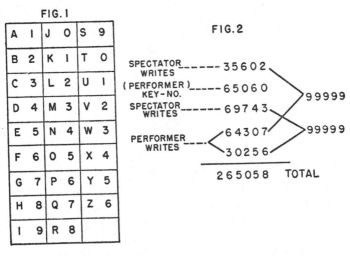

FIG. 1

A	1	J	0	S	9
B	2	K	1	T	0
C	3	L	2	U	1
D	4	M	3	V	2
E	5	N	4	W	3
F	6	O	5	X	4
G	7	P	6	Y	5
H	8	Q	7	Z	6
I	9	R	8		

FIG. 2

SPECTATOR WRITES	35602
(PERFORMER) KEY-NO.	65060
SPECTATOR WRITES	69743
PERFORMER WRITES	64307
	30256

99999
99999

265058 TOTAL

PRESENTATION: Say to the audience that you will now attempt to do some mysterious and lightning calculation. You will predict the result of the addition of unknown numbers. On a piece of paper write the prediction, which in this case will be 265058. Fold the paper and hand it to a spectator to hold, without looking at it. On the top of the first page of the pad, have another spectator write any five-digit number, for example, 35692. After he has done this, write your key number, 65060, under it. Have another spectator write any other five-digit number, such as 69743, under this. Then you (the performer) add two more five-digit numbers immediately under the other three. For this example, the numbers you write at this time are 64307 and 30256.

Note: If you add the first of these numbers to the first number written by the spectator, you get a five-digit number composed of all 9's. If you add the latter of these numbers to the third item on the list, you also get a five-digit number composed of 9's. So, when you choose your numbers, make sure that they will lead to these results (Fig. 2).

Immediately upon writing the last two numbers, hand the pad to the spectator whose name you are going to work with, and tell him to add the figures. When he has written the result, ask the spectator to whom you gave the paper on which the prediction was written, to read off the result ot the addition and compare it with the predicted number. These are, of course, the same.

You now tell the spectator, who did the addition, to tear off the first page of the pad, and to note the formula of the letter-number code on the second page. Tell him to substitute the corresponding letters for the last five digits of the result. He and the audience will be extremely surprised to find that it finally spells out his own name.

10. *Cigarette from Nowhere*

EFFECT: The performer removes an imaginary pack of cigarettes from his pocket. He removes an imaginary cigarette from this imaginary pack, and places it in his mouth. He then lights it with a real match. When he removes his cupped hands, he is seen to be smoking a real cigarette.

PREPARATION: Take a match box, of the type that holds wooden matches, and cut out one-third of the end of the drawer. Into this opening insert a cigarette so that most of it is in the box, with only about three-quarters of an inch protruding (see illustration). Fill the remaining part of the box with matches and close. Place this in your right-hand pocket.

PRESENTATION: The entire action is done in pantomime, as it is more impressive that way. First, call the attention of the audience to yourself. Place your left hand in your left pocket, take it out and cup it as if you are holding a pack of cigarettes. Make all the motions that are necessary to remove one of the cigarettes. Replace the imaginary pack, and place the imaginary cigarette in your mouth. All these motions must be done in such manner that the audience knows what you are doing. Place your right hand in your right pocket, and remove the prepared box of matches. Make sure your hand covers the protruding end of the cigarette. Open the drawer by pulling out the opposite end. Remove a match and close the drawer. Strike the match against the box, and immediately after the match lights, cup your hands, holding the box in the left hand and the lighted match in the right hand. Make sure the protruding end of the

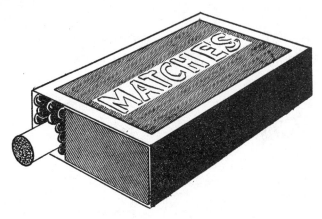

cigarette is toward you. Under cover of your cupped hands, have your lips grasp the end of the cigarette and pull it out of the box. Then light the cigarette. Bring your hands down and replace the box in your pocket. The audience will be extremely surprised to see you actually smoking a cigarette.

11. Find the Pellet

EFFECT: Three small screw-on bottle tops, the mouths of which are closed by tape, are placed on the table. One of these has a metal pellet in it which rattles when the top is shaken. The other two are empty. No matter how many times the performer changes their positions on the table, the spectator never is able to pick out the one that rattles.

PREPARATION: (*For the smoker*) Get three small screw-on bottle tops, easily obtainable at a drugstore. In one of them place a small metal pellet (buck-shot or steel bearing). Tape up the mouths of these bottle tops so that there are no openings. Now insert into a cigarette, or cigar (so that it is not visible), a small medicinal capsule, or an empty .22 caliber shell which is plugged up, into which you have put one of the small pellets. Make sure that the pellet can move freely.

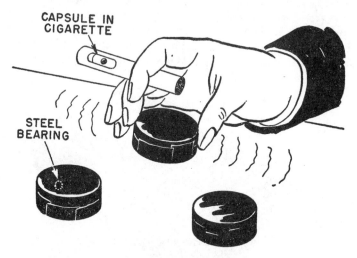

CAPSULE IN CIGARETTE

STEEL BEARING

PRESENTATION: Place the three bottle caps on the table. Place the cigarette, or cigar, in your mouth, lit or unlit. Allow the spectator to examine the three bottle tops, and to make sure that only one of them rattles. Tell him that you will mix them up, by changing their positions on the table. Now ask him whether he is able to discern where you placed the top that rattles. Undoubtedly he will be able to do this, since you have not made it too difficult. Now tell him that you will use a bit of hypnotic influence so that he will not be able to pick the right one hereafter. Mix the cap tops again, and tell him to point to the one he thinks rattles. No matter which one he points to, remove the cigarette, or cigar, from your mouth, and with the same hand pick up one of the empty tops and shake it. Hearing the rattle, he is convinced his choice was wrong. Of course, what really happens is that when you shake the empty top, you are also shaking the loaded capsule in the cigarette, or cigar, which simulates the sound of the loaded bottle top. Repeat this once or twice and you will certainly frustrate the spectator. You may show him your hands are empty, except for the cigarette or cigar, at all times.

PREPARATION: (*For the non-smoker*) If you do not smoke, prepare a fourth bottle top with a pellet enclosed. Tape this just above the wrist on the palm side of the hand. Use either cellophane tape or regular tape, and make sure that your sleeve covers it at all times.

Thus, when you shake an empty top, the top on your wrist will rattle as if the pellet were in the empty one.

12. *Is He Alive?*

EFFECT: Each person in a group of people prints on a piece of paper the name of a person unknown to the performer. One is chosen to print the name of a dead person, and the others are to print the names of living people. By studying the printed names, the performer immediately reveals the name of the dead person.

PRESENTATION: Have several pencils in your hand, one of which has a sharp hard point, the rest having dull and fairly soft-lead points. Hand out sheets of paper, all the same size, and then say, "It is a peculiar thing, but it has been shown several times that the dead may influence the living. To prove this, I am about to do the following experiment. It is important that you follow my instructions. On the sheet of paper in front of you, in the center, you will print the name of a person totally unknown to me. However, you, Miss ——, will print the name of a dead person. I have you print these names so that I will not recognize anyone's handwriting. I also pick a female to print the name of the dead person, because it has been found that females are more mediumistic than males." (Picking the female on your part is a subterfuge, since a female rarely carries a pencil on her person.) Now you say, "I notice, Miss ——, you have no pencil, please take this one." (Hand her the pencil with the sharp point.) Wind up your patter by saying, "Does anyone else need a pencil? If you do, I have several here I can lend you."

When the participants announce that they have finished their part in the experiment, ask one of them to collect all the sheets of papers and mix them thoroughly. He is to hand them to you, and you proceed to study each one. It is easy to locate the name of the dead person because of the lightness and the sharpness of the printing. Reveal this name and prove your point.

13. *The Rope and Bracelet*

EFFECT: The performer's wrists are tied with the ends of a rope or string. A solid ring, the size of a bracelet, is handed to him. He turns his back for a moment, and when he turns around, the ring is hanging on the string.

PREPARATION: Obtain two fairly large rings or bracelets, exactly alike. These must be the solid type with no openings or means of opening. They must be of such size that they can be slipped over your hand, and held by friction fairly tight on the arm above the wrist. Take one bracelet, slip it over one hand, and bring it up the arm as far as it will go. The friction will hold it there, and when your coat is on it will be hidden by the sleeve. Have the other bracelet handy to give to a spectator.

RING
ON ARM

PRESENTATION: Hand a spectator a piece of string or rope, and have him tie your wrists snugly and tightly, using one end of the string or rope for each wrist. There should be about a foot of string or rope between the tied wrists. Hand the available bracelet to a spectator. Tell him to examine it thoroughly, and when he is perfectly satisfied that there are no openings in it, have him hand it back to you. You turn your back and place this ring, without the spectator being aware of it, into a pocket in your vest or shirt, or some other hiding place, and allow the bracelet on your arm to slip down over the string. You turn around and show that you have accomplished a magical feat.

14. *Key on a String*

EFFECT: A key is threaded on a string. Two spectators hold the string, one at each end. The key and the center of the string are covered by a handkerchief. The performer, under cover of the handkerchief, then removes the key from the string.

PREPARATION: The performer requires two identical keys, a string two or three feet long, and a handkerchief.

PRESENTATION: Keep the duplicate key in your left-hand coat pocket. The other key and the string may be passed around for examination. Now request a spectator to thread the key on the string and hold both ends of the string. Or he may hold one end and have another spectator hold the other. You (performer) reach for a handkerchief and throw it over the center of the string, thereby concealing the key from view; and, at the same time, remove the duplicate key with your left hand and bring this hand under the handkerchief. Now pretend that you are attempting to take the original key off the string, but, instead, push part of the string through the hole in the duplicate key and loop it over the top part of the

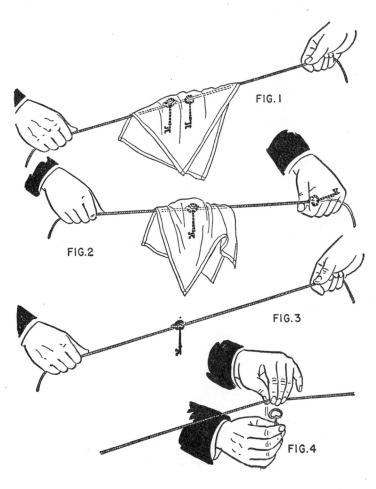

FIG. 1

FIG. 2

FIG. 3

FIG. 4

key (Fig. 1). The key, in this position, will hang by itself, and at a quick glance will look as if it is threaded on the string.

Now, take hold of the key which is threaded on the string and cover it with your left hand. Tell the spectators who are holding the string that in order to remove the key from the string it is necessary to swing the key back and forth, and you will show them how it should be done. With your left hand, slide the key to the end of the string, which you now take from the spectator for a moment (Fig. 2). Hand the end back to the spectator and tell him to swing the key back and forth for a while. (Of course, all these manuevers are done under cover of the handkerchief.) Naturally, you have slipped the key off the string and have hidden it in your pocket, while the spectators are swinging the duplicate key which is looped on the string. After the spectators have swung the key several times, remove the handkerchief and state that you will now remove the key visibly (Fig. 3). Place your cupped left hand over the key, take the loop off, and then, as though it were being done with a great deal of effort, finally show the key (Fig. 4). If done properly, people will rarely remember that you held the end of the string momentarily.

Note: If you are careful in your presentation, you can perform this trick with only one key. Instead of putting the key in your pocket, bring it back under the handkerchief and loop it on the string.

15. *The Magic Toothpick*

EFFECT No. 1: The end of a toothpick is rubbed on the sleeve and then held close to a cigarette on the table. The cigarette moves away from the toothpick, demonstrating the power of negative static electricity.

PRESENTATION: Place a cigarette on the table in front of and horizontal

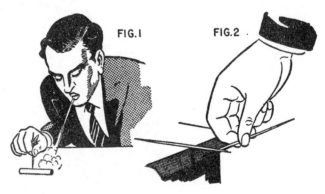

FIG.1   FIG.2

to you. Take a toothpick and rub one end vigorously on your sleeve. Then slowly bring this end close to the cigarette, in front of and toward its horizontal side. The cigarette will start to roll away from it before contact. This continues as the toothpick is moved toward it. What you actually do, as the toothpick approaches the cigarette, is to blow gently through a small opening in your mouth so that the cigarette is moved by the draft (Fig. 1). This, of course, is done so that it is unnoticed by the spectators.

EFFECT No. 2: The end of the same toothpick is brought to the end of another toothpick and the latter jumps away, sometimes as much as several feet.

PRESENTATION: A toothpick is placed on the edge of the table so that less than half of it juts out over the edge. Another toothpick is rubbed, as described above, and its end is brought slowly up to the unsupported end of the toothpick on the table, barely touching it. The toothpick (on the table) jumps suddenly into the air for a distance of about two feet. Actually, as you approach the end of the tabled toothpick with the "magnetized" end of the toothpick in your hand, the nail of the second or third finger flicks the opposite end of the toothpick in your hand, suddenly and very slightly (Fig. 2) which motion causes the tabled toothpick to jump on contact. The action of the flicking is hidden by the hand holding the other toothpick.

16. *Releaso*

EFFECT: The wrists of the performer's hands are tied tightly together with a handkerchief. A rope is passed through the space between the hands and behind the tied handkerchief. Both ends are held by the spectator, and in front of the performer. The spectator now gives a sharp tug of the rope, toward himself, and the rope passes through the handkerchief which is still tied tightly around the wrists of the performer.

PRESENTATION: Tell the audience that you are about to demonstrate the magical process of passing a solid through a solid, contrary to all scientific principles. Place the palms of your hands together, face to face, and request a spectator to tie your wrists together with a handkerchief. Tell him to make it good and tight, and to tie it with a double knot. During the tying, hold your hands slightly cupped, and you will obtain the necessary slight slack needed for this trick. Now have the spectator insert one end of a soft rope, about ten feet long, between the arms and behind the handkerchief tying the wrists. After he has done this, he is to take both ends of the rope and stand directly in front of you, as far as the rope will allow. Tell him to slacken the rope a bit so that you can move your arms up and down, and demonstrate this action.

While this action is taking place, and the rope is slackened, bring the fingers of one of the hands down between the wrists, engage the loop of the rope with your fingers, pull it through and bring it over one of the hands (Fig. 1). With a bit of practice, and the proper slackness, you will find that this is not difficult at all. Of course, the spectator must not see what is going on. After you have accomplished the above, hold the hand steady, and out in front of you, and tell the spectator to pull on the ends

FIG. 1

FIG. 2

of the rope, suddenly and hard. He will be astonished to find the rope loose in his hands (Fig. 2). The handkerchief and your wrists may now be examined, and they are found tied as tightly as before.

17. *Color by Sense of Touch*

EFFECT No. 1: While the performer's back is turned, one of three differently colored discs is placed in his hands, and by the mere sense of touch, he announces the color.

PREPARATION: Prepare three differently colored cardboard discs, red, green and blue, for instance. Through the center of each disc punch a hole. Each of these holes must vary slightly in size. Get a small stub of a pencil, making sure that it is well sharpened. Make the hole in the red disc so that when the point of the pencil is placed through it, only about two-thirds of the point penetrates; make the hole in the green disc so that almost the entire point penetrates; make the hole in the blue disc so that the entire pencil goes through it (see illustration). Hide the pencil in your back pocket.

PRESENTATION: Tell the audience that you have developed the sensitivity of your fingers to such an extent that by mere touch they can distinguish colors. Hand the three discs to a spectator; turn your back to him and tell

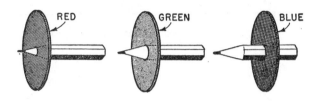

him to place any one of the discs in your hand. Face the audience again, keeping the discs behind you, and assume an attitude of deep concentration. At this time, remove the pencil from your back pocket and insert the point into the hole of the disc. Depending upon how far the pencil enters, you can name the color. Hide the pencil again in your back pocket so that you may repeat the effect.

EFFECT No. 2: Any one of four safety pins, to each of which is tied a differently colored ribbon, is placed in the performer's hands while his back is turned. The performer, by mere touch, names the color.

PREPARATION: Have four fairly large safety pins. Dull the pin points of two of them by filing them down. To one of the sharp pins, on its solid side, tie a small red ribbon. To the other sharp pin, on the pin side, tie a small green ribbon. To one of the dull pins, on the solid side, tie a small blue ribbon. To the other dull pin, on the pin side, tie a small yellow ribbon. All pins should be closed.

PRESENTATION: Use patter, as in Effect No. 1, and give the four pins to a spectator. Have him, while your back is turned, place any one of the pins in your hands. Face the audience again, assuming a thoughtful attitude. Open the pin behind your back, and by noting where ribbon is tied and by feeling the point, you can name the color. Close pin before returning it. Repeat once or twice.

EFFECT No. 3: Any one of several crayons, each of a different color, is handed to the performer while his back is turned. By mere touch he names the color.

PRESENTATION: Hand a pack of crayons to a spectator, and tell him to place one of them in your hands, behind your back. Face the audience, concentrate for a moment, and then name the color. This is done as follows. Using the nail of the thumb of the right hand, nick the crayon slightly, leaving a slight amount of the crayon under the nail. Holding the crayon in the left hand, behind your back, bring your right hand forward, slowly, to your forehead as if you are concentrating. This will give you ample opportunity to observe the color under your nail. Bring your hand back and name the color.

It is advisable to use crayons of distinctive and solid colors. Gradations may confuse you.

18. *Swallowing a Goldfish*

EFFECT: The performer dips his hand into an aquarium, takes out a goldfish which he places in his mouth and swallows.

PRESENTATION: This effect, actually not a trick in the true sense of the word, is more or less a gag, which will produce consternation and plenty of laughs. Of course, this may only be done where an aquarium is present. Prepare yourself by cutting a piece of carrot to the shape of a small goldfish, and hide this in your right hand. When you are ready, dip this hand into the aquarium and move it about as if you are trying to catch a goldfish. Remove your hand with the carrot dangling in it. With a slight back and forth movement of the hand it will look like a real live fish. Open your mouth and let it drop in, then swallow it. The look of amazement on the faces of the audience, and the general hilarity that will prevail, is worth this little bit of mischief.

Now, if you do not mind exposing the *modus operandi* of this little bit of chicanery, you may proceed as follows after doing the above, or this may be done as a separate effect.

EFFECT: Explaining the use of a bit of carrot in simulating the swallowing of a goldfish, the magician slices a small piece off a carrot, places it in water, and it becomes a genuine live goldfish.

PREPARATION: In your right pocket place a wet blotter or a ball of wet tissue paper. It may be advisable to line your pocket first with some waxed paper, to prevent soaking your clothing. Into the same pocket place a small live goldfish. Under these conditions the fish will live about five or ten minutes. Also, place a small jackknife in the same pocket. Have a glass of water and a carrot on the table.

PRESENTATION: Pick up the carrot and explain the fraudulent method used by publicity seekers in the past in swallowing goldfish. Place your hand in your pocket and remove the knife. Slice a small elongated piece of the carrot, and replace the knife in your pocket. At this time, while you are replacing the knife, conceal the goldfish in your hand and remove it from the pocket. With the same hand pick up the piece of carrot, and show how, even at fairly close range, it looks like a goldfish. Bring it to the glass of water as if to drop it in. However, at this point, you bring the piece of carrot into your closed fist next to the fish, and allow the gold-fish to drop into the glass instead, at the same time concealing the piece of carrot. The fish naturally will begin swimming around and the audience will be nonplussed.

19. *Extrasensory Perception*

EFFECT: The performer lays several ordinary objects on the table. The spectator "thinks" about one of the objects. The performer finally points to the object mentally selected by the spectator, without a word ever having been said.

PRESENTATION: Put about eight or ten objects on a table, scattered so that each can be seen separately. The objects are ordinary and not distinctive in any way; but there is one important requirement: the spelling of the names of the objects should vary in count by one letter, the shortest word to be comprised of three letters. The following list of objects will explain this.

Key (3 letters)   Ashtray (7 letters)
Ring (4 letters)   Bracelet (8 letters)
Watch (5 letters)   Cigarette (9 letters)
Wallet (6 letters)   Dictionary (10 letters)

The above list is just an example. Any other objects which follow this rule may be used. After putting the objects on the table in haphazard fashion, ask a spectator to note mentally one of the objects and concentrate on it. Tell him that you will point to one object at a time, and as you do so he is to spell out in his mind the object he thought of. But he is to use only one letter at a time—this to be used as you point to another object, in other words, a letter for each action of pointing. When he comes to the last letter of the word, he is to say, out loud, "Stop."

The performer starts pointing at any object, then points a second time to any other object. However, the third time he points to the three-letter object (Key), and then to the four-letter, five-letter, etc., up the line. When the spectator says "stop," naturally your finger will be pointing to the object he has selected. If it happens that you do not have an object with a certain number of letters, let us say one with eight letters (for example, bracelet), when you point to the eighth object it may be any one of those on the table. It will never occur to the spectator that the spelling of the objects has anything to do with this effect, and so it becomes quite mysterious.

20. *The Magnetized Knife*

EFFECT: A table knife is picked up by the clasped hands of the performer. When all visible means of support are eliminated, the knife still clings to the hands as if it were magnetized.

PRESENTATION: Tell the audience that because of your magical ability, your hands have attained a peculiar magnetic power. Proceed to demonstrate, as follows. Clasp the fingers of your hand in alternate positions, except for the second finger of the right hand, which you curl in toward the palm. When you show the backs of the hands in this position, the missing finger cannot be seen and the fact that it is missing from the clasped arrangement is not noticed (Fig. 1). With the hands in this position pick up a table knife from the table, and hold it up behind the hands in a vertical position. Hold the knife up by means of the curled-in finger. (This, of course, cannot be seen by any spectator.) When you hold the knife in this way, bring the thumbs down behind the hands. This

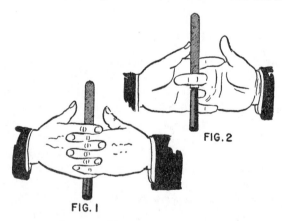

FIG. 2

FIG. I

makes it appear as if you are holding the knife with your thumbs. When anyone in the audience begins to heckle you because of this (and they will), look surprised and bring one thumb up. The spectators will not be satisfied with this, so bring the thumb down again and bring the other thumb up.

Repeat this several times, until the audience seems to be pretty much disappointed with you. At this time slowly raise both thumbs, and the hilarity of the audience will change to embarrassed consternation, because the knife will cling to the hands without any visible means of support (Fig. 2). Allow the knife to be dropped and unclasp your hands, showing that they are empty. The knife may be examined, if anyone wishes to satisfy himself that it is not "magnetized."

21. *Houdini Escape Trick*

EFFECT: One red-colored card and three green-colored cards are placed in a hat. Two of the green cards and the red one are taken out of the hat and placed in the performer's pocket. After a short magical pause, the hat is turned over, and out falls only the red card. The hat is then shown to be empty. The performer places his hand in his pocket and withdraws three green cards, instead of the two green ones and the one red one which he had placed there previously. A mysterious transposition has taken place.

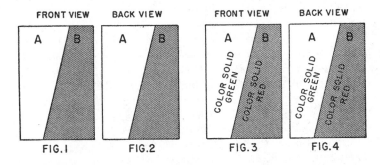

PREPARATION: Prepare five blank cards, about the size of ordinary playing cards, as follows. Color three of the cards a solid green on both sides, with crayon or water color. Color one of the cards a solid red. Place the fifth card on the table with the smaller edges horizontal to you, that is, in the same position as you would place and look at a playing card. Starting at about three-quarters of an inch to the left of the upper right-hand corner, on the smaller edge, place a dot. Three-quarters of an inch to the right of the lower left-hand corner, on the lower side, place another dot.

Connect these two dots with a straight line. Turn the card over and do exactly the same with the opposite side. If the card were transparent and were held toward the light, the two lines would look like a big X. (Note Figs. 1 and 2.)

(The sides of the cards in illustrations are lettered to help you understand how they are to be colored. Letter A is the left side of the card, letter B is the right side. Now, color (both back and front) in solid green the portion of the card on the side of the diagonal line marked A. Color, in solid red, the other side of the diagonal line. See Figs. 3 and 4.)

Place one of the green cards in the right-hand pocket of your coat. Place an empty hat on the table. Place the specially prepared card between the other two green cards and have these cards lying on the table, placed together in a stack.

PRESENTATION: Pick up the hat on the table and show that it is quite empty. Place it back on the table with the crown down. Take the red card, show it on both sides, and say, "All of us remember Houdini, and what a great escape artist he was. I am going to demonstrate his prowess by means of these cards, the hat, and my pocket. The hat will represent the stage on which he is performing. Into this hat (or the stage) I am going to place the red card, which will represent Houdini. Three people from the audience challenge him. And they are invited on the stage."

The performer now picks up the packet of three cards and fans them so that only the green part of the middle card shows. He shows this fan of three green cards, back and front, and continues his patter. "These three cards will represent the three challengers, and I will place them in the hat, too. Houdini and the three challengers are momentarily hidden by a curtain, and then with a shout of glee, two of the challengers bring Houdini out between them and carry him into the audience." In order to demonstrate this the performer removes from the hat the three fanned cards he had placed therein, but in a reverse fan, showing only the red part of the middle card. One green card is presumably left behind. However, actually the solid red card is the only card left in the hat.

Place the fanned cards, after showing them front and back, in your right-hand pocket, saying, "My pocket will represent the audience of the theatre. While this commotion is going on, the curtain on the stage is suddenly raised, showing Houdini still on the stage." At this time the performer turns the hat over, and out falls the red card representing Houdini. The card and hat may be freely examined. Now place your hand in your right-hand pocket, remove the three solid green cards and leave the bi-colored card behind, saying, "When the two challengers, who thought they had Houdini between them, looked again, they found that actually they had the third challenger between them, and not Houdini as they thought, proving again the invincibility of Houdini." The performer may now hand the three green cards out to be examined.

22. *Solid Through Solid*

EFFECT: Two ordinary safety pins are linked together by a spectator. The performer is able to unlink these by pulling them apart, without opening the pins.

PRESENTATION: Hand two pins to a spectator and have him link them together. It doesn't matter how he links them, provided he doesn't link through the small openings in the head or at the bottom of the pin. Explain that by dint of your magical powers you are able to pass solid through solid. Take the pins from the spectator. With thumb and forefinger of your left hand, take hold of one of the pins by the small end, with the opening of the pin facing upward. With your right hand, take hold of the other pin, and maneuver it around the pin held in the left hand until both pins are in the position shown in Fig. 1.

Still holding the pin with your left hand, grasp the other pin by its head with the thumb and forefinger of your right hand. If you have followed the directions properly, you will be holding the pins in the same

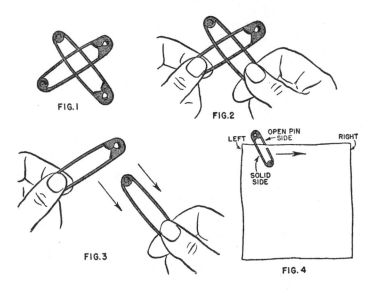

FIG.1

FIG.2

FIG.3

FIG. 4

manner as shown in Fig. 2. Take a firm hold on both pins and pull them apart with a sudden jerk. The pins will come apart, as in Fig. 3. What actually has happened is that the pin held in the left hand has opened and closed instantaneously, and this cannot be seen by the eye. A bit of practice may be required. After the pins are separated, hand them to anyone in the audience to try it. Unless he knows the secret, he will not be able to do it. Be sure to use fairly large safety pins that are undamaged in any way.

EFFECT No. 2: Take one of the safety pins, pin it through the top edge of a handkerchief. Move the pin from left to right along the border of the handkerchief. This will simulate a tearing noise, but when the handkerchief is examined, it is seen to be quite whole.

PRESENTATION: Along the same lines of patter—of passing the solid through a solid—borrow a handkerchief and insert one of the safety pins near a corner and over the edge of the handkerchief (Fig. 4). Hold the pin by the small end and place pin in position, as shown in illustration. The pin side should face the right, and the solid side must be completely over the border.

Have two spectators hold the two upper corners of the handkerchief. Take hold of the small end of the pin and swing it up almost parallel to the upper border. Pull the pin steadily but quickly to the right. It will sound as if the handkerchief is being torn. But when the handkerchief is examined it is found to be completely whole. The pin is still through the handkerchief and still closed. Actually, what happens is that the pin opens slightly, allowing the handkerchief to pass through; the pin automatically closes again when the sliding motion stops.

Better practice this with discarded pieces of cloth until you are adept at it. Otherwise, an embarrassing accident may happen. Linen handkerchiefs of the heavier type are preferable. Very thin handkerchiefs, such as silk, are dangerous.

23. *The Rising Cigarette*

EFFECT: The performer holds a pack of cigarettes in one hand. As he waves his other hand over it, a cigarette mysteriously rises from the pack without any obvious means of motivation.

PREPARATION: Open a pack of cigarettes by exposing one half or one third of the end of the pack, leaving the rest of the wrapping and cellophane paper intact. Take a few cigarettes out of the pack. Take one of these cigarettes and insert it between the cellophane and paper wrap-

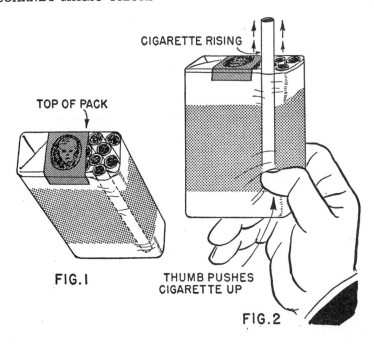

CIGARETTE RISING

TOP OF PACK

FIG. I

THUMB PUSHES
CIGARETTE UP

FIG. 2

ping in the open side of the pack (Fig. 1). Hold this side toward you; the pack of cigarettes will look perfectly innocuous.

PRESENTATION: If for any reason a cigarette is needed for an effect you may wish to do, or if you or someone else wishes to smoke, remove the "fixed" pack from your pocket. Hold it up with the inserted cigarette toward you and casually engage the spectators' attention. In holding the pack of cigarettes, place the tip of your thumb against the cellophane, directly under the cigarette. Wave your other hand over the pack, and by means of a slight pressure of the thumb under the cigarette, and a slow, upward sliding motion, the cigarette will rise (Fig. 2). If done slowly and smoothly, this will look very weird and mysterious to the audience. If the pack is flattened slightly, it may be done at fairly close range. Though simple, a bit of practice is advisable.

24. The Flame Prediction

EFFECT: The performer hands a spectator a number of cards, each of which is blank except for a small spot of color in one corner. The performer turns his back while the spectator selects one card and with a match burns off the colored mark. The performer now takes the card and examines the flame, almost immediately announcing the color with which the card was marked.

PREPARATION: Take about ten blank cards (standard index cards are excellent for this purpose), about five by three, and place a colored mark on one of the corners of each card. This can be done with crayons, and each color should be different. About one third of the distance up from this corner, and near the opposite corner on the same side of the card, write the name of the color with lemon juice. On the other side of the card, exactly opposite this writing, write it again with lemon juice (see illustration).

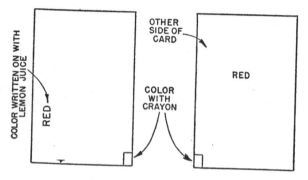

PRESENTATION: Explain and show to the spectator that you have about ten cards, each marked at the corner with a different color. Tell him to take the cards and select any one he wishes, while your back is turned. Place your hand behind you and tell him to place the card in your hand, with the marked corner toward him. Then tell him to light the marked corner with a match. When he is sure that the color is completely burnt off, he is to give you a signal. This should not take more than a minute. Bring the card forward and act as if you are studying the flame. At the same time, casually, direct the flame toward the invisible writing. You will find that the heat of the flame makes the writing quite visible. After the card is more than half burnt, drop it into an ashtray and announce the color. Make sure that the interval between the time the spectator lights the card and the time you look at it is short, otherwise too much of the card will be burned. The reason for writing on both sides of the card is to prevent your having to turn the card in your hand while it is in flames.

25. *The Disappearing Coin*

EFFECT: The performer places a coin in a fold of his trousers. Then, by means of a magical pass, the coin vanishes.

PREPARATION: Empty your right trouser pocket, and place a coin, either a quarter or a half dollar, in it. Take another coin of similar denomination and attach it to an elastic about a foot long. This may be done by boring a small hole through the coin near its edge, or by soldering a small metal loop to its edge. Pin the other end of the elastic on the inside lining of your right coat sleeve, high enough that when the coin hangs loose it is two or three inches above the edge of the cuff.

PRESENTATION: Take the coin out of the sleeve and hold it, with the tips of the thumb and first finger, so that the elastic cannot be seen. Engage

the attention of the spectator, and place the coin on the trousers, immediately above the coin in your pocket. With your left hand grasp the cloth of the trousers, so that you also include the coin in the pocket, and fold completely over the coin on the elastic. Leaving the fold as it is, release your right hand, which will automatically cause the coin on the elastic to vanish up your sleeve (see illustration). This action must be done smoothly and without arousing suspicion.

In order to prove to the spectator that the coin is still present, have him feel the fold of the trousers. Of course, he will be satisfied that the coin is still there, though he is actually feeling the coin in the pocket. Pass your right hand over the fold in a magical sort of way, slowly release the fold, and with your hand brush the area, showing that the coin has completely vanished. You must show your empty hands immediately.

26. *Initial in Fire*

EFFECT: While a spectator holds a lighted match and concentrates on the initial of his last name, this initial mysteriously appears on the burnt-out match head.

PREPARATION: Secretly find out the initials of the name of a spectator, preferably unknown to you. Print these initials, with a pencil, on the head of a paper match, still attached to the packet; use heavy strokes.

PRESENTATION: Say to the spectators, "I am going to demonstrate the power that mental concentration sometimes has. You know the old saying of 'mind over matter'; I am going to prove this right now." Approach the spectator, whose initials are on the match, and say to him. "We have never met before, have we?" The spectator will, of course, say, "No." Then tell him, "I am going to light a match. I want you to hold it for a moment and I want you to gaze into the flame and concentrate on the initials of your name. Then blow the flame out."

Take the packet of matches out of your pocket, tear out the match with the spectator's initials on it, light it and hand it to him. After he blows the light out, tell him to look carefully at the head of the match, and he will be greatly surprised to find his initials imprinted there.

27. Sensitive Fingers

EFFECT: Several dollar bills are borrowed from several spectators. The number on one of them is recorded for identification. All the bills are folded and placed in a hat, where they are mixed thoroughly. The performer now places his hand in the hat, and without looking, almost immediately removes the recorded bill.

PREPARATION: All the performer needs is a small pellet of sticky wax stuck to the tip of his thumb. Use yellow wax, as this color is least noticeable.

PRESENTATION: Tell the audience that you have developed the sensitivity of your fingers to such degree that with them you are able to read numbers on a bill even though the bill is folded. Have five or six spectators lend you bills. Take one of the bills, look at it, and say, "I am going to fold this bill, and I want you to fold yours the same way. However, before I do this I would like someone to write the number of this bill for future identification." Read the number off and have someone check it. Now proceed to fold the bill into eighths. However, before you actually begin to fold, press the wax which is on your thumb tip onto the center of the bill. After all the bills have been folded exactly alike, drop them into a hat and have them thoroughly mixed. Have someone hold the hat up high so that you cannot see inside it. Place your hand into the hat and feel for the "marked" bill. Usually you can feel the pellet of wax without unfolding the bill. If you cannot, unfold each bill until you find the wax. Take the bill out of the hat, folded if possible, and have it checked for identification.

Note: This effect may be performed with similar coins of different dates. When you read the date of the coin for identification, press the wax to its edge. When the coins are mixed in the hat, the proper coin is easily identified by feeling for the one with the wax on it. In both cases, for the bill and the coin, before you hand it out to check for identification, remove the wax with your thumbnail.

28. The Liquid Tells

EFFECT: Six glasses, each containing a differently colored liquid, are placed on a table. A spectator places one of these glasses in the performer's hand, which is behind his back. By testing its weight, the performer announces the color of the liquid in this particular glass.

PREPARATION: Fill each of the six glasses about a third full with water. Into each glass, drop some differently colored vegetable dye, or any other easily obtainable dye. On the bottom of each glass, in the center, place a small smear with the same dye or with chalk of the same color.

The color of the mark must be the same as the color of the liquid in the glass.

PRESENTATION: Tell the spectator that you have developed your senses to such fine degree that you are able to tell color by weight. Place the six glasses in a row on the table and turn your back. Ask the spectator to place any glass he wishes in your hand, which you have placed behind your back. Go through the motions of testing its weight; then ask him to remove the glass and replace it in its previous position. While you are going through the "weighing" process, rub the center of the bottom of the glass with one or two fingers, which will of course pick up the color of the smear. After the glass has been replaced, turn around, and bring your fingers toward your forehead, as if you were in deep thought. You can now easily glimpse the color on your fingers. You say, "The weight of that glass shows me that the liquid in it is—" and announce the color.

29. *Drinking Smoke*

EFFECT: Smoke is poured from one glass to another. The performer then startles his audience by drinking a glassful of smoke. Smoke is then made to appear in a glass, merely by a wave of the performer's hands.

PRESENTATION: Fill your mouth with some smoke from a cigarette, and by very gently blowing over the edge of a glass, fill the glass with smoke. Make sure that there are no breezes in the room. Pick up the glassful of smoke in one hand, and an empty glass in the other. Bring the mouth of

the full glass to the mouth of the empty glass, and by gently and very slowly tilting the full glass, the smoke from this glass will pour into the empty glass. This looks quite weird when done correctly. Since smoke is heavier than air, it will pour. Pick up the glass that is filled, and if necessary add more smoke. Tell the audience you will drink it. Bring the mouth of the glass to your own mouth, and simulate the drinking of a glass of water. Remember that all these actions must be done very slowly and gently, otherwise, you will lose the smoke before the effect. When you are "drinking" the smoke, you actually (very gently) blow air into the glass as you tilt it. You must do this in such fashion that the audience is not aware of it. This action dissipates the smoke. You may inhale some of the smoke through your nose so that when the glass is empty, you can prove that you drank the smoke by slowly exhaling some. You may wait a moment or two to do this, after you have placed the empty glass down.

Now take an empty glass and place it, mouth down, in the center of a saucer. Wave your hand over the glass—and it fills completely with smoke. You must prepare the glass and saucer beforehand for this effect. Place a few drops of ammonia in the glass and a few drops of hydrochloric or muriatic acid in the center of the saucer. When you invert the glass over it, the vapors of the two chemicals combine to form a heavy smoke.

30. *Lightning Addition*

EFFECT: A spectator adds any two numbers. He then adds the total to the second of the numbers, after which he adds the new sum to the previous total, and continues to do this until he has eight totals in addition to the two original numbers. The spectator adds these figures, but before he can announce the result, the performer predicts the currect total.

PRESENTATION: Hand a pencil and a piece of paper to a spectator. Tell him to write any two numbers, one under another, at the top of the paper. (You are not to see this.) Then instruct him to add these together and place the result immediately under the numbers. He is now to add this result to the number above it and place the answer underneath. He is to continue in this way, adding each result to the number above it until he has ten numbers written down. (It would be a good idea to tell the spectator to itemize these numbers by jotting down the figures 1 to 10 at the side of the paper, so that he will know when he has acquired the ten numbers. This also makes it easier for the performer to note the figures quickly.)

When he has completed this computation, tell him to cover, with his hands, all but the three middle items, the fifth, sixth and seventh. Explain that the reason for this is that you wish to see if he has understood and followed your directions. You glance at the exposed numbers for a moment, and say everything is all right. All you need do is notice the seventh number. Multiply the seventh number by eleven, and mentally note the result. Now ask the spectator to add all ten numbers together. But before he can arrive at his answer, tell him what you think the result should be. He will be surprised to find that you are correct. The following is an example:

1	. . . .	6	6	33
2	. . . .	3	7	54
3	. . . .	9	8	87
4	. . . .	12	9	141
5	. . . .	21	10	228
			Total	594

You will notice that the first number is added to the second, resulting in 9. The 9 is added to the 3, resulting in 12. The 12 is added to the 9, resulting in 21, etc. The seventh number in the column is 54. This multiplied by 11 gives the total of all the numbers, 594.

31. *The Spiritual Glass*

EFFECT: A glass tumbler is made to pass through a solid table top.

PRESENTATION: Put a coin on the table and place the mouth of a glass tumbler directly over it. Now say, "When I have the coin in this position, of course you are able to see it through the glass. You may also hear it against the sides of the glass when I slide the glass from side to side." Proceed to demonstrate this. "Let us take a sheet of paper and wrap it around the glass so that the entire glass is covered and the coin cannot be seen." When you wrap the glass, wrap it so that even if the glass were not there the paper would stand up and make it appear as if it were. "However, you still may hear the coin when I slide the glass back and forth. You may even see it if I pick the wrapped glass up."

Pick the glass up, very inconspicuously bring it to the edge of the table, and allow the glass to fall into your other hand, which is resting in your lap. If you do this at the level of the table it cannot be seen. Meanwhile, you are bringing the attention of the audience to the coin which is now

visible on the table. Bring the wrapping (which appears as if it still has the glass) forward to the coin, and cover it as before. Lift the paper two or three times very slightly and bring it down on the table, always covering the coin. The effect is made even more convincing by simulating the sound of a glass hitting the table. Just as the paper touches the table, raise the glass—which is in your other hand under the table—so that its edge hits the under side of the table. If the actions are thoroughly synchronized, it seems to the spectator, and convinces him, that the glass is still in the wrapper. Suddenly release the paper and bring the same hand down hard on the wrapping paper, crushing it flat. Follow this action by immediately bringing up the glass with the other hand, showing that it must have penetrated the table top.

32. *Crossed Digit*

EFFECT: From a series of digits, composing a large number made up of five or more digits, one is eliminated by the spectator. Learning the digits that remain, the performer immediately tells him which digit was eliminated.

PRESENTATION: Hand out several slips of paper to some spectators in the audience. Tell each of them to write on his slip of paper a number, composed of five or more digits. They may use the serial number of any bill. Then ask them to total the digits and subtract the sum so obtained from the original large number. Tell them to cross out any one of the digits of the result so obtained. Tell them now (one at a time, of course) to read off slowly each digit of the result, except the one crossed out. They may read these digits backward, forward, or in any order they wish. After they have done this, surprise them by telling them immediately which number has been crossed out.

EXPLANATION: When the spectator reads the numbers to you, add them mentally. Subtract the result so obtained from the next larger multiple of nine. For instance, if the result you arrived at mentally was thirty-seven, the next larger multiple of nine would be forty-five. Subtract thirty-seven from forty-five and the answer will be the number crossed out, or, in this case, eight.

33. *The Tricky Spoon*

EFFECT: A spoon is apparently bent by the performer, but as soon as it is thrown down on the table top, it is seen to be in perfect condition. Then the spoon vanishes mysteriously.

PRESENTATION: Hold the spoon by its handle with both hands, the handle pointing at you, the belly of the spoon resting on the table as a fulcrum. In holding the spoon, keep the backs of the hands up, one over the other. Have the little finger of the lower hand, the hand adjacent to the spoon, under the handle (Fig. 1). Make a motion as if bending the spoon handle

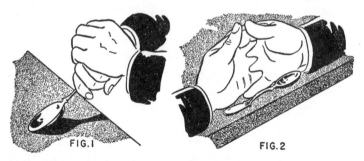

FIG.1   FIG.2

upward, using a bit of false effort to simulate the actual process. Of course, you do not bend the spoon handle; you slowly bring the hands to a vertical position to the spoon. Do not move the spoon upward at all. Remove the upper hand and lift the spoon off the table as if you are holding the bent end with the other hand. The little finger under the spoon actually does the lifting. The remaining part of the hand hides the end of the spoon. Immediately drop the spoon to the table, showing that it has not been bent at all.

Place the spoon on the table, about six inches from the edge and parallel to it. Interlocking the fingers of both hands and with the backs of the hands up, place hands over the spoon, covering it completely. At this time you seemingly lift the spoon from the table, with the backs of hands toward the audience, blow on your hands, turn them slowly around and show that they are empty. The spoon has vanished! This is accomplished as follows: As you proceed to lift the spoon from the table, slowly and imperceptibly bring it right over the edge of the table, at the same level as the table top. At this time, since the action cannot be seen, drop the spoon into your lap, and continue raising your hands (Fig. 2). This must be done smoothly and without any hesitation.

34. The Talking Cards

EFFECT: Several people are given blank cards on which they write anything they wish. When the cards are shuffled and thoroughly mixed, the performer, by looking at the participants, can tell who wrote what. In other words, the performer demonstrates his ability to identify handwriting by studying the individual's physical characteristics.

PREPARATION: The secret of this effect is that each card is marked to indicate one to ten, but this mark, of course, is imperceptible to the spectator. Index cards that have lines on one side and are blank on the other are excellent for this experiment. Since the performer will probably repeat this effect several times, in different places, it is advisable to prepare a few sets of cards, as shown below.

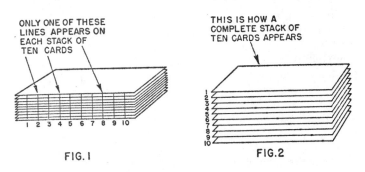

ONLY ONE OF THESE LINES APPEARS ON EACH STACK OF TEN CARDS

1 2 3 4 5 6 7 8 9 10

FIG. 1

THIS IS HOW A COMPLETE STACK OF TEN CARDS APPEARS

1 2 3 4 5 6 7 8 9 10

FIG. 2

Make up ten stacks of ten cards each, keeping all the lined surfaces up. Take a stack, square it, and hold the long edge toward you. With a sharp pointed pen, draw a line on the edge, vertically and to the extreme left. Take another stack, hold it the same way, and make the same mark at the extreme right. A third stack, mark in the middle. Mark the remaining stacks by dividing the edges accordingly (Fig. 1). The mark on the extreme left represents number one. The one on the extreme right represents number ten; the one in the middle, number five, etc. You now have enough cards prepared to work this effect ten times. If you take any of these cards and hold it with the lined surface up, you will see an inked dot on one of the long edges, and according to its position you can tell what number it represents. Stack the cards from one to ten in rotation, from top to bottom, number one being on top (Fig. 2). With this stack you are now ready for the experiment.

PRESENTATION: Hand out the cards from top to bottom, one each to an individual, "dealing" from left to right. In other words, the person at the left will get card number one, the next one will get card number two, etc. Now tell the audience that you have made a study of handwriting, in reference to a person's physical characteristics, and that you are about to test your ability. Tell them that you will turn your back, or leave the room, while each of them selects any short sentence from any book or periodical available, and writes it on the card. One of the participants is to collect the cards and mix them thoroughly. When he has done this, you turn around, or come back into the room, and take over the cards. Choosing one, you act as though you were making a careful study of the handwriting on it, and every once in a while, you look up and study some individual in the room. While you are doing this, it is easy for you to find the dot on one of the long edges of the card. This immediately tells you which number it is and therefore identifies the person who wrote the item. You then hand the card to that individual, who verifies his own handwriting.

If the audience is a stationary one, this is a fairly simple process. However, if this trick is performed at a party or some place where people may move around a great deal, it becomes more difficult. In that case, it would be necessary to connect something about the individual with the number of the card you hand him, so that you will not make an error.

35. Scarne's Bank Night

EFFECT: The performer states that he is going to play a game called Bank Night, and that he is going to give a ten-dollar bill to some lucky contestant. He calls upon a spectator from the audience to act as his assistant. The performer has the assistant put blank pieces of paper into each of four pay envelopes and seal each envelope. Then a ten-dollar bill is placed by the assistant in the fifth pay envelope, which is also sealed. Each of these envelopes is in turn put into a larger envelope, and sealed. The assistant now holds five envelopes, one containing a ten-dollar bill, and the other four containing blank pieces of paper. The assistant is asked to mix these thoroughly and then to distribute four of them to members of the audience. The last remaining envelope is given to the performer. All those receiving an envelope are asked to step up with the performer to see which one of them is going to win the ten-dollar bill. The performer states that if anyone of the participants desires to exchange envelopes with any other participant or with himself, he may do so. A series of exchanges takes place. Finally, when all the participants are satisfied with the exchange, each participant is asked to open his or her envelope. On doing so, they find they have all drawn blanks. The performer hands his envelope to his assistant to open, and to the surprise of everyone, his envelope also contains a blank. Now, the performer tears open a cigarette which he has been smoking and from it he extracts the ten-dollar bill.

PREPARATION: To perform this trick you require: ten small envelopes; five blank pieces of paper to fit inside the pay envelopes; five regular letter-size envelopes; two ten-dollar bills or any two bills of the same denomination that you prefer to use; a package of cigarettes. Take one of the blank pieces of paper and seal it inside a pay envelope. On the face of this envelope (the side used to write the address) write a large and bold number 5, on or about the center. Place this envelope into one of the larger envelopes (which has the open side facing you) with the number 5 facing upward. Close the flap but do not seal this envelope. Mark the faces of the other pay envelopes from 1 to 9. When writing the number 5, take particular care to make it resemble the number 5 marked on the pay envelope which you have placed into the large envelope.

Now arrange the envelopes and papers in your left hand as follows: first, the pay envelopes, the pay envelope marked number 1 resting on the palm of your hand, envelope marked number 2 on top of envelope marked number 1, number 3 on top of number 2, etc. Next, on top of the nine pay envelopes, place the large envelope which contains the hidden pay envelope. This is placed so that the flap is facing upward and away from your body. The four large unprepared envelopes, with their openings facing, are placed on top of the large envelope containing the hidden pay envelope. And on top of these are placed the four pieces of paper (Fig. 1). A large rubber band is placed around the envelopes and paper to hold them in position until the time arrives to perform the trick.

Place one of the bills in your right trouser pocket. The other bill must be inserted into a cigarette. This is done as follows: First, take the bill and fold it in half the long way. Then fold it in half again the opposite way. Roll this into a compact bundle. Take a cigarette and roll one end of it between the fingers of both hands until enough tobacco loosens up and falls out so that it will be easy for you to push the rolled bill into the cigarette. After pushing the rolled bill into the cigarette, take a pair of scissors and clip off any excess tobacco that may protrude from the cigarette. Then place the cigarette back into the pack of cigarettes, but let it remain about one-eighth of an inch above the rest of the cigarettes so that you can get at it immediately without fumbling for it. Place the pack in your pocket.

PRESENTATAION: When ready to perform the trick, step forward with the envelopes and papers in your left hand, papers uppermost. Remove the rubber band from around the envelopes and state that you are going to give away a ten-dollar bill, and the manner in which you intend to do

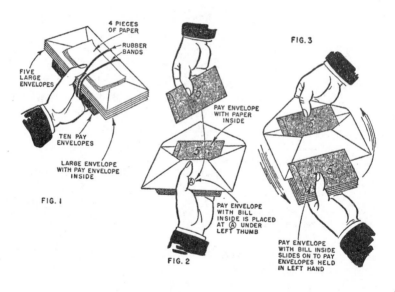

this is by playing a game called Bank Night. To play this game you need a member of the audience to assist you. So, you ask someone from the audience to be your assistant. Hand him the pay envelope marked number 1, and a piece of paper. Ask him to seal the paper inside the envelope. Then hand him a large envelope and have him insert the pay envelope into this and seal it, also. He may hold it in his hand or place it on the table. Repeat the above with envelopes marked numbers 2, 3, and 4. When this has been done, you will have four sealed envelopes, each containing a numbered pay envelope (1 to 4) in which there is a blank piece of paper.

Hand the assistant the pay envelope marked number 5, and reach into your right trouser pocket and extract the ten-dollar bill. This is also handed to the assistant, with instructions to seal it in a pay envelope. While your volunteer assistant is busy sealing the bill in the pay envelope, you are also busy. With your right hand, open the flap of the last large envelope held in your left hand. Then, with the fingers of your right hand, pull out the pay envelope (which you placed there before the start of the trick) until the number 5 is in view. Remove your right hand, and hold the large envelope, with the pay envelope protruding from it, with the thumb and fingers of your left hand. Naturally, you must not permit your audience to see this. Therefore, as you do this, hold the open side of the envelope toward your body. The crucial part of the trick is after your assistant has sealed the bill in the pay envelope. Here is where the trickery comes in.

You are holding the large envelope with the opening toward your body. Take the pay envelope from your assistant and pretend to place it in the large envelope, but, instead, place it under your left thumb outside the envelope (Fig. 2). The right hand releases this pay envelope; the thumb of the right hand is placed on the prepared number 5 envelope, with the four fingers behind the flap of the larger envelope (Fig. 3). The large envelope is pulled away from the left hand, leaving the envelope containing the bill on top of the few remaining pay envelopes in your left hand. The right hand then holds up the large envelope, showing the prepared envelope (containing the blank piece of paper and marked number 5 on its face). After you have shown it, push it into the larger envelope and hand it to the assistant to be sealed. The dirty work is now finished. All the envelopes contain blank pieces of paper. The few pay envelopes remaining in your hand (including the one containing the bill) are placed in your pocket, since they are not needed any more.

No matter how the envelopes are mixed up and handed out, no one will get the bill, so have the assistant shuffle them and pass four of them out to the audience, leaving one envelope for you. After they are handed out, invite those holding envelopes to step up in order to see which one holds the lucky one. Ask them if they wish to exchange envelopes with you. If they do, comply with their wishes until they are completely satisfied—it doesn't make any difference to you which envelope anyone gets. Then act a bit nervous, presumably because of the excitement..

Take out your pack of cigarettes. Offer it to the spectators, making sure that no one gets the cigarette with the bill in it. Have each person open up his envelope, and as the first person opens his, light your cigarette. Once it is lit, don't puff or draw on it, since you must make certain that it will not burn the bill before you are ready to expose it. Just hold the cigarette between your fingers as each person opens up his envelope. When all the envelopes have been opened, hand yours, with some dramatic gesture, to the assistant to open. When he opens it, your envelope also contains a blank—to everyone's surprise. The bill has disappeared. Remark that the cigarette you are smoking has something wrong with it, it just doesn't smoke right. Tear open the cigarette and produce the duplicate bill.

36. *The Knotted Coin*

EFFECT: A coin vanishes and then is found mysteriously in the knot of a handkerchief, which was shown to be empty and tied visibly in full view of the audience.

PRESENTATION: Show a small coin to the audience. Place it on the back of your left hand, and rub it from side to side with your right hand. "Accidentally" drop the coin to the floor, apologize, and bend over to pick it up. As you come up with the coin, let your hand approach your trouser leg just above the cuff, and allow the coin to drop into the cuff. Keep bringing your hand up, seemingly still with the coin, and make as if you were placing it, as before, on the back of your other (right) hand. Rub again and show that the coin has vanished. The above moves must be done smoothly and without hesitation, to make them appear spontaneous.

Now borrow a handkerchief from anyone in the audience. While someone is looking for a handkerchief to lend you, surreptitiously get another coin, of the same denomination as the one in your cuff, into your hand near the tips and behind the first and second fingers of the right hand, holding it with your thumb. You may casually get this coin from your pocket or any other convenient place. Take the handkerchief by two opposite corners, and place the coin at one of the corners, on the side away from the audience, and hold it there with your thumb (Fig. 1). Holding the handkerchief taut, by the two opposite corners, twirl it toward yourself several times, until it becomes similar to a thin tube (make sure it is loose) (Fig. 2). Bring the two corners together and hold by one hand. At

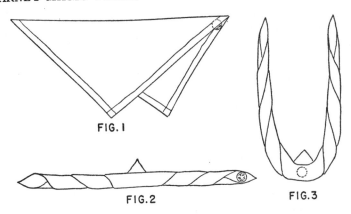

FIG. I

FIG. 2

FIG. 3

the same time release the coin, which will roll into the folds of the hand-kerchief and settle at the looped portion (Fig. 3). Shake it once or twice to make sure the coin has dropped to the correct position. Tie a knot, enclosing the coin. Hand the handkerchief to a spectator to hold by the ends. Make a magical pass and then tell him to untie the knot—he will be extremely surprised to find the vanished coin within it.

Always make sure that the coins you use are of the same date and similar appearance.

37. *It's in the Ashes*

EFFECT: When ashes are rubbed on the arm of the performer, the name of a spectator, chosen at random, mysteriously appears, written or printed, on the arm.

PRESENTATION: Tell your audience that you are about to demonstrate the power of mind over matter. Proceed to ask for about ten first names of people in the audience. If your audience is composed of less than that number, have them all call out their first names. As they do so you write each name on a separate piece of paper. However, what you actually do is write a name you have picked previously on each piece of paper. You are of course actually writing the same name over and over, although your audience believes you are writing a different one each time. When this phase is completed, fold the pieces of paper and throw them all into a hat. Mix them thoroughly, and have anyone in the audience pick one at random.

Say to him, "I do not wish to see the name on the piece of paper; so,

will you please unfold it, look at the name, remember it, and now burn
the piece of paper. Here is an ash tray because I wish you to save the
ashes." After the spectator has done this, tell him to concentrate on the

ASHES

name. Roll up your sleeve and bare your arm. Approach the spectator
and tell him to take some of the ashes and rub them on your arm. Slowly
and mysteriously the name he is concentrating on appears, written or
printed, on the surface of the arm.

EXPLANATION: Prepare your arm previously by taking a thin piece of soap
and writing or printing, as you wish, the name of the individual whom
you have selected before the experiment. Rubbing the ashes on this will
bring the name out very clearly.

38. *The United Shreds*

EFFECT: A piece of cigarette paper is torn into bits and then completely
restored.

PRESENTATION: Show a piece of ordinary cigarette paper, or a piece of
ordinary tissue paper of that size. Tear it openly into small bits and roll
them into a small ball. On it drop some ash, which you represent as being magical, from a cigarette or cigar, whichever you are smoking. Now
spread open the balled-up paper, and show that it is completely restored.

METHOD: Prepare, beforehand, a cigarette paper or a piece of tissue, similar to the one you are going to tear, as follows. Roll it into a small ball
and place it between the first and second finger of the right hand, so that
it is completely hidden. When you roll the torn pieces of paper into a

ball, at the same time substitute the balled-up paper, which is hidden between the fingers, for the torn one, and secretly place the torn batch between the fingers. Lift up your hand for the cigarette or cigar, which all this time is in your mouth, and allow the secreted ball of torn paper to drop into your mouth. Then proceed, as mentioned above, to throw some ash on the paper in your hand, after which take it apart and show that it is restored. You can at this time casually show that your hands are empty.

The following is a version for non-smokers. The preparation and switch is the same, except that in order to better roll the torn pieces into a ball, you come to your mouth with the index finger of your right hand and wet it with your tongue. You do this several times, and during one of these actions you drop the torn pieces into your mouth. After which you make your magical pass, and show the paper completely restored.

In dropping the ball of paper into your mouth, make sure you place it somewhere in the mouth—such as under the tongue—so as not to interfere with your talking.

39. *Three to One*

EFFECT: Two pennies are picked up by the performer, one in each hand, and the hands are closed over them, forming fists. Two more pennies are placed on the hands, one on each fist, at the fingertips. The performer quickly turns his fists over, and a mysterious transference is found to have taken place. When the hands are opened, three pennies are found in one, and only one penny in the other.

PRESENTATION: Place four pennies on the table. Pick up one penny in each hand, and keeping the palms up, close the fingers over the pennies so as to form fists. Ask the spectator to place a penny on each closed fist, right at the juncture of the fingertips and the palms (see illustration). Rapidly turn your fists over. At the moment of turning, have the fingers of the left hand grasp the penny the spectator placed on it and enclose it in the fist. This is easily accomplished by opening your left fist approximately half an inch, and rapidly closing it again. At the same time, let both the penny that the spectator placed on your right hand and the penny enclosed in that hand drop to the table. This should be done with no perceptible opening of the right fist, for the spectators are not to know that both pennies come from the same hand. You should create the illusion that the pennies the spectator placed on your fists fell to the table when you turned your hands. This illusion can be strengthened by keeping the fists fairly close together, and by permitting the penny which was on your right hand to fall under your left hand.

At this time excuse yourself, saying that the pennies dropped off prematurely. Turn your closed fists palms up again, and ask the spectator to replace the pennies on your fists, as before. Quickly turn the fists over again, drawing these pennies into both fists in the same manner as you drew the penny into your left hand before. Turn your fists palms up again, open your hands slowly, and show one penny in the right hand and three in the left. Apparently one penny traveled from your right hand to your left.

40. *The Dollar That Wouldn't Burn*

EFFECT: A dollar bill is, apparently, burned up. It reappears, totally restored, between the pages of a magazine selected by a spectator.

PREPARATION: Memorize the numbers on a dollar bill. If you can't memorize the numbers, write them in ink on one of your thumb nails. Add the digits of this number together. Take any magazine and open to the page number which corresponds to this sum. Fold the dollar bill into eighths; spread it out again and then insert it at that page. Close the magazine and place it with two others on a table or any place which is rather inconspicuous but convenient.

Take an ordinary-sized envelope, and on its address surface make a horizontal slit about an inch and a half or two inches long. Place this slit at about the center of the envelope (Fig. 1). Have this envelope handy.

PRESENTATION: Borrow a dollar bill from someone in the audience. Begin folding the bill two or three times, but suddenly remind yourself of something. Say to the audience, "I would like to identify this bill for checking purposes later. Will someone please write down on a piece of paper the number of the bill, as follows." You now repeat the number of the hidden bill, which you have memorized or written on your thumb nail. The audience, of course, thinks you are reading the number of the bill that is in your hand. Good presentation can make this very convincing.

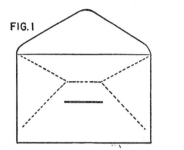
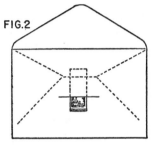

After you have made sure that someone has written the number down, proceed to fold the bill into eighths. Pick the prepared envelope up with the flap-side toward the audience. Insert the folded dollar bill into the envelope, but as you insert it you allow it to slip halfway through the slit on the other side of the envelope. Of course, the audience does not see you do this. They see it actually going into the envelope (Fig. 2). Seal the envelope, but keep the face of it covered with your hand. Reach into your pocket for a packet of matches, but at the same time take the dollar bill, from the envelope and slip it into your pocket in order to get rid of it. Since the bill is partially out of the envelope it is easy to steal it out. Take the matches out, light one and burn the envelope.

Now turn to the spectator who had written down the number of the bill, and ask him to add together the individual digits of that number, but not to announce the total as yet. Pick up the three magazines, approach another spectator, and ask him to point to two of them. If neither of these is the one that contains the dollar bill, you say you will use the one that is left. If one of the two magazines the spectator points to is the one that has the dollar bill, you ask him to keep one and give the other one to you. If the one he keeps is the one with the dollar bill, tell him, "All right, we will use the one you have selected." If the magazine that he has given to you is the one with the dollar bill, pick it up and use the same statement. Turn to the person who has totaled up the digits of the number and tell him to announce the result. Hand the magazine to another spectator and ask him to turn to the page number which corresponds to that sum. He does this, and surprisingly finds the dollar bill at that page. The bill can now be checked against the number which had been recorded.

41. *Divination of Age*

EFFECT: The performer tells an individual his correct age by means of some arithmetical maneuvers with the individual's personal telephone number, which is unknown to the performer.

PRESENTATION: This is a good stunt when a group of people is present. Have someone, preferably unknown to the performer, volunteer for this experiment. Begin your patter with, "It is a peculiar thing how fate takes a hand in our daily lives. For instance, no one here, I am sure, is aware of the fact that the telephone number which has been assigned to him by the telephone company has fatalistic characteristics, since by means of that number his age can be arrived at."

Addressing the spectator who has volunteered, say, "Will you please place on paper the four basic numbers of your telephone number. For instance, if it is WA 8-5847—the basic numbers will be 5847. Now, under this write the number with the digits in any position you wish. For instance, if your number were 5847, you may change their order to 4587, or any order you wish. Have you got that down? Now subtract the smaller of these numbers from the larger. Add the individual digits of this result together. You should have a single digit left. If not, keep adding the digits of the results until you do. When you have finally arrived at the single digit, please add to it the number of days in the week which, of course, is seven. To this result add the number equivalent to the last two digits of the year in which you were born. For instance, if you were born in 1923, add 23. Will you please now state the result." Of course, you immediately tell him his age.

METHOD: The manipulation of the numbers in the telephone number, as above, will always give the result of nine. To this nine you add seven, which gives sixteen. This is your key number, which you subtract from the result the spectator gives you. The result is the number forming the last two digits of the year he was born in. This easily gives you his age.

42. *Tricks with Sugar*

EFFECT: A lump of sugar is made to pass mysteriously through a table top.

PRESENTATION: Secretly and carefully remove the wrapping from a lump of sugar, taken from a bowl on the table. Rewrap the empty paper so that it looks as if the sugar is still in it, and place it back on top of the other lumps in the bowl. Make sure you know which one it is. Conceal the lump of sugar in your left hand.

Now call the attention of your audience to the fact that you are going to do a trick, and remove the empty wrapper from the bowl. Place it before you on the table and slam the palm of your right hand down, flattening the paper completely. Meanwhile, bring up your left hand, which has been under the table, and show the lump of sugar. Now you may proceed with another trick, as shown below.

EFFECT: The initials of a spectator are printed on the surface of a piece of sugar. The sugar is dropped into a glass of water, and after a moment the initials disappear from the sugar and appear on the surface of the spectator's hand, which is held, during the experiment, over the mouth of the glass.

PRESENTATION AND METHOD: Across the wide surface of a piece of sugar print the initials of a spectator, using a pencil with soft lead. While talking to the spectator, secretly press down hard, with the end of the thumb of your left hand, on the initials, picking up an imprint of them on the thumb. Say to the spectator, "It is a very peculiar thing, but if I

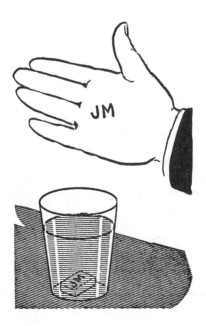

were to drop this lump of sugar into this glass of water, with the initial side up, a very mysterious and magical thing would occur. If you were to rest your hand palm down on the mouth of the glass, the initials would vanish from the sugar and appear on your hand." Now proceed to drop the sugar into the glass of water.

Take the spectator's right hand with your left hand, and place the thumb, on which the initials are imprinted, on the back of the spectator's hand. A slight pressure of the thumb will mark the initials on his hand. At the same time, with your other hand, take the spectator's left hand. Now place spectator's right hand over the mouth of the glass and cover it with the left hand. Do not release your thumb on the spectator's right hand before covering with his left hand, or the initials might be exposed prematurely.

Tell the spectator to watch the sugar in the glass as the initials gradually disappear, and to note the bubbles as they rise, which is part of the magical process. When the initials have disappeared from the sugar, raise both his hands from the glass, quickly turning them palms up. Act very surprised at not seeing the initials on the palm of the spectator's right hand. With a puzzled expression, casually turn the hand over, and add surprise to surprise by finding the initials on the back of the hand. Explain that the magical force, at this time, must have been so powerful that the initials penetrated the hand, and came to rest on its back.

43. The Reappearing Match Heads

EFFECT: The heads of two paper matches are dropped into the left hand of the performer. A third is put in the performer's right-hand coat pocket. When the left hand is opened, the heads of three matches are found. This is repeated, with the same effect. At the climax, the performer throws away the three match heads, and in their stead, the three headless matches mysteriously appear.

PREPARATION: Tear the heads from three paper matches. Place the three headless matches in the right-hand coat pocket. Take one of the heads that was torn from the matches and place it in the small change compartment of your right-hand coat pocket. The other two match heads are discarded. You are now ready to perform the trick.

PRESENTATION: Remove a packet of matches from your pocket. This packet must have matches of the same color and size as those secretly placed in your pocket before the start of the trick. Tear out three matches. Then tear the heads off, and place them on the table. Throw the three headless match stems out the window, or some other place where they cannot be retrieved. While you are moving the three match heads about the table with your left hand, casually place your right hand in the small change pocket of your right-hand coat pocket and pick up the match head you placed there before the start of the trick. The match head is picked up and held between the first and second fingers of the right hand so that the match head cannot be seen from the back of the hand. Holding the match head in this manner, pick up a match head from the table by using the tips of the forefinger and thumb of the right hand. Drop this match head into the left palm, counting "One" as you do. Repeat the same procedure; pick up the second match head with the right hand and drop it into the left palm, counting "Two," but as you drop this match head, drop the one concealed between your first and second fingers as well, and immediately close the left hand over the match heads.

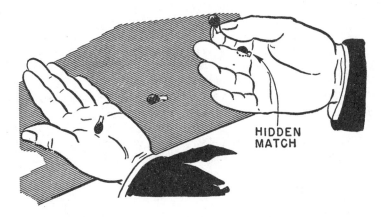

HIDDEN
MATCH

Spread the fingers of the right hand and pick up the third match head, between the thumb and forefinger. Then say, "I will place the third match head in my pocket." As you do this, and while your hand is in the pocket, conceal the match head between the first and second fingers and withdraw your hand, then slowly and casually place your right hand on the table. Open the left hand and show the three match heads in it. Now, repeat the above once more, but when you say, "I will place the third match head in the pocket," actually drop the match head in the pocket with the right hand and take hold of the three headless match stems you had placed in the pocket before the start of the trick. This is done as you are showing the three match heads in the left hand and placing them on the table.

Withdraw the right hand from the coat pocket with the three match stems concealed in it. With the left hand, pick up the three match heads from the table and throw them away, preferably in the same spot as the original match heads were thrown. After this has been done, cup your hands together and tell the spectator that you are going to make the heads of the matches reappear in your left hand. You repeat the magic words, "Matches, matches," then open your left hand, and there are the three headless matches instead of the three heads. Say to the spectator that you should have used the magical words, "Heads, heads," instead of "Matches." Really a startling trick.

44. *Magic Dates and Days*

EFFECT: The sheets of a calendar are distributed, one to an individual, throughout the audience. The calendar may be of any year. Any one of the spectators is asked to add any three, four or nine dates together. The spectator announces the result; the performer unscrambles the sum and tells the spectator which dates were added. One of these spectators is then asked to name the day on which any date falls. The performer then tells him on which days the month starts and ends.

PRESENTATION: Have the first spectator circle any three contiguous dates, either vertically or horizontally. Instruct the second spectator to circle any four dates by forming a square (two dates by two dates). Instruct the third spectator to circle any nine dates forming a square (three dates by three dates). For clarification, see diagrams below.

M A R C H
SUN	MON	TUE	WED	THU	FRI	SAT

SUN	MON	TUE	WED	THU	FRI	SAT
				1	2	3
4	5	6	7	8	9	10
11	12	13	14	15	16	17
18	19	20	21	22	23	24
25	26	27	28	29	30	31

J U N E
SUN	MON	TUE	WED	THU	FRI	SAT

SUN	MON	TUE	WED	THU	FRI	SAT
					1	2
3	4	5	6	7	8	9
10	11	12	13	14	15	16
17	18	19	20	21	22	23
24	25	26	27	28	29	30

D E C E M B E R
SUN	MON	TUE	WED	THU	FRI	SAT

SUN	MON	TUE	WED	THU	FRI	SAT
						1
2	3	4	5	6	7	8
9	10	11	12	13	14	15
16	17	18	19	20	21	22
23/30	24/31	25	26	27	28	29

The performer now addresses the spectator who has circled three contiguous dates, and asks him for the total sum of these dates. The performer must find out if the three contiguous dates fall on the same day or on three different days in order to ascertain the dates circled. The performer merely asks that spectator, "Do the circled dates fall on the same day?" If the answer is "Yes," the performer divides the sum of the three dates by three. The result is the middle date. By subtracting seven, then adding seven to that number (the middle date), he determines the other two circled dates. If the spectator answers "No," the performer divides the sum of the three dates by three to ascertain the middle date. He subtracts or adds one to determine the other two dates. The performer now addresses the spectator who has circled four dates, and asks for the sum of these dates. He mentally divides the sum by four, and subtracts four from this total. This gives the performer an answer, which is the lowest date in the circled figures. By adding seven to this answer, and seven to the answer plus one, he arrives at the four dates.

The performer now follows through with the spectator who has circled nine dates, except that this spectator does not have to add all the dates, only the highest and the lowest. When performer is told this total, he mentally divides by two, which gives him the center date of the group. Add seven and you get the eighth date, subtract seven and you get the second date, subtract one and you arrive at the fourth date, add one and you arrive at the sixth date. The mathematics of the rest is obvious. You arrive at the remaining dates by adding or subtracting ones and sevens where necessary.

After you have completed this routine, turn to another spectator with a sheet and ask him to call off the day on which any date falls. Almost immediately, you announce the days on which the month begins and ends.

The explanation for this is that the fifteenth of the month always falls on the same day as the first of the month. All the performer has to do is to figure forward or backward, from the date and day the spectator has called out, to the fifteenth. This gives him the first day of the month. If the month has thirty days, the month will end one day after the day it starts. If it has thirty-one days, two days are added. In the case of February, if twenty-eight days, the month ends one day before the day it starts. If it has twenty-nine days, it ends at the same day it starts.

For clarification, let us take an example. Let us suppose the spectator announces that Tuesday falls on the twentieth. Going back to the fifteenth, we find that this latter date falls on Thursday. Therefore, the month begins on Thursday. If there are thirty days in this month, the month ends on Friday; if thirty-one, it ends on Saturday; if twenty-eight, it ends on Wednesday; if twenty-nine, it ends on Thursday.

45. *The Six-Cent Trick*

EFFECT: While the performer's back is turned, he requests a spectator to hold a nickel in one hand, a penny in the other. By indulging in a bit of mathematics, the performer correctly tells which hand holds the penny and which hand holds the nickel.

PRESENTATION: Ask a spectator to remove a nickel and a penny from his pocket, and tell him that while your back is turned he is to place the nickel in one of his hands and the penny in the other. Now, tell the spectator to multiply by 13 the value of the coin he holds in his left hand; then, to multiply by 13 the value of the coin in his right hand. Then request him to give you the total of the two answers. This total really has nothing to do with the trick. You merely must be observant while asking the spectator to multiply. If the spectator hesitates on the multiplying of the coin in the left hand, you will know that is the hand which holds the nickel, as it takes longer to multiply 5 times 13 than 1 times 13. The spectator will think the trick is based on a mathematical formula. But let him try to figure it out by mathematics, the total will always be 78, no matter which coin is in either hand. Should you desire to perform this trick some other time for the same audience, it is suggested that you use another number, instead of 13; for example, any one of the following numbers: 9, 15, 14, 11, 12, etc. And if you desire, a bit of patter may be used when performing this trick. The following is very appropriate:

"Einstein is famous for his many theories and in proving what mathematics can do. Here is one he worked that really never did have an explanation. It has to do with items we all know about, and it is so simple one wonders why it has amazed people for so many years. I am pleased to say I was one of the first to have it explained to me, by an old-time magician who put on a show for Einstein several years ago. In return for this favor Einstein taught him this. Here are a common nickel and a penny. You, sir, take them, and while my head is turned place a penny in one hand and the nickel in the other—*but*—so I cannot know which is in which hand. You are set? Very well. Multiply the coin you have in your left hand by thirteen. You have it? Now multiply the coin in your right hand by thirteen. You have it? Fine. Now give me the total of the two answers. That, my friend, tells me you have the nickel in your left hand and the penny in your right hand. Is that correct? Do it again? Sure, I will do it again and again. As you will see, the answer is always the same. So how can I tell which is which? That is the sixty-four dollar question!"

46. *The Famous Penny*

EFFECT: Some coins are picked up by both hands, seemingly in equal amounts, but when the hands are finally opened, the number of coins in the right hand is obviously out of proportion to those in the left hand.

PRESENTATION AND METHOD: Have a spectator place six pennies in a row on the table and then two more pennies below them, one on each side. Then tell your story, as follows.

"There were three thieves who had stolen six bags of gold, and ended up with the gold in their hideout. The six pennies in a row represent the six bags of gold. The two pennies below them represent two of the crooks. At the present time the third crook is away on a trip. The two crooks who have remained behind have, after some discussion, decided to double-cross the third crook, by dividing the gold and deserting the hideout."

While you are talking, pick up the coins representing the crooks and place one in each hand. Then, starting with the right hand and alternating with the left, pick up a coin at a time until one is left. At this time stop and say, "Just as the crooks were dividing the gold and one bag was left they heard footsteps outside, became panicky and immediately replaced the gold." Now replace the coins that are in the hands, one at a time, but be sure you start replacing them with the left hand. This will actually leave you with nothing in the left hand and two coins in the right hand, but, of course, do not reveal this to the spectator. Now say, "The crooks immediately investigated and found that the footsteps they heard were made by a stray cow that passed the hideout. So they began to divide the loot again."

Now start picking the pennies up again, first with the right hand, alternating with the left, and one at a time. Do this again until one penny is left. At this time, say to the spectator, "Just as they were about to reach for the last bag of gold, this time they heard unmistakable sounds of the third crook returning. They knew that their lives were not worth anything if they were caught in the position they were in. So, making a grab for the last bag of gold [the right hand picks up the remaining penny], they quickly maneuvered into position [make phony and quick movements with both hands], just as the door was flung open by the third crook, who demanded an explanation of what was going on. The two crooks nonchalantly said, 'Why, nothing.' [At this time open the left hand and throw the two pennies that are there on the table, signifying that they are the two crooks.] "We have just placed the bags of gold in the closet for safekeeping." This time you open your right hand and throw the six pennies on the table.

47. Mathematics Plus

EFFECT: By the number of people in a room, the performer mysteriously is able to tell the result of the addition of several quantities unknown to him.

PRESENTATION: Have any of the spectators volunteer, and give him a piece of paper upon which he is to write the following items, one under another as for adding. The year of his birth, the year in which a great event happened in his lifetime, the number of people in the room (the only number the performer knows), the spectator's age, and finally the number of years ago the great event took place. The spectator adds this, and to his surprise you announce the answer before he is finished.

EXPLANATION: Actually, this is what is done: you multiply the present year by two and add the number of people in the room. The year of birth plus the age equals the present year. The year of a great event plus the number of years ago it took place equals the present year. The only other number used in the addition is the number of people in the room.

48. Cut and Tied

EFFECT: A piece of string or rope is visibly cut in two and then mysteriously restored.

PRESENTATION AND METHOD: Cut off about three or four inches from the end of a piece of string about two or three feet long. Loop this small piece and place it between the first and second fingers of the left hand, loop toward the fingertips. Hold the two fingers together so that this piece of string cannot be seen. This is to be prepared before the start of the trick. Now take the large piece of string, show it to the spectators or hand it out for examination. Now take it and hold it up by the center, in the left hand, letting the ends hang loose. Good comedy patter is useful at this time. With the other hand make as if to pull up the center of the string so that the loop can be seen, but instead pull the small loop from between the fingers and hold as if it were a continuation of the large string (see illustration). Hand someone a pair of scissors and have him cut through the center of this loop. This seems as if the large string has been cut in two. Of course, it is only the small loop which has been cut. Take the scissors and snip off these ends, meanwhile getting rid of the pieces of the small loop. Make some magical passes and grab the string by its ends and show that it is completely restored.

If you wish to do this trick with a rope, have a short loop of rope tied to an elastic which is attached to the inside of your sleeve. The looped end of this piece is toward the hand. The elastic is just long enough so

←FAKE LOOP

that the loop is hidden when not in use. Show large piece of rope, as above, presumably with its loop on top and ends hanging free. However, you are actually holding the false loop and the center of the rope together in the hand making it look like one piece. Cut the loop in the center. Release your hand from the rope quickly, grabbing it by an end with the other hand and show that it is completely restored. The cut loop springs up the sleeve so rapidly that it cannot be seen.

49. Two Minus Two Equals Two

EFFECT: Fifteen coins are placed in a hat by the performer. They are counted by the spectator, and the number is verified. Two of these coins are borrowed by the performer, who makes them vanish. Yet, when the spectator again counts the coins in the hat, he finds that there are still fifteen there.

PREPARATION: Sew a pocket in one of the corners of a man's handkerchief, and place in it two twenty-five cent pieces, or any two coins of like denomination. The pocket is formed by a piece of material of the same texture and color of the handkerchief. This pocket is then sewed completely around the coins (Fig. 1). Place this handkerchief in your breast pocket. Have a small flat plate ready.

PRESENTATION: With your right hand hold the small plate, fingers on the bottom and thumb on top. Hidden by the fingers, and held against the bottom of the plate, are two twenty-five cent pieces. These must not be seen by the audience (Fig. 2). Have fifteen other twenty-five cent pieces

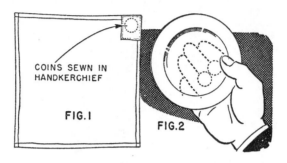

COINS SEWN IN HANDKERCHIEF

FIG. I

FIG. 2

ready, and drop them one at a time on the plate, counting them as they drop. Now ask a spectator to come up to assist you. Tell him to take one of the men's hats, and hold it up with the crown down. Tip the plate so that the money falls into the hat, and tell the audience that now the fifteen coins are in the hat. However, to satisfy any skeptics in the audience, have the spectator recount the coins onto the plate. When everyone is satisfied, tip the coins into the hat again, but this time release the two hidden coins with them. Be sure that you tip the plate toward the audience so that they cannot see the back. Though the audience at this time is sure that there are fifteen coins in the hat, there are actually seventeen.

Put the plate down and ask the spectator to give you two of the coins from the hat. Take the coins in the right hand, and at the same time, with your left hand, remove the handkerchief from your breast pocket. Hold the handkerchief by the center, allowing the corners to drape down, with the loaded corner toward you. With the right hand bring the coins under the handkerchief, but as you pass the loaded corner grasp this corner with your fingers, and bring it up to the center of the handkerchief, underneath, of course. With the fingers of the left hand, and through the handkerchief, grasp the loaded coins, drop your right hand to your sides with the two borrowed coins still in it but concealed. Hand the handkerchief to a spectator to hold up exactly as you are holding it. The feel of the faked corner with the two coins therein convinces everyone that the borrowed coins are in the handkerchief. Casually place your hand in your pocket, getting rid of the coins in your hand. Turn to the spectator, who is holding the hat with the coins in them, and ask him how many coins should be left in the hat. His reply will, of course, be "Thirteen." Wave

your hand toward the hat, and say to the audience that you have magically transported the coins from the handkerchief back to the hat. The
spectator holding the handkerchief will deny this, since he still feels the
coins.

Joke a bit and tell him that he is not feeling too well, and at the same
time grasp the handkerchief by one of its corners and jerk it out of the
spectator's hands. Hold it up with the tips of the fingers at the corners,
showing both sides of the handkerchief and your empty hands, proving
that the coins have really vanished. Tell the spectator with the hat to
take the coins out, one by one, dropping them on the plate and counting
them at the same time. To the surprise of everyone he counts fifteen
coins.

50. *Up in Flames*

EFFECT: A borrowed coin is wrapped in a piece of paper. The entire
packet is burnt into ashes and the coin vanishes. The same coin is then
mysteriously reproduced.

PRESENTATION: Have a square piece of paper ready. This should be
about four by four. Borrow a half dollar from a spectator, and place it on
the paper with its lower edge a little below the center line. The coin is
centered from the sides. At the coin's lower edge, fold the lower part of
the paper up over the coin (Fig. 1). This will leave a free edge formed by
the upper edge of the paper. Hold the coin through the paper, with the

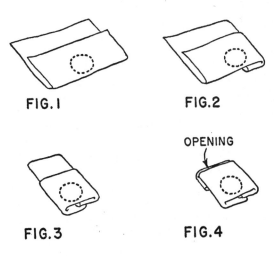

FIG. I   FIG. 2

OPENING

FIG. 3   FIG. 4

thumb and first finger of the left hand. Now fold the paper to your right, at or near the coin's edge, completely over and away from you (Fig. 2). Place the packet so formed in the right hand, held by the thumb and first finger. Now repeat the same fold with the left side of the paper (Fig. 3). As you fold with the left hand, retain packet in that hand, held by the fingers, the free flap pointing upward. With the right hand, fold this flap downward and away from you. To the audience this looks exactly as if the coin is fully enclosed. However, the upper edge is really open (Fig. 4). Transfer the packet to the fingers of the right hand, but reverse it so that the flap is down and facing the palm of the right hand. Have a few spectators feel the packet to make sure that the coin is still there.

When they have been fully satisfied, release the pressure of your fingers from the coin (through the paper). This will cause the coin to drop into your hand. If the packet is held with the back of the hand toward the audience, this action will not be seen. Have a spectator light a match, and with it light the corner of the packet. Hold it, flaming thus, until it is almost all consumed. Then drop the ashes and the remains into an ash tray. Pass the ash tray out to the spectators so that they may verify that the coin has vanished. You may reproduce the coin in any way you please. A simple way would be to walk across the room and lift up any flat object and pretend to find the coin under it.

51. *The Knife That Doesn't Cut*

EFFECT: Two spectators hold a borrowed handkerchief between them and spread out in full view of the audience. A sheet of paper is placed over the center of the handkerchief. The performer penetrates both the handkerchief and paper with an open pocket knife. Blade and handle go completely through without any harm being done to the handkerchief.

PRESENTATION: Conceal a small nail in your right hand. Borrow a large handkerchief from a spectator, and have two spectators hold the handkerchief, spread out, one hand at each corner. One spectator stands to the left and one to the right. The surface of the handkerchief should be at about a forty-five degree angle toward the audience. The front edge of the handkerchief, that is, the edge toward the audience, must be in the lowest position. In this way, everything that goes on on the upper sur-face can be seen readily, but any action below the handkerchief cannot be seen. Borrow a pocket knife and open one of its blades. Hold this knife, with blade upward, in the right hand (together with the concealed small nail). In the left hand hold a square sheet of paper, about one third

the size of the handkerchief. Bring the left hand to the edge of the handkerchief closest to your body, so that the paper rests on this edge, half on
and half off. This looks as if you are just steadying the handkerchief.

Now explain to the audience what you are going to do, and place the
right hand, with the knife, under the handkerchief. Raise the center of
the handkerchief with the point of the blade of the knife, and tell the
audience that you are going to penetrate the handkerchief with the entire knife, and yet the handkerchief will remain unharmed (Fig. 1). Bring

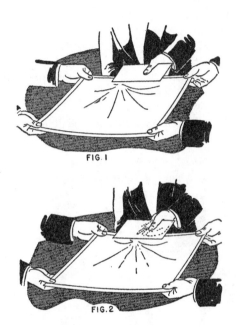

FIG. 1

FIG. 2

the knife out from under the handkerchief. Then tell them that you must
cover this spot, since the magical process will not work unless it is kept
secret. Put your right hand again under the handkerchief, but this time,
as the hand moves under the paper, grasp the knife with the fingers of the
left hand, which is under the paper. This must be done smoothly and
with no hesitation, and, of course, this action must not be seen by the
audience. Continue moving your right hand to the center of the handkerchief, and with the point of the concealed nail, which is hidden in your
right hand, raise the center of the handkerchief (Fig. 2). Immediately
bring the paper over the center of the handkerchief, and through the
handkerchief grasp the handle of the knife. Force the blade through the

paper, as if it were difficult going; force the handle through likewise. Remove the paper and the knife, and show that the handkerchief is completely unharmed. Then secretly put the hidden nail into your pocket.

52. *Stringing a Ring*

EFFECT: A string is cut into two pieces and then completely restored with the aid of a borrowed ring.

PREPARATION: For this effect the best type of string is the fairly thick kind, which is made up of several thin strands. Take about three feet of such string and lay it flat on the table. Separate the strands in the middle of the string, just about equally, as shown in Fig. 1.

Pull these separated strands taut in a direction perpendicular to the string, and twist them so that they look like ends (Fig. 2).

Now pick up the string by the middle and pull the twisted ends taut, until they look like two ends which are a continuation of two strings (Fig. 3).

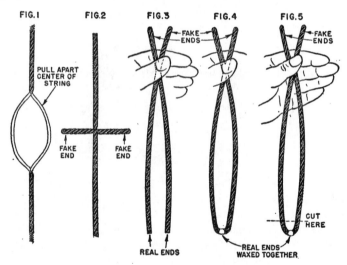

Now, wax the two real ends together with a small piece of white wax, so that they look like a continuation of one string (Fig. 4).

Now you are ready to proceed with the effect.

PRESENTATION: Hold the string by the faked ends, in your left hand (Fig. 5). Do not be afraid that the twisted ends will give themselves away. They look just like the ends of the string. (Try it beforehand and you will see.) Hand someone a pair of scissors and have him cut the looped end (waxed end) off, apparently cutting the string into two pieces. Nonchalantly put the cut end piece into your pocket, with the scissors, as you do not want it to be examined. Now borrow a ring from any one of the spectators, and ask him which pair of ends he wishes you to use. No matter which end he selects (since you are going to use both pairs), proceed as follows.

Thread the ring over one of the cut ends, and when the ring is close enough to the twisted ends, lay the ring and the twisted ends on your left palm; close the left hand, hiding both the ring and the twisted ends. Now have two spectators hold the cut ends, one at each side. Tell them that if you released your hand the ring would drop; however, as you say the magic word, they are to pull their ends gently but firmly. As they do this, run your hand, holding the ring, back and forth along the string to flatten the strands. Remove your hand, show that it is empty—and the string is seen to be completely restored with the ring hanging safely. (When the string is pulled by the spectators, the twisted ends straighten out and resume their original positions in the string.)

53. *Change for a Five-Dollar Bill*

EFFECT: A one-dollar bill is held in the right hand, and is freely shown. A five-dollar bill is held in the left hand, and is also freely shown. The bills are folded into eighths. The five-dollar bill is enclosed in the right fist. The one-dollar bill is enclosed in the left fist. After a magical pause— when the hands are opened the situation is found to be reversed. The dollar bill is in the right hand, and the five-dollar bill is in the left.

PREPARATION: Cut out the circled number five on the green side of a five-dollar bill. Carefully cut the numeral five, including the circle, so that you have what is pictured in the illustration. Stick this to the right-hand upper corner of the green side of a one-dollar bill, covering the numeral one completely. Stick it to the bill by means of a very small piece of wax. Hold this dollar bill in the right hand with the thumb covering this faked five-spot. Have a five-dollar bill handy.

PRESENTATION: Holding the dollar bill (as described above) in the right hand, casually show both sides. Then wave about a five-dollar bill, which you hold in the left hand, also showing both sides. Fold the dollar bill into eighths. Keep the green side on the outside, and end up with the faked five-spot facing upward. Fold the five-dollar bill into eighths, also keeping the green side outward, and ending up with the circled number five upward. In folding the dollar bill make sure your thumb is continually hiding the faked five-spot. Place the one-dollar bill on top of the five-dollar bill, both numerals facing you. Turn the bills completely over so that the five-dollar bill is now toward you, and the faked five-spot on the one-dollar bill is facing away from you, toward the spectator. Do this during a pause, while moving the hands so that the spectator cannot see this reversing action. He now sees the one-dollar bill, which, of course, he thinks is the five-dollar bill, since he sees the faked five-spot.

Slide the upper bill (actually the five-dollar bill) into the left palm. You may show this movement quite freely, as there is no numeral on the upturned surface. At the same time, say, "I am placing the one-dollar bill in my left hand and the five-dollar bill in my right hand." Close your fingers over the bill which you have slid into your left palm, and hold up the other bill (with the faked five-spot) so that the spectator is sure to see the number five. Let it fall into the right palm, five-spot down, and close the fingers over it. Now say, "Unless your senses were false to you, you actually saw the five-dollar bill go into the right hand and the one-dollar bill into the left hand." The spectator will confirm this statement since he actually saw the number five on the bill in the right hand. Continue the patter: "However, your senses were actually lying to you, because, as you see, I now have the five-dollar bill in my left hand and the one-dollar bill in my right hand!" Open the left hand and unfold the bill therein. It is easy to do this with the left hand only. Show the five-dollar bill, both sides, and lay it on the table or hand it to the spectator. Now open the right hand, unfold the one-dollar bill—covering the faked five-spot with the thumb or first and second fingers of the right hand—and show both sides. If you wish, you may secretly remove the faked five-spot from the bill with a finger nail, conceal it in your hand, and then give the one-dollar bill to the spectator for him to examine.

54. Ghost Match

EFFECT: A book of matches is opened and the matches are counted by a spectator. The performer removes one of the matches, lights it, blows out the flame, and then makes the used match vanish. While this occurs, the spectator's hand is tightly closed over the book of matches. He is now told to open the book of matches. To his surprise, he finds not only the same number as was originally placed there, but one of them is burnt.

PREPARATION: Take a packet of matches which contains two or more matches. Take one of the top surface matches and bend it outward from the pack (do not tear off) and close the cover. Light this match by striking it on another packet. Blow out the lighted match and place the packet in the left-hand coat pocket of your jacket. You are now ready to perform the trick. (Fig. 1 shows how the packet of matches looks in the pocket.)

PRESENTATION: When the opportune time arrives to light a cigarette, reach into your left-hand coat pocket and take hold of the prepared packet of matches (the thumb of the same hand hides the used match, see Fig. 2). A bit of practice is required to place the packet of matches in

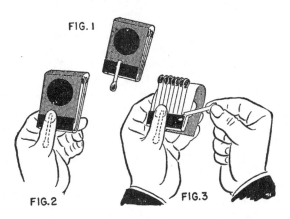

FIG. 1

FIG. 2   FIG. 3

this position without any fumbling. Open the packet with your right hand. Have a spectator count the matches in the book (except, of course, the one you are hiding, which he must not see). When you have done this, tear a match from the packet with the right hand (Fig. 3). While holding the loose match in the right hand, bend the matches over to the level of the hidden match so that the hidden (used) match is back in the book. Then close the match book cover. Light the match you are holding in your right hand by striking it on the space on the match cover provided for this purpose. Hand the match book to the spectator, instructing him to hold it in his closed fist.

Now shake the lighted match back and forth briskly to put it out. On one of the back strokes, get rid of this match by releasing it and letting it fall behind you. Immediately and without hesitation, place your hand—in which, to all appearances, the used match is still present—palm down on the back of the spectator's closed fist, and rub his hand briskly. Turn your hand, palm up, and show that the used match has vanished. Tell the spectator to open the packet and count the matches. If he had twelve originally, he will count eleven unused matches and one used one, showing that the used match which disappeared has found its way mysteriously back into the closed book of matches.

55. A Life-Saving Dollar

EFFECT: The performer borrows a dollar bill from a spectator. The number is recorded by the spectator for identification. The bill is made to vanish by the performer, and is then found in a new and unopened package of Life Savers. The bill is identified as the original one.

PREPARATION: Obtain a new package of Life Savers and a piece of elastic about eighteen inches long. Tie one end of the elastic around the package of Life Savers, near one of its ends, and carefully open the tin foil at the other end of the package. Now pin the opposite end of the elastic to the back of your vest, or shirt, so that even when the package of Life Savers hangs loose, it does not show when your coat is on. If it does, shorten the elastic accordingly. Place the package in your left pants pocket.

PRESENTATION: Borrow a dollar bill from a spectator, and ask him to record its number so that he can identify it later. He may even put another identifying mark on it, such as his signature. Tell him to fold the bill into eighths, and then to roll it up tightly. While the spectator is doing this, secretly remove the package of Life Savers from your left pocket. Take the rolled bill from the spectator by one of its ends. Bring your left hand up, closed into a fist around the package of Life Savers, and insert the bill through the open end into the space formed by the holes of the candy. This should look as if you are inserting the bill into an empty left fist.

When you have fully inserted the dollar bill, release your hold on the package. The package will fly behind your coat and hang there. With a little practice this can be done so that it is not discerned by the spectator. Now bring your hands together in a brushing motion, and then show that your hands are empty, proving that the dollar bill has vanished. Bring your right hand under the back of your coat, as if reaching into your hip picket. It will take only a moment to fold down the opened end of the package, and to push off the elastic from the other end. Take the package, so released, as if it were coming from your hip pocket, break it in the middle, and act surprised when you find the dollar bill. When the spectator checks the number and his signature, he finds, of course, that it is the same dollar bill he originally loaned to the performer.

56. *Mind Over Matter*

EFFECT: The performer suggests to one or more spectators that they have temporarily lost their strength. To demonstrate this, the performer holds a cane in front of himself with both hands, and the spectators push

against the cane, using all their strength to attempt to throw the performer off balance. They are unable to make him budge.

PRESENTATION: To be most effective, it is suggested that you treat the entire procedure with real seriousness, in order to impress your audience with your ability to hypnotize and your achievement of remarkable strength. Discourse a few moments on the powers of suggestion and the science of hypnosis. Also, touch indirectly upon your attainment of remarkable strength, due to your magical prowess. Proceed to demonstrate, as follows.

Hold a cane in front of you in a horizontal position, one hand near each end of the cane. Bend your elbows at almost right angles, so that your forearms are almost parallel to each other (see illustration). Get several strong-looking spectators from the audience to assist you with the experiment. Tell them that during this performance not only will they lose some of their strength, but you, due to your peculiar powers, will gain in strength. Then have one of the spectators stand directly in front of, and facing, you. He is to grasp firmly the ends of the cane, outside your hands. He is to brace himself with his feet solidly on the floor, and to push his entire weight with all his strength against the cane, toward you in a horizontal direction only (picture). He must not use any sudden or jerky moves, but the pressure must start and continue very smoothly. He will find that even by using all his strength he cannot throw you off balance. Ask one or two of the other spectators to help him—it will avail them nothing.

The secret of this demonstration lies in the fact that in the above positions, the force of the spectator is dissipated. As he presses against you, all you must do is to exert enough upward pressure against the cane to keep it in position. This deflects almost all of the spectators' pressure into space, rather than against you. It may be necessary to practice this several times in order to perfect it.

57. *The Coin Vanishes*

EFFECT: A handkerchief is folded over a borrowed coin. When the handkerchief is lifted suddenly by its edge, the coin has vanished.

PRESENTATION: Under the nail of the thumb of your right hand conceal a small piece of soft sticky wax. Borrow a handkerchief from a spectator and spread it out flat on the table. Borrow a coin, preferably a dime, from another spectator, and place it in the center of the handkerchief. Grasp the corner nearest your right hand. Press the wax onto the surface of this corner, and then fold it down so that the corner rests on the coin. Press this corner with your thumb, so that the coin will stick to the wax. Do not make this move too obvious (Fig. 1). Now take the other three corners of the handkerchief and fold them down over the first corner. The handkerchief is now folded so that the four corners are resting on the coin (Fig. 2).

To convince the more skeptical individuals in the audience, have several spectators feel the coin through the handkerchief, to make sure it is still there. After they are thoroughly satisfied, place the fingers of each hand under the folded edge of the handkerchief, toward you (Fig. 3).

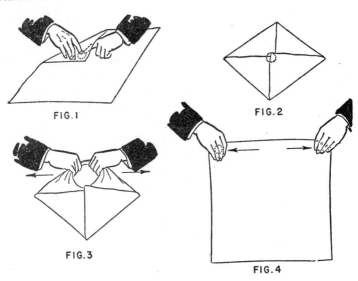

FIG.1

FIG.2

FIG.3

FIG.4

With a quick outward movement, straighten this edge and grasp the corners, lifting up the handkerchief and showing that the coin has vanished. What has really happened is that the coin, being stuck to the corner of the handkerchief, is carried into the right hand (Fig. 4). You may now make the coin reappear any way you wish.

58. *The "Cut-Up" Tie*

EFFECT: The performer cuts up his own tie, right up to the knot. Passing his hand from the knot downward, the tie is seen to be miraculously restored.

PREPARATION: Get two identical inexpensive ties. Put one on in the normal manner, but tuck the entire tie up to knot into the shirt, so that only the knot is visible. From the other tie cut the wide end off, which piece should be the same length as the portion of the tie tucked into the shirt. Tuck the cut end of this piece into the forepart of the knot, so that it looks like a complete tie. You are now ready to cut and restore your own tie.

PRESENTATION: Tell the audience that inasmuch as you are a magician, no matter what you destroy you are able to restore magically. For instance, if you were to cut your own tie to pieces, you could, by magic, restore it to its former condition. You now proceed to prove this. Begin cutting pieces off your own tie from the bottom up. When you get to the top, pull out the tucked-in piece in the knot. (What you have actually done, of course, is cut to pieces the false portion of the tie which was tucked into the knot.) When you have completed the cutting, it looks to the audience as if all that is left of the tie is the knot. Bring your right hand up, fingers over the knot and thumb under it. In this way, with a quick downward and forward motion, you are able to pull the hidden portion of the tie from behind the shirt. This appears to the audience like a miraculous restoration.

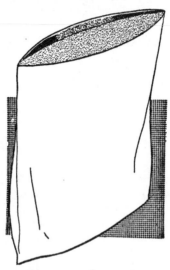

Before you restore the tie, get rid of the pieces you have cut off. You may make them disappear by placing them in a false pocket in an empty paper bag. You may prepare this bag, as follows: Get two duplicate grocery bags (paper). Cut the side completely away from one. Paste this side into the other bag, pasting the sides and bottom only. This will produce two pockets (see illustration), one narrow, one wide. Show that the bag is empty by pressing the false piece to the side of the bag. Place the pieces into the bag as they are cut off, but place them in the narrow side. When you are again ready to show the bag, press the false side to the side of the bag, then show the empty bag. The pieces cannot be seen because they are enclosed by the false side against the side of the bag.

59. In Your Hat

EFFECT: The performer borrows a spectator's hat. Presumably meaning to pour some water into a paper cup, he pours it into the hat instead, to the consternation of the hat's owner. Eventually, to his relieved surprise, he finds everything to be all right.

PREPARATION: Get two medium-sized paper cups. Do not use those made of soft paper; they should be fairly hard and firm. Cut off the top rolled edge of one of the cups. Make this edge even all around (Fig. 1). Cut the bottom completely off the other cup (Fig. 2). Place this second cup within the first cup. This should now look like one complete cup (Fig. 3). Place this cup next to a glass about half full of water.

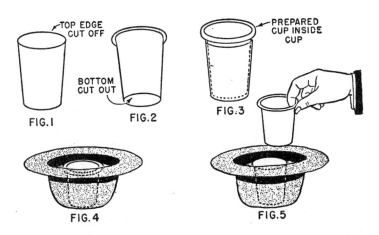

PRESENTATION: Borrow a spectator's hat and place it on the table, mouth up. Now say to the audience, "I am going to show you a little magical effect with water. If I were to take this cup and place it in the hat [do this], and then if I were to pour water into the hat, of course, it would go into the cup [Fig. 4]. If I were to remove the cup from the hat [do this], and then pour the water in, I don't think the owner would like it."

At this time, when you remove the paper cup from the hat, remove only the cup which has its bottom cut out. Thus, unbeknownst to the audience, you still have the other cup in the hat (Fig. 5). You may at this time patter a bit about practically anything, after which you pick up the glass of water and pour it into the hat.

Naturally, the audience does not know that the water is going into the cup, which is secretly in the hat. The discomfort of the hat's owner at this time will cause some laughs. After you have poured the water, do a double-take, scratch your head, and dismally say, "Gee but I'm sorry. I forgot to put the cup back in." This will get another laugh. Keep looking into the hat, at the owner, back and forth. You must do a bit of good acting here. Suddenly brighten up, and say, "Well, since I am a magician, let us see what I can do by means of a bit of magic." Take the bottomless cup and place it in the hat; actually, of course, you insert it into the cup full of water. If you wish to make it funny at this time, recite several funny lines of magical patter, the more nonsensical, the better. Reach into the hat, take the combined cups out, pour the water into the glass, return the dry hat to the owner, and heave a sigh of relief.

60. *The Animated Match Box*

EFFECT: The performer places a match box on the palm of his hand. At a command from him, it rises and stands on one end. At another command, it falls back to its original position.

PRESENTATION: Open the drawer of a match box slightly. Place the open end on the palm of your hand, and bend the fingers slightly toward the palm. The greater part of the box should rest against the fingers; the open end rests on the palm (Fig. 1). The slight bending of the fingers loosens the skin on the palm. Now close the box with the other hand, and in so doing apply sufficient pressure so that the box will pinch a bit of the skin between the drawer and cover of the box. Then slowly straighten out the fingers of your hand and the box will rise (Fig. 2).

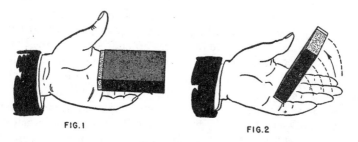

FIG. 1   FIG. 2

It is suggested that you wave the forefinger of your other hand, in a beckoning motion, as the box is rising. Or merely command it to rise, by saying, "Up, up." When the box has risen to its full height, command it to fall. This is done merely by bringing your hand back to its original position. To release the skin from the box, straighten the hand out to its fullest extent, and you will feel the skin slowly extricating itself from the box. The box can then be handed around for examination.

61. Magnetic Hands

EFFECT: A half dollar is balanced on its edge on the finger tips of the performer's left hand. Apparently the magnetic power of the tips of the fingers of the right hand keep the coin upright. When these finger tips are moved down toward the palm of the left hand, the upper edge of the coin follows them slowly, and ends up lying on the fingers.

PRESENTATION: Pick up a half dollar with the right hand. (You may hand it around for examination.) In the left hand, between the first and second fingers, an ordinary straight pin is hidden. This pin should lie in the crevice formed by the fingers when they are close together, the head of the pin facing the tips of the fingers, the point resting on the palm side of the hand. Take the coin by its edge and balance it on these two finger tips (first and second fingers). With the thumb of the right hand, raise the

PIN HELD BETWEEN
FINGERS

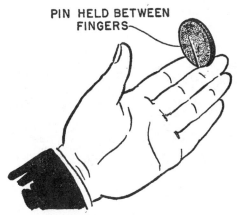

point of the pin to a vertical position against the coin. This action will not be seen by the spectator, since it takes place behind the coin. Press the two fingers of the left hand tightly together, grasping the head of the pin. The coin, leaning against the pin so held, will appear to the audience as if it is resting on its edge. Raise the fingers of the right hand about an inch above the coin and hold them there for a short interval, explaining that the magnetism in your finger tips is keeping the coin upright. Slowly move the finger tips toward the palm of the left hand, and slowly release the pressure of the fingers holding the head of the pin. The coin will slowly describe a backward arc, and finally lie flat on the fingers, as shown in illustration.

This is an excellent illusion if done correctly. At the finish, throw the coin to a spectator to be examined, and at the same time release the pin to fall where it may.

62. Scarne's Cellophane Tear

EFFECT: The performer takes off the cellophane wrapping of a cigar, flattens it, and very easily tears it in half. He gives one half to a spectator, and holds the other half. The performer tears his portion quite easily. The spectator cannot, no matter how hard he tries, tear his piece of cellophane.

PREPARATION: Remove the cellophane wrapping from a cigar. Flatten it, and with the fingernail of one of your thumbs tear two notches on the edge of the cellophane, one in the middle and the other dividing one of the halves (Fig. 1).

PRESENTATION: Up to this time you have not said a word to the spectators about doing a trick. Now you announce that because of your magical

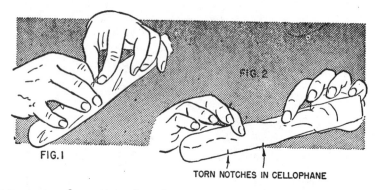

FIG. 2

FIG. 1

TORN NOTCHES IN CELLOPHANE

prowess you have strengthened your fingers to such an extent that you are able to perform feats of strength which the ordinary person cannot.

Hold the cellophane with the notches facing downward (Fig. 2). Pretend to tear the cellophane from the top down, but instead, with a slight downward move, start tearing upward at the middle notch. You will find that this is easy to do, since you have a start with the notch. Hand the un-notched half to a spectator and tell him to try to tear it as you are tearing the other half. You will tear your part without any effort whatsoever, because of the notched edge. The spectator will try and try, but he will probably hurt his fingers before he is able to tear it, if he can tear it at all.

63. Dry Water

EFFECT: The performer shows a bowl of water. He drops a coin into it and then dips his hand in to retrieve the coin. When his hand is examined, it is found to be thoroughly dry.

PRESENTATION: Fill a fairly deep bowl with water, almost to the top. Have a spectator drop a coin into it. Challenge any spectator to remove the coin with his bare hand and keep his hand dry. No one, of course, is able to do it. However, you say that you are able to do it by using a bit of magical powder. Dust the surface of the water with some Lycopodium powder (obtained at any drug store). Insert your hand, remove the coin, and then show that your hand is perfectly dry.

Lycopodium has no adhesive powers for water, so that when your hand goes into the water through this powder, it keeps the water away. The water will flow off your hand as off a duck's back, which is protected in the same way by an oily secretion. If you wish to make the effect more unbelievable, use very hot water. The feeling of heat will remain, but scalding or burning will be prevented by the powder. However, if you use very hot water, be careful.

64. Multiplying Dimes

EFFECT: The performer rubs a dime along the edge of a table. He removes the dime, and two coins are found in his hand.

PREPARATION: On the underside of the table, near its edge and about a foot apart, stick two dimes by means of bits of wax.

PRESENTATION: Tell the audience that magic, at times, is very handy. If a magician is in need of a bit more change, all he needs to do is— Place a dime near the edge of the table, right over one of the hidden dimes. Show that your hand is empty, and then place your thumb over the dime on · the table. The fingers of the same hand are curled under the table edge in reach of the hidden dime. Rub the dime against the table top, by moving the thumb briskly back and forth. During this action your fingers have loosened the hidden dime and allowed it to fall into the palm. Remove the dime from the table top with a sudden movement, so that it also falls into the palm. Bring your open hand up and show two dimes. You may repeat this effect again with the second hidden dime.

65. Scarne's Coin Vanish

The author has mystified many of the nation's top magicians with this trick.

EFFECT: The performer indulges in a little game with a coin, requesting the spectators to guess whether it will fall heads or tails. The climax is quite surprising. The coin disappears from under the performer's hand.

PRESENTATION: Seat yourself at a table. Rest your left elbow on the table and lean your head sideways on the palm of your left hand. Now rest your right elbow on the table, at such a distance that without lifting

your right elbow from the table, your right hand can swing to the left and touch the edge of your left sleeve which is near the left side of your face. This is done merely to get the range, prior to performing the trick. Swing your right hand back to the table, pick up the coin and don't say a word about making it vanish. Merely slap the coin on the table with your right hand and ask a spectator if it is heads or tails. Do this once or twice more; if the spectator guesses correctly, tell him he is lucky; if not, he is unlucky.

The third time pick up the coin by the edge with your right hand, and turning to a spectator, say, "What do you guess this time, heads or tails?" At the same time, the right hand pivots up to the left sleeve (see illustration), drops the coin into the sleeve. Now, immediately bring your right hand palm down onto the table, pretending you still have the coin there. Drop your left hand onto the table, look the spectator in the eye and ask him if the coin is heads or tails. After the spectator has called, slowly turn the palm of your right hand over, and the spectator will be amazed to see that the coin has vanished.

Note: There should be no hesitation when dropping the coin into the sleeve.

66. *Time Machine*

EFFECT: A spectator calls out any date in history, and the performer, in a very short time, tells him the day of the week upon which the date fell.

METHOD: Let us say the date called is July 4, 1778. Take the last two digits of the year and divide that number by 4. In this case the last two digits are 78. Divide this by 4. The result is 19½. Disregarding any fractions, add the whole number, which in this case is 19, to the last two digits of the year, 78. Now, using Table No. 1, look up the month, in this case July, and add the number designated, which happens to be 0. To the total add the day of the date, which is 4. Look up Table No. 2, and add the number designated by the period in which the year falls, which in this case is 4. Add together all the numbers so obtained. The result in

TABLE 1		TABLE 2	TABLE 3	
MONTH	KEY NO.	YEAR KEY NO.	DAY	KEY NO.
JAN ___ 1	LEAP	1900 to 2000 — 0	SUN ___ 1	
FEB ___ 4	YEAR	1800 to 1900 — 2	MON ___ 2	
MAR ___ 4	0	1752 to 1800 — 4	TUE ___ 3	
APRIL ___ 0	3	1700 to 1752 — 1	WED ___ 4	
MAY ___ 2		1600 to 1700 — 2	THUR ___ 5	
JUNE ___ 5			FRI ___ 6	
JULY ___ 0		ADD 1 FOR EACH	SAT ___ 0	
AUG ___ 3		CENTURY FURTHER		
SEPT ___ 6		BACK		
OCT ___ 1				
NOV ___ 4				
DEC ___ 6				

this case will be 105. Divide this result by 7. You get a result of exactly 15. In this instance you have no remainder left over, therefore you make use of a "zero." Look up in Table No. 3 the day of the week designated by the remainder in this result. The remainder being 0, the day so designated is Saturday. For example, should the result be 107, you divide this amount by 7. You get a result of 15 plus a remainder of 2. In this instance, the day designated in Table No. 3 would be Monday.

67. *Through Stick and Pin*

EFFECT: A small stick is stuck on a safety pin, and appears to go through the opposite bar of the pin.

PRESENTATION: Through the center of a small stick of soft wood, slightly thicker than a match stick, insert the point of a safety pin. Bring it all the way through and lock the pin. (If you are careful, you may use a headless wooden match stick.) Place the stick in the center of the pin. Hold the pin tightly by either end with the fingers of one hand (Fig. 1). Swing

FIG.1   FIG.2

the stick around so that its free end is resting on the opposite bar of the pin, away from you, as in Fig. 1. Bring the forefinger of the other hand under the lower tip of the stick, and snap it toward you with a sudden movement of the finger (Fig. 2). If this is done properly, the upper end of the match will now be on the other side of the safety pin. Swing the stick back to its original position and repeat. The movement is so fast that the illusion of the stick going through the pin is perfect.

68. *Cross Your Palm*

EFFECT: A line is drawn on the palm of the hand with the end of a burnt match. The hand is closed into a fist, and another line is drawn on the back of the hand, in another direction. After a bit of hocus-pocus, the line on the back of the hand is erased. When the hand is opened, it is found that the line which was drawn on the back of the hand has mysteriously penetrated the hand and crossed the line on the palm.

PRESENTATION: With the burnt end of a match, draw a short line so that it crosses the natural line in your palm (see illustration). Close your hand into a tight fist (do not curl the fingers in, but lay them flat in the palm) and turn it, back up. On the back of the hand, draw another line of simi-

MARK

lar length, directly over the line on the palm. Draw this line in an opposite direction from the line on the palm. Place the fingers of your other hand on this mark and rub it in a rotary motion, making some sort of magical incantation. Pick up your hand and show that the mark has been erased. Open the hand and turn it palm up. It will be found that the original line on the palm is now crossed by a similar line, which, apparently, was the line drawn on the back of the hand.

The explanation, of course, is that the line is crossed automatically by itself when the fist is closed.

69. Telepathic Coins

EFFECT: Five coins are placed on the table. A spectator touches one of them. The performer's assistant names the coin, though he is out of the room.

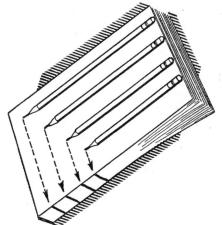

PREPARATION: Place five pencils in your upper vest or shirt pocket. Four of these pencils should be of one color. These pencils should be of graduated sizes: the smallest a half inch shorter than the second, the second a half inch shorter than the third, and the third a half inch shorter than the fourth. On the edge of a pad, mark off from the bottom of the pad the sizes of these pencils, as shown in illustration.

Place this pad in your side pocket. Along with these four pencils put a pencil of another color, and of any size, into the same pocket.

PRESENTATION: Ask several spectators to place five different coins on the table, so that you have one penny, one nickel, one dime, one quarter, and one half dollar. Tell the audience that you are going to demonstrate an experiment in telepathy. Hand the pad to your assistant and tell her, or him, to go into another room. When the assistant has gone, ask anyone in the audience to touch one of the coins. Then tell the audience to concentrate mentally on that coin. Now say in a loud voice, so that your assistant may hear, "Will you please write down the denomination of the coin we are thinking of."

After a slight hesitation the assistant comes in to borrow a pencil. Hand her, or him, the appropriate pencil: the smallest designating the penny, the next the nickel, the third the dime and the largest the quarter. The fifth and odd pencil designates the half dollar. The assistant leaves the room with the pencil, and all that she, or he, has to do is measure the pencil according to the mark on the edge of the pad. This will tell her, or him, what coin has been selected. Of course, the fifth indifferent pencil does not have to be measured, but always designates the half dollar.

70. Breaking a Pencil with a Dollar Bill

EFFECT: The performer folds a dollar bill in half. With it he hits the center of a pencil, which is held in the spectator's hands, and the pencil breaks in two.

PRESENTATION: Give a long pencil to a spectator and ask him to hold it tightly with both hands out in front of him, and in a horizontal position. Borrow a dollar bill from another spectator, and fold it in half lengthwise; rub the finger of the other hand over its edge as if you are testing

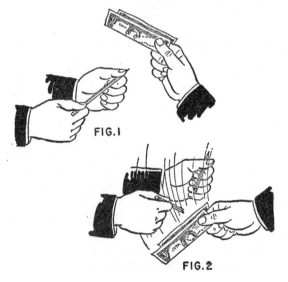

FIG. I

FIG. 2

its sharpness. Grasp the end of the dollar bill with the thumb and fore-finger (Fig. 1). Raise it up high over the pencil and bring it down on the center of the pencil with a sharp blow. The pencil will easily break in two. What really happens is that when you come down on the pencil with the bill, you quickly extend your forefinger under cover of the bill. Though it seems to the audience as if the bill itself broke the pencil, the finger does the actual work (Fig. 2).

Challenge any spectator to do this. His frustration and exasperation will increase with each effort.

71. *Replacing a Button without a Needle*

EFFECT: The performer tears off a button from a spectator's vest, and by a mere wave of the hand restores the button to its original position.

PRESENTATION: The buttons on men's vests are usually of three colors, black, brown, or gray. They are of uniform sizes. Prepare yourself by placing three such buttons in your side change pocket. Having noticed a spectator in the audience who is wearing a vest, observe the color of the buttons, and secrete the proper button in your left hand.

Now call up the spectator as a volunteer. Unbutton the lowest button on his vest and place the thumb of your left hand over the lower edge of the button, at the same time secreting the loose button under the tip of the thumb (Fig. 1). The loose button should overlap the real button slightly. With your right hand, pick on the sewed button a few times, and during one of these motions cover the button with the hand. Under cover of this hand, slide the loose button upward, making it visible, and cover-ing the actual button with the tip of your thumb (Fig. 2). Remove your

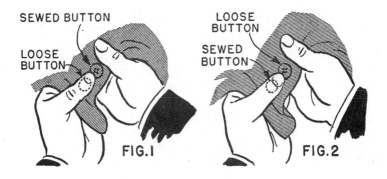

SEWED BUTTON   LOOSE BUTTON
LOOSE BUTTON   SEWED BUTTON
FIG.1   FIG.2

right hand and everything appears to be all right. Take hold of the loose
button with the fingers of your right hand, and with a sudden snap, remove it from the vest. This should look as if you have actually torn the
button off. Before the spectator is able to regain his composure, wave
your right hand toward the vest, remove the thumb of the left hand, and
show that the button has been magically replaced.

72. Spots Before the Eyes

EFFECT: The blade of a knife is shown on both sides, several times.
Sometimes two spots are seen on each side, sometimes one, and sometimes they completely vanish, after which they are magically restored.

PREPARATION: For this effect you need a small butter knife, the blade of
which is uniformly shaped (Fig. 1). However, if this is not available, cut
a paddle out of a piece of soft wood. A doctor's tongue depressor is ideal
for this (Fig. 2). Cut out two circular dots from a piece of black tissue or
crepe paper. Affix them with a bit of moisture to the blade of the knife,
or paddle, on one surface (Figs. 1 or 2).

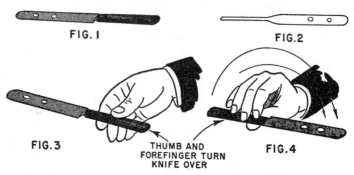

FIG. 1   FIG.2

FIG.3   THUMB AND   FIG.4
                    FOREFINGER TURN
                      KNIFE OVER

PRESENTATION: Hold the handle of the knife, or paddle, with the thumb
and forefinger of the right hand. The tip of the thumb should be on the
right edge of the handle, and the tip of the forefinger on the left edge of
the handle. Hold the blade horizontally, pointing away from you, with
the surface showing the two spots facing up (Fig. 3).

Now say, "As you see, I have a paddle [or knife] in my hand, and
there are two spots on it. As a matter of fact, there are also two spots on
the other side." As you say this, turn the paddle over, following an arc
toward you, but as you do this move the tips of the thumb and forefingers, the thumb forward and the first finger backward, rotating the

paddle so that when you apparently show the other side you actually
show the same side. If done correctly, the rotation of the paddle cannot
be seen, and it should look as if you are showing the other side. This may
require a bit of practice (Fig. 4). Bring the paddle down to its original
position, reversing the movement of the fingers. This will show the same
side with the spots again.

Now say, "You have seen two spots on each side of the blade. However, if I pass my hand over it you will notice that the spots disappear."
Under cover of the hand, as you bring it over the paddle, rotate the paddle, bringing the empty surface of the blade up. Remove your hand and
show the empty blade. Repeat the move, as above (Fig. 4), showing the
other side, which is also empty. Bring the paddle down again, pass your
hand over it, restoring the spots with the same undercover move. You
may, if you wish at this time, scrape off one of the spots and tell the spectator that if you scrape the spots off one side, the corresponding spots on
the other side will also vanish. Demonstrate this with the above moves.

73. *The Match Box Coin Vanish*

EFFECT: A borrowed and marked coin is openly placed in a match box.
After a magical wave of the performer's hand, the box is opened and
the coin is found to have vanished.

PREPARATION: Get a match box that holds wooden matches. Take the
drawer out, and in the bottom of one of its ends, cut a slit through
which a coin may pass easily (Fig. 1). Fill the drawer with loose matches
and insert it back into its cover. Place this box in your pocket.

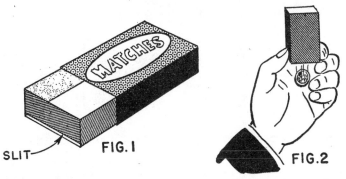

PRESENTATION: Borrow a coin from a spectator and have him mark it for
future identification. Do not handle this coin, but let the spectator hold
it. Tell the audience that the coin will be put some place where you are

unable to touch it. Place your hands in your pocket as if you are looking
for something. Remove the match box from your pocket, and say, "This
is just the thing."

Open the unslotted end of the box and dump out all the matches. Hold
the box with thumb on top and fingers on bottom. Tell the spectator to
drop the coin into the empty box. Close the box, shake it a few times to
prove that the coin is still there, but at the end of this action, hold the
box vertically in your hand and allow the coin to slide through the slot
into your hand (Fig. 2). This will not be seen by the audience. Place the
box on the floor or on a table. Wave your hand over the box in a magical
way, and then tell the spectator to open the box. He will be surprised to
see that the coin has vanished. You may make the coin reappear any way
you wish.

74. Scarne's Think of a Number

EFFECT: A card, upon which there are sixteen numbers, is handed to a
spectator. He is told to think of any number on this card. The performer
taps the numbers on the card with a pencil, and stops at the mentally
selected number. (A recent creation by the author.)

PREPARATION: Make up a card with numbers on it, as shown in illustration.

1	15	3	11
5	11	7	1
9	3	5	13
13	7	15	9

PRESENTATION: Hand the card with the numbers on it to a spectator. Tell
him to think of any number on this card, and place it face up on the
table. Tell the spectator that as you tap your pencil or finger on the numbers shown on the card he is to count the taps mentally, but is to begin
with the number he is thinking of, and count up from there. For example, if he selected number 7, he would count your first tap as 8, your sec-

ond tap as 9, and so on. Tell him to say, "Stop," when his count reaches 25. Your pencil will be resting mysteriously on the number he was thinking of.

EXPLANATION AND METHOD: The performer may point his pencil to any numbers on the card he desires for his first nine taps. But for his tenth tap, his pencil must be pointed at number 15. Thereafter, he must tap his pencil on the numbers in the following order.

TAPS		TAPS	
ELEVEN	any number	EIGHTEEN	number 7
TWELVE	number 13	NINETEEN	any number
THIRTEEN	any number	TWENTY	number 5
FOURTEEN	number 11	TWENTY-ONE	any number
FIFTEEN	any number	TWENTY-TWO	number 3
SIXTEEN	number 9	TWENTY-THREE	any number
SEVENTEEN	any number	TWENTY-FOUR	number 1

If the performer follows the instructions listed above, whenever the spectator says, "Stop," the pencil will be resting on the selected number. *Note:* The performer should tap the pencil slowly, so that the pencil will still be resting on the number when the spectator says, "Stop."

75. When a Break Is Not a Break

EFFECT: A wooden match is placed in a handkerchief. Under cover of the handkerchief the match is broken. When the match is uncovered, it is found to be magically restored.

PREPARATION: The performer requires a handkerchief with a hem which has an opening on each end. Into the opening of the hem, the performer inserts a wooden match. Then he places the handkerchief in his breast pocket. Also, he must carry some spare matches.

PRESENTATION: Remove the handkerchief from your pocket and spread it on the table. Ask to borrow a wooden match. If one is not forthcoming, use one of your own. Place the match in the center of the handkerchief (see illustration), and roll the handkerchief around it. Pick up the handkerchief and have a spectator feel the match through the handkerchief, but be sure you allow him to feel only the match which is hidden in the hem of the handkerchief. Ask the spectator to break the match in two through the handkerchief. You then complete the job by breaking the match into quarters. The spectator will hear the sound of the breaking pieces. Place the handkerchief on the table and unroll it slowly; at the same time repeat the magical words, "Scarne, Scarne." After the

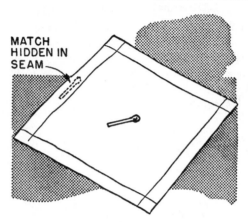

MATCH HIDDEN IN SEAM

handkerchief is unrolled, have the spectator pick up the unharmed match, then immediately place the handkerchief back in your pocket.

76. Disobeying Gravity

EFFECT: The performer holds his hand up, fingers extended and palm vertical. He places the metal blade of a table knife in various positions on the palm or fingers of the hand. The knife sticks to the hand in any position.

PREPARATION: The hand is prepared before the trick by applying to the surface of the hands and fingers a very weak solution of glue. This is allowed to dry. If the hand is cool, it can be examined and felt without arousing suspicion. Use only a very thin layer of glue.

PRESENTATION: Announce that you are going to demonstrate the magical

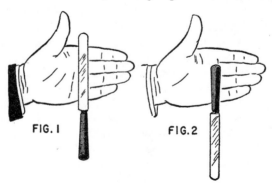

FIG. I   FIG. 2

magnetism of your hand. Hand a table knife to the spectators for thorough examination. Have them look your hand over to make sure that you have nothing hidden in it. Hold the hand up in front of you, fingers extended and palm vertical. Place the surface of the blade of the knife on the palm or fingers, and it will stay there. Two positions are shown in Figs. 1 and 2.

Note: When the hand is examined, make sure it is fairly cool. To moisten and warm your hand again before the experiment, close the fingers into the palm, and hold that way for a short while until you are ready to do the trick.

77. *A Cigarette Production*

EFFECT: The performer shows that his hand is empty, and then proceeds to produce a cigarette from his elbow.

PRESENTATION: Secretly place a cigarette in your collar at the back of your neck. Show that your hands are empty. Raise your right hand, bending your elbow, and with your left hand feel below your elbow as if you are looking for something. At the same time, your right hand reaches behind your collar, removes the cigarette, and secretes it in the hand. When you do not get anything from your elbow, look surprised, and say, "I'll try the other one." Bend your left elbow, raising your arm as before. Bring your right hand under the elbow, visibly removing the cigarette. The reaching of your hand to the back of the neck will not be noticed, as everybody will be concentrating on your elbow. This is a short, quick trick, but very effective.

78. *The Famous Belt Trick*

The Belt Trick, or Find the Loop, was a favorite of carnival grifters several years ago. Plenty of gullible people were taken for their last dollar by this innocent-looking swindle.

EFFECT: A belt is laid on the table by the performer in rolled-up fashion. The spectator is handed a pencil and requested to insert it into the center loop of the belt, which he does. The performer pulls the belt by its two ends, and the belt clears the pencil or is caught in the center loop. Either of these results is controlled by the performer.

PRESENTATION: Double a belt in half, then roll it and lay it on table. Request a spectator to insert a pencil into the center loop, which will catch the belt when the belt is withdrawn. He does as directed, and you with-

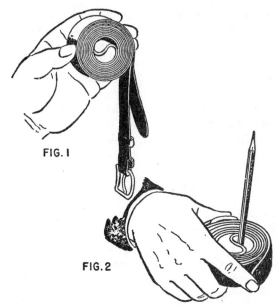

FIG. I

FIG. 2

draw the belt by pulling the two ends away from the pencil. Naturally, the belt is caught by the center loop. Now loop it again, and say to the spectator that you will bet him a cigar that he cannot find the center loop again. He tries, but always fails. The secret lies in the fact that when you roll the belt up, you must do as follows in order to control the result.

Double the belt, but the buckle side must be a little longer and must be rolled toward the center (Fig. 1). The belt is rolled until the unbuckled tip of the belt is reached and held by the forefinger of the right hand (Fig. 2).

Now have the spectator insert the pencil in the loop. If he guesses wrong, merely pull both ends of the belt with the right hand. If he guesses the correct loop, release the tip of the belt held by the forefinger. It will swing around to the buckled end. Then pull. This way he's wrong every time, and you have a game that can't be beat. But, don't play unless *you* pull the belt.

79. *Houdini's Coin Vanish*

EFFECT: This is a little trick that was made famous by the great Houdini. The performer places a coin in the palm of his hand. This is covered with a handkerchief. The spectators feel for the coin under the handkerchief to verify its presence. Yet, when the handkerchief is removed, the coin has vanished.

PRESENTATION: To make this trick more effective, remove your coat and roll up your sleeves. Place a large coin in the palm of your right hand. Keeping the palm up, drape a handkerchief over the hand. Pass among several spectators and ask them to verify the presence of the coin in your palm, by placing their hands under the handkerchief and feeling the coin. After they have all been satisfied, step back and ask one of the spectators to tie the ends of the handkerchief around your wrists. This produces, you say, almost impossible conditions under which the coin may vanish. However, you brazenly announce that you will make it do so. After a couple of seconds, ask one of the spectators to untie and remove the handkerchief from your hand. The coin has completely vanished.

EXPLANATION: All you need to work this trick is a confederate in the audience. He is the last spectator to feel for the coin under the handkerchief. He actually removes the coin. If this is done without arousing suspicion, the trick becomes extremely effective.

80. Strip Tease

EFFECT: A strip of paper with a message on it is torn to pieces by the performer, and then is restored almost immediately.

PREPARATION: Print two identical messages on two strips of thin paper, of exactly the same size (about five inches by sixteen inches). The message may be anything: a funny saying, foreign lettering, someone's name, in fact, anything to which you can fit appropriate patter. When completed, the two strips of paper and the printing thereon should look exactly alike. Take one of the strips and fold it along its length in a series of small pleats. This will give you a small thin packet. Straighten out the bottom-most pleat (Fig. 1). Place some paste in the middle of the second

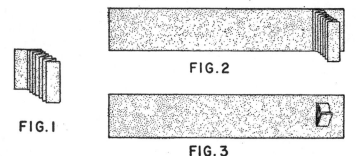

FIG.2

FIG.1

FIG.3

pleat, and glue this onto the back and to the right of the second strip of paper. This should be glued about two inches from the end and equidistant from the long sides (Fig. 2). When this has set, fold the free pleat over the packet. Fold the upper part of the packet down, and then fold the lower part upward (Fig. 3).

PRESENTATION: With your thumb over the packet in the rear, pick up the unfolded strip, with the message facing the audience. Patter along appropriate lines, and then begin to tear the paper. You may tear down the middle first, putting the pieces together so that the packet is always in the rear. Keep tearing until you have several approximately square pieces in your hand. Fold these pieces together, toward the audience, into a small square packet. Wave your hands up and down once or twice, and during this action reverse the entire package so that the torn pieces are facing you and the untorn strip is facing the audience. Unfold the packet facing the audience, always keeping the packet of torn pieces toward you. When you have the strip fully extended, the audience will not be able to see the torn pieces that are held in place in back with the thumb, and this will look like a miraculous restoration.

Note: In gluing the folded strip on the back of the duplicate strip, the lettering should be inverted as compared to the other strip. This is necessary so that when the entire folded packet is turned over, immediately before restoration, the restored message will be readable.

81. *Ring Levitation*

EFFECT: The performer holds a pencil in a vertical position. A ring is placed over it. The ring rises or falls, according to the command of the performer.

PREPARATION: Take an unused long wooden pencil, the type without an eraser on it, and cut a slit with a razor across one of its ends. Make this slit a quarter-inch deep. Take a piece of fine but strong black thread about the length of your arm, and knot one end. Place this end into the slot of the pencil. The knot will prevent its slipping out, as shown in illustration. Tie the other end of the thread on the lowest button of your vest or coat, and place the pencil, thus prepared, into your upper vest or coat pocket.

PRESENTATION: Tell the audience that you are about to demonstrate the power of mind over matter. Borrow a ring from a spectator. Remove the pencil from your pocket, and holding it vertically in front of you, with

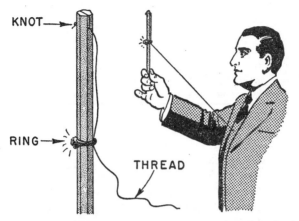

the slit end upward (holding it fairly close to your body), drop the ring over it. This will appear quite innocuous, as the thread cannot be seen and the ring will fall naturally to the bottom of the pencil. Command the ring to rise. Slowly moving the pencil away from your body, the ring will rise because of the tightening of the thread. By gauging your movements, you may command it to rise to the top, or stop anywhere along the pencil. You may also command it to fall at any time.

82. *A Drink on the House*

EFFECT: Water is poured from a pitcher into several glasses. At a command from the performer, the water in each glass either becomes wine or remains water. Repeated pourings into the glasses, and back and forth into the pitcher, produce either wine or water at a command.

PREPARATION: Fill a transparent glass pitcher with warm water, and add two teaspoons full of tannic acid (powder); stir until dissolved. Have six empty glasses on the table. Place a pinch of Oxalic Acid crystals into one. Pour a small amount of hot water into this and stir until dissolved. Into each of three other glasses, put three to four drops of Tincture of Iron. Two glasses remain empty.

PRESENTATION: Tell the audience that you have discovered the very ancient magical secret of changing water into wine, and vice versa. Ask them which they would prefer, wine or water. If they say they want wine, fill a glass containing the drops of Tincture of Iron with the water from the pitcher. This will immediately appear red, and will look like wine. If water is called for, fill the glass containing Oxalic Acid. This will remain clear. Fill the other glasses and you will end up with three glasses of wine and three glasses of water. Empty the contents of all the glasses, except the one with Oxalic Acid, into the pitcher. The water in the pitcher immediately turns red (wine). Fill the empty glasses again, and you will have five glasses of "wine." Now pour the water from the Oxalic Acid glass back into the pitcher, and then follow with the wine from the other five glasses. All the liquid in the pitcher turns to "water." With the proper patter this experiment can be made quite entertaining and mysterious.

83. *A Cigarette Changes to a Dollar Bill*

EFFECT: A cigarette is soaked in water and then rolled between the hands. The cigarette disappears and a dollar bill appears in its place.

PREPARATION: Remove the tobacco from the paper of a cigarette. Roll up a dollar bill and place it within the paper so that it looks like a whole cigarette. Place this in an open pack of similar cigarettes.

PRESENTATION: Say to the audience that you smoke the most expensive cigarettes in the world. Remove the open pack from your pocket and take out a cigarette. This, of course, unbeknownst to the spectators, is the prepared one. Dip the whole cigarette into water for a moment and

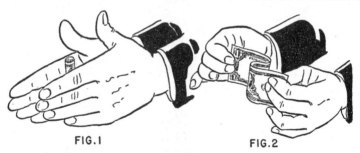

FIG. I   FIG.2

then remove it, placing it between your hands. Roll the cigarette briskly between the hands a few times (Fig. 1). When you open your hands, all traces of the cigarette paper are gone, but in its place is a rolled-up dollar bill (Fig. 2), which you unroll and show to the audience. Naturally, you also show that your hands are empty. The secret of this effect lies in the fact that the wet cigarette paper, when rolled and rubbed as above, will practically disappear.

Note: To remove tobacco from cigarette, loosen tobacco by rolling cigarette between hands, then push tobacco out with a pencil.

84. *Stick Through Hat*

EFFECT: The performer removes his hat and passes a stick through its crown, yet it remains absolutely undamaged.

PREPARATION: The performer must secure a soft felt hat, either his own or one borrowed from a spectator, and a stick about eighteen inches in length and about one-fourth to one-half inch in diameter.

PRESENTATION: Straighten out the crown of the hat and place the stick in the hat. With the right hand twirl the hat on the end of the stick several times (Fig. 1). The left hand grasps the brim of the hat with the four fingers. Apply pressure on the left thumb and form sort of a ditch in the

FIG.1   FIG.2   FIG.3   FIG.4   FIG.5   FIG.6

hat on the side facing you (Fig. 2). Place the thumb of the right hand where the left thumb is, fingers of right hand grasping stick and the inside of the hat. Now the left hand grasps the inner folds of the ditch and makes an inside crease of this ditch by applying pressure on the inner folds of the ditch. This forms an externally deep crease (Fig. 3). Hold the inner folds of the crease between the thumb and forefingers of your left hand, and remove your right hand, holding the stick (Fig. 4). Strike the stick on the table with your right hand, showing it is solid. Now bring the stick up and push it through the crease from the outside (Fig. 5). Push the stick up and down several times, finally bringing the stick out from the top of the crown (Fig. 6). This will appear to the audience as if the stick has completely penetrated the crown of the hat. Straighten the hat out and pass it around for examination.

85. *Classical Rope Trick*

EFFECT: A rope is cut right through its middle. Two ends are tied together. At a magical command by the performer, the rope is restored and the knot vanishes.

PREPARATION: Get a soft rope, similar to an indoor clothesline, approximately three to four feet in length. If a rope of this type is not available, a length of heavy string may be used. The performer will also require scissors.

PRESENTATION: Pick up the rope, and hold it in the left hand, one end between the thumb and forefinger (this end will be referred to as A) and the other end between the tips of the forefinger and second finger (this end will be referred to as B) (Fig. 1). The palm of the hand is facing you.

Place the four fingers of the right hand around the lower loop facing you, the hand being held below the loop (Fig. 2). Bring this loop up, draped over the four fingers of the right hand. The right hand almost reaches the palm of the left hand, and the second and third fingers of the

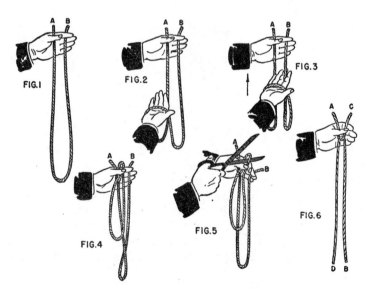

FIG.1   FIG.2   FIG.3   FIG.4   FIG.5   FIG.6

right hand grasp the rope seven inches below end A (Fig. 3). Holding the rope firmly between the second and third fingers, pull the rope through the loop, which is resting on the palm of your right hand, and continue to bring the rope up to meet your left hand. Form a loop with the rope held in your right hand, about the size of the end of the rope held in your left hand. Transfer this loop to the left hand, where it is held between the thumb and forefinger, as is end A (Fig. 4). Now take the scissors in your right hand and cut through the loop held in the left hand (Fig. 5).

You are now holding four ends in your left hand. The end held between the thumb and the palm of the hand is end A. There are two ends between the thumb tip and forefinger. The end nearest A is end C, the end nearest B is end D. You now apply pressure with the thumb and firmly hold ends A and C. Allow ends D and B to fall (Fig. 6). Tie ends A and C together with a double knot (not too tightly) and show the rope now, full length and tied together.

Starting with either one of the two hanging ends, wind the rope around your left hand, and as the rope slides through the right hand, retain the knot in it, finally removing the knot with the right hand. Done in a fast motion, the removal of the knot is not seen by the audience. Unwind the rope from the hand, throw it out to the audience, showing it to be completely restored, and while they are examining it, secretly place the knot in your pocket to get rid of it.

86. *Spin the Coin*

EFFECT: The performer tells a spectator to spin a coin on a table top, and by mere concentration is able to tell whether the coin falls heads or tails. This may be repeated, and the performer never misses.

NICK
IN COIN

PREPARATION: Use a nickel, and with a sharp knife, upon one of its surfaces right at the edge, make a fairly large nick, but not large enough to be seen except upon close examination (see illustration). You will find that the sound of the spinning nickel, while it is coming to rest, is now different on the nicked side as compared to the other side. Spin it yourself a few times and you will notice the difference. If the nick is on the tail side of the coin, when this comes to rest it sounds flat and clicky. Therefore, the side that turns up is heads. If the head falls, it will sound clear and ringing, and a spin will last slightly longer. Therefore, the coin will turn up tails.

PRESENTATION: Hand the nickel to a spectator and tell him to spin it while your back is turned. Tell him that by concentration alone you will be able to call it correctly when it comes to rest, heads or tails. Wait a moment after it stops spinning, and with a very thoughtful attitude, announce the result.

87. *Roll Your Own*

EFFECT: The performer removes a sheet of cigarette paper from a packet, pours in imaginary tobacco, rolls it into a cigarette, lights it casually, and smokes it. (The cigarette is fully packed and smokable.)

PREPARATION: Place a cigarette between two sheets of cigarette paper. Paste together the edges of these sheets so that it contains the cigarette but from a short distance looks like one sheet of paper. Place this back in the packet of cigarette papers and cover it by another sheet.

PRESENTATION: Remove the packet of cigarette papers from your pocket and take out the top single sheet. Go through the actions of rolling a

cigarette with imaginary tobacco, but somehow you have difficulty and do not succeed. Crush the paper and throw it away. Now remove the second sheet (the loaded one). Hold it cupped between your fingers, ready for the tobacco (see illustration). Held this way it looks perfectly innocent. Pour in some imaginary tobacco, going through the actions that you often see a cowboy do in westerns. A little bit of acting is required. Roll the cigarette, lick it, and place it in your mouth. Bring a lit match to it, light it, and casually puff away. Instead of the paper flaring up, as your spectators expect it to do, you casually continue smoking it. They will be surprised and may even examine the cigarette (not too carefully, of course).

88. *Vest Through Coat*

EFFECT: The performer challenges any man in the audience to remove his vest without removing his coat first. The spectators will concede finally that this is impossible, as it would require the passing of a solid

FIG.1. FIG.2 FIG.3

FIG.4 FIG.5

through a solid. The performer now calls up one of the spectators, who is wearing a vest, and proceeds to do the impossible.

PRESENTATION: Stand in front of the spectator. Have him remove all objects from the pockets of his coat and vest. Unbutton his coat and vest. Bring the right-hand lower front corner of the spectator's coat up and through the right armpit of the vest, from the outside in. Bring the armpit over the (Fig. 1) right shoulder, and pull his arm completely through (Fig. 2). Swing the armpit around the back and toward the left side; at the same time keep pulling his coat through (Fig. 3). When the armpit of the vest reaches the left shoulder, bring it over the shoulder and pull his left arm through. Then pull the entire left side of the coat through this armpit, from the inside out. The vest is now hanging by its left armpit, inside the coat, on the left shoulder (Fig. 4). Bring the loose end of the vest through the left coat sleeve, and pull the vest right through and off. It will come off easily as there are no encumbrances now (Fig. 5). Do these actions quickly, so that the spectators, even if they watch closely, will be confused and will not be able to repeat the moves.

89. *Animated Cigar Band*

EFFECT: The performer places a cigar band over the tip of one of his fingers. Moving the hand in a quick up and down motion, the cigar band seems to jump from the tip of one finger to the tip of the other.

PRESENTATION: Remove a cigar band from a cigar and place it on the tip of the second finger of your right hand. Tell the audience that you have the power, because of your magical abilities, to give life to the band so

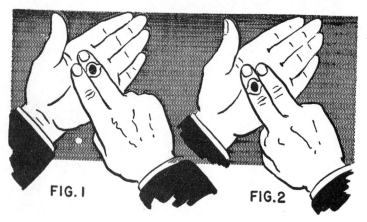

FIG. 1   FIG. 2

that it is able to fly instantaneously from one finger tip to another. Place your index finger and the second finger (with the band) close together at the edge of the palm of your left hand (Fig. 1). Curl the other fingers in. Bring the hand up and down with short sudden movements, and at the same time curl your index finger into your hand and bring up the third finger. This move cannot be seen by the audience, as the up and down movement is too fast (Fig. 2). It now appears as if the band jumped from one finger to another. Actually, you have just substituted the third finger for the first one. Repeat the movements several times, and the band actually appears to jump from one finger to another. With proper movements and timing, this is an excellent example of visual deception.

90. Salivary Repair

EFFECT: The performer has a string cut into two, places two ends in his mouth, takes hold of the other ends, and after a bit of chewing, removes the string from the mouth fully restored.

PRESENTATION: Announce that inasmuch as you are a magician even your saliva contains magical qualities. Take a piece of string about three feet long and tie the two ends together. The string is held by the four fingers of the right hand and the four fingers of the left hand. The right hand holds the knot and is facing palm upward. The left hand is facing palm downward (Fig. 1). You now reverse the position of the hands by turning the wrists. The right hand now faces palm downward, the left palm faces upward. This movement twists the string between the

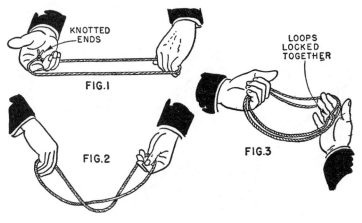

FIG.1 KNOTTED ENDS LOOPS LOCKED TOGETHER FIG.2 FIG.3

hands (Fig. 2). Then bring the right hand over to meet the left hand, in the above described position, and let the string fall from the right hand onto the left hand. Immediately place the knuckles of the right hand against those of the left hand, then pull both hands apart, thereby forming a double loop. This action has caused two loops to be locked together in the right hand, forming a lock (Fig. 3 shows this, as viewed by the performer).

Hold the string covering the "lock" between the thumb and forefinger of the right hand. With the left hand, grasp both pieces of string about an inch away from the locked position. Now ask a spectator to take the scissors and cut the two strands of string between the fingers. After the string has been cut, allow the left ends to drop, and still covering the locked position with the thumb and forefinger of your right hand, show the two pieces of string.

Place the ends and the loop held in the right hand into the mouth. Take hold of the opposite ends with each hand and go through the movement of chewing, in the meantime manipulating with your mouth to remove the small piece. Hide the piece so removed under your tongue, and take the string from the mouth, showing it to be completely restored. Hand it out for examination, if you wish.

91. *The Unstickable Pin*

EFFECT: The performer makes an ordinary straight pin stand up vertically by sticking its point lightly into a hard surface. Then he challenges

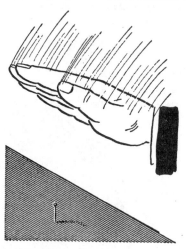

anyone in the audience to make the pin penetrate the surface by giving it a sharp blow with the palm of his hand. No one will have the courage to do this. You then proceed to do it yourself. Even though the pin does not penetrate the surface, but is merely bent in two, the palm of the hand remains completely undamaged.

PRESENTATION: Stick the point of an ordinary pin into a hard surface, making it stand up vertically, as shown in illustration. Tell the audience that due to your magical powers, the skin of your palm is absolutely impenetrable. You can, with one blow of the palm of your hand, drive the pin into the table. Emphasize this statement by bringing your palm down with a real sharp blow on the surface of the table. This helps to harden the surface of the palm momentarily. Challenge someone in the audience. No one will volunteer, being afraid that the pin will penetrate the palm. Now bring the palm down with a sharp blow on the head of the pin. When the hand is lifted the pin has not penetrated the table, but it is bent in two. You will barely feel the pin on your palm. Even after you have done this, no one else will have the courage to try to duplicate your feat.

92. Flexible Pencil

EFFECT: The performer holds a pencil horizontally between the thumb and forefinger of his hand. When he waves his hand up and down, the pencil becomes flexible and bends as if it were made of rubber.

PRESENTATION: Take hold of a pencil with the thumb and forefinger of your hand, about one-third the distance from one end. Hold it extended and in a horizontal position. Hold it very lightly and loosely between the fingers. Move your hand up and down in short, rapid, brisk moves, and allow the ends of the pencil to seesaw up and down. As the pencil seesaws in the hand, an illusion is created—it looks as though the ends are flexible and bend and flap like the ends of a soft rubber bar. Try this, it is very mystifying and amusing.

93. The Non-Burning Shoelace

EFFECT: The performer exhibits what looks like an ordinary shoelace. He holds up one end and asks someone to burn it. After it has burnt for quite a distance, the performer passes his hand over the damaged end, and the lace is shown to be completely restored.

PREPARATION: Obtain a pair of shoelaces, the type that has hollow strands. Make a small hole in one side of the center of one of the laces. Thread the end of the other lace through this hole and up one end, bringing its metal tip out near the metal tip of the other lace. Cut off the remaining half, leaving a small end protruding at the center, and sew this end to the first lace (Fig. 1).

PRESENTATION: Hold up the prepared lace for the spectators to see, covering the double end with the fingers of your left hand. With the thumb

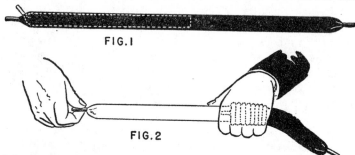

FIG. I

FIG. 2

and forefinger of the left hand, grip the protruding tip of the inserted half lace. Bring the other hand to this end, and gripping the end of the whole lace, bring it with a sliding motion to the center of the lace. This portion of the whole lace will pleat itself within the right hand like an accordion. When the right hand reaches the center, hold it there in order to hide the pleated portion (Fig. 2). Hold up this end, so uncovered, and have someone hold a lit match to it until it burns. Allow it to burn about halfway, releasing and dropping the left hand. Bring the left hand over to the right, and with the thumb and forefinger of this hand, grasp the metal tip enclosed in the right hand. Pull this out sharply. This movement will straighten out the pleated end and will enclose any remnant of the burnt end. You show the restored lace and may even pass it around for superficial examination.

94. The Match from Nowhere

EFFECT: The performer takes a box of matches out of his pocket. He opens the drawer of the match box, removes a match and closes the box. Striking the match on the side of the box he finds that it is a dud, and throws it away. He brings his right hand to the box as if to open it to remove another match. Mysteriously a lit match appears in his hand.

PREPARATION: On the striking side of a match box, with a small piece of wax, stick one of the matches. Stick it parallel to the side and along its lower edge. The head of the match should face toward the left (see illustration).

PRESENTATION: Remove the match box from your pocket and hold it in your left hand, faked match toward you with match head to the left. Open the drawer of the box and remove a match. Close the box. Secretly reverse the removed match and strike the wrong end against the side of the box a few times. After a few tries, look at it in disgust, and throw it away as a dud. Bring your right hand toward the box as if to open it for another match, but, instead, grasp the end of the fixed match, break its seal, and with the same move strike it. Mysteriously, seemingly from nowhere, a lit match makes its appearance.

Make these moves without hesitation and the trick will be very effective.

95. Fourth-Dimensional Knot

EFFECT: The performer challenges anyone to tie a knot in a string that is being held at both ends, without letting go of either end. After some unsuccessful attempts by several spectators, the performer proceeds to perform this feat.

PRESENTATION: Lay the string on the table. Fold your arms, one above the other, with your left hand over the right upper arm and your right hand under the left upper arm. While your arms are thus folded, grasp one end of the string with one hand, and grasp the other end of the string with the other hand. Separate your arms by pulling them in opposite directions. A knot will appear in the center of the string, demonstrating the performer's superior prowess.

Another more elaborate and much more baffling method is shown below. Holding the string as in Fig. 1, go through the movements of loop-

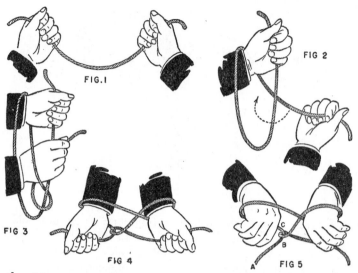

FIG.1

FIG 2

FIG 3

FIG 4

FIG 5

ing the string, as in Figs. 2 and 3. The string and your hands will be looped together, as in Fig. 4. Turn your hands down, allowing the loops to fall off the hands. However, here there occurs a subtle move. As you allow the loops to fall, release end A (Fig. 5), and allow it to slip through loop B, and at the same time grasp part C of end A. This move sounds more difficult than it is—it really is almost automatic and cannot be seen when executed without hesitation. Follow the diagrams and instructions with a piece of string or rope in your hand.

96. Rope Through the Neck

EFFECT: A rope is wound around the neck of the performer. Grasping both ends, he pulls at the rope and it appears to go completely through his neck.

PRESENTATION: Take a piece of rope about five or six feet long and drape it on the back of your neck, letting the ends hang loosely on your chest. The end that hangs over your right shoulder should be about a foot longer than the other end (Fig. 1). With your right hand, grasp the shorter end of the rope (the one over your left shoulder) (Fig. 2). Bring your left hand under your right, grasp the longer end of the rope, and form a loop (Fig. 3). Bring the loop over your left shoulder and around your neck, stopping midway behind your neck, and tuck the loop under your shirt collar. Immediately thereafter, bring your right hand (holding

FIG.1 FIG.2 FIG 3

FIG.4 FIG.5

the shorter end of the rope) completely around the neck in the same direction. The function of the loop tucked under your shirt is to prevent the loop from slipping. From the front it looks as though the rope is wound completely around the performer's neck (Fig. 4).

All you have to do now is pull forward with both ends of the rope, and it will clear the neck (Fig. 5), appearing as if the rope had gone through the neck.

Note: The above moves should be practiced so that you can do this trick neatly and without hesitation.

97. *Cut-Up*

EFFECT: A string is placed lengthwise in a piece of paper, which is then folded over it. The paper and the string are cut in half. Yet, when the string is held up, it is seen to be unharmed.

PRESENTATION: Use a fairly heavy piece of string. Fold a piece of stiff paper with two folds and lay the string in it (Fig. 1). Fold over the wider side of the paper, and then fold the narrower side over this. However,

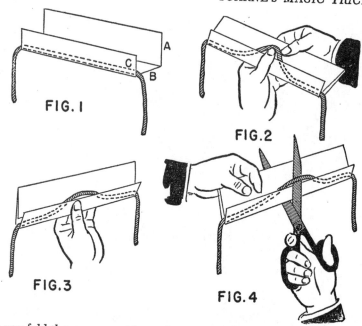

FIG. I

FIG.2

FIG.3

FIG.4

as you fold the narrower side, with the tip of the thumb push the center
of the string out over the wider side (Fig. 2). This move should not be
seen by the spectators. Hold the entire thing now, as shown in Fig. 3,
thumb side toward yourself. Proceed to cut, as shown in Fig. 4. What
occurs is obvious. After the cut, allow the two pieces of paper to fall to
the floor, revealing that the string is still intact.

98. He Knows Your Number

EFFECT: The performer sends his assistant out of the room. A number,
between 1 and 100, is selected by any spectator in the audience. It is
written on a slip of paper, which is then folded. The assistant comes back
into the room, and after a bit of concentration, announces the number.

PREPARATION: Have a square or rectangular table in the room (or on the
platform). Mentally place the numbers from 1 to 10 on two edges of the
table (Fig. 1). The other two edges of the table are noted as zeros. This
placement is, of course, mutually worked out beforehand by both the
performer and his assistant.

PRESENTATION: Send your assistant out of the room. Ask the spectators
to decide on any number between 1 and 100. After this is done, write the

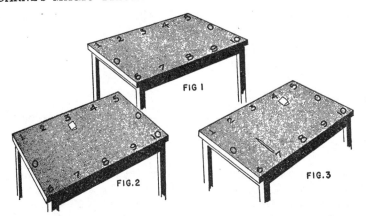

number on a slip of paper, and fold it so that the number cannot be seen. For a one-digit number—for example, 3—place the folded piece of paper on the table at the spot mentally designated as that number (Fig. 2). If a two-digit number—for example, 47—is chosen, place the paper at the position of the first digit and the pencil at the second (Fig. 3). If the number ends in zero—for example, 50—drop the paper at the proper spot and place the pencil at right angle to the "zero" edge of the table. Call the assistant back into the room. He concentrates a moment, looks at the table, and announces the number. Before the assistant returns, you may leave the room to obviate any suspicion of collusion.

99. Color-Changing Shoelace

EFFECT: The performer holds up, and shows freely, a black shoelace. The lace mysteriously changes from black to white, after the performer runs the lace from one end to another through his closed fist.

PREPARATION: Obtain a pair of shoelaces, one black and one white. The

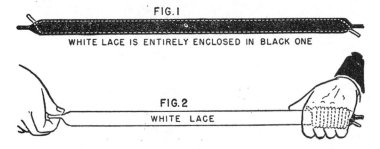

strands of these laces must be hollow. Make small openings right near the two tips of the black shoelace. Insert the tip of the white shoelace into one opening and thread it all the way through the black shoelace up to its tip. Bring the tip of the white lace through at one end (Fig. 1). Cut off the tip of white lace at other end, and sew this end to the black lace.

PRESENTATION: Hold up the prepared lace with thumb and forefinger of left hand, covering the two tips, and allowing the rest of the lace to hang loose. Call attention to its color—black. Say some "magic" words, and now enclose end with your right fist. With the fingers of the left hand grasp the protruding tip of the white lace, and holding the end of the black lace with the right hand, slide the hand down, pleating the black lace all the way to the other end, which will fold like an accordion within the right fist and will be hidden by it. Only the white lace will show now (Fig. 2). This is a very effective color transposition.

100. *Changing Checkers*

EFFECT: Two stacks of checkers are shown. One is all red and the other all black. Each of these is covered by a paper cone. At a command by the performer, the stacks change places: the red becomes black and the black becomes red.

PREPARATION: Take a black checker and paint its bottom red, or paste a piece of red paper on it so that when it is held toward the audience it looks like a red checker. On the bottom of a red checker do the same with black paint or paper. Arrange a stack of six or seven black checkers, the prepared black one on the bottom. Arrange another stack of six or seven red checkers, with the prepared red one on the bottom. Make two paper

cones by wrapping a piece of paper loosely but snugly around the stacks, and twisting the top of the paper, as shown in illustration.

PRESENTATION: Have the two stacks, red and black, standing in front of you on the table. Visibly cover each stack with a prepared cone. Now say to the audience, "If I were to move these stacks around a few times, you would probably not be able to follow the movements, and finally would wonder which stack is red, and which is black. This would not be magic, but sheer confusion." (Move the stacks around quickly so as to confuse the audience.) "Can anyone now tell me which is red and which is black?" Whether someone guesses or not, tip each stack back without removing the cone, and let the audience observe the bottom of each stack, the color of which is actually the reverse of the checkers. Continue, saying, "Now, as you see, this stack is the black one, and this is the red one. If I were to command each stack to change places—that would be magic. Let us try." Make a magical pass and command the checkers to change places. Remove the cones from the stacks, and lo and behold! the checkers actually have changed places. If presented properly, this effect will really worry the audience.

101. *Sleight of Foot*

EFFECT: The performer places a coin under the left toe of his shoe. Upon command, it vanishes from that position and appears under the toe of the right shoe.

PRESENTATION: This effect, for best results, should be done while sitting down. Hide a coin under the heel of the right shoe. Now, by swinging your feet to the side, on your heels, you may show that there is nothing under each toe. Show a coin to the audience. (This coin should have the same appearance, and, if possible, date, as the one hidden under the right heel.) Bring the coin down toward the left toe. As you pass the cuff of your trouser leg, allow the money to drop into this cuff and, without hesitation, bring your hand to the toe and make it appear as if you place the coin under it. Make sure that this is done smoothly, and without any jerky movements. Practice it awhile before performing. After doing this, carelessly show that the hand is empty. As you do this, move your right foot back so that the coin under the heel will now lie under the toe. Command the coin to move from where it is, under the left toe, to under the right toe. Raise your left foot, showing that the coin has vanished. Now raise your right foot, showing that the coin has been mysteriously transposed from under the left shoe to under the right shoe.

102. *Transposed Colors*

EFFECT: A red checker is placed in one match box, and a black checker is placed in another match box. The match boxes are marked accordingly. At a command from the performer, the checkers change places.

PREPARATION: Obtain two match boxes. On one end of one drawer mark a red cross. On one end of the other drawer mark a black cross. Have the drawers open at the opposite ends as the boxes are lying on the table. In addition, have one red and one black checker on the table.

PRESENTATION: Announce that you will attempt, by magical means, to have two checkers of different colors change places. Place the red checker into the drawer of the box marked by the black cross, and the black checker into the drawer of the box marked by the red cross. These marks are invisible to the audience, being hidden by the cover when the drawers are open. Close the drawers, and holding the previously marked ends down so that they cannot be seen, have a spectator mark the blank ends of the drawers appropriately, red cross for the red checker, and black cross for the black checker. Pick the boxes up in one hand, and in the process of explaining what you are about to do, reverse them, so that the previously marked ends face the audience. This action must not be noticed by the audience.

Place the boxes on the table, with the marks that you have prepared previously facing the audience. Pick up the boxes one at a time, and say, "As you have seen, the black checker was placed in this box marked by the black cross, and the red checker in this one marked by the red cross." Place them on the table again, wave your hand over them, and order the checkers to change places. Open the drawers on the side facing the audience, and dump out the checkers—which are found to be in reversed positions. The marks made by the spectator cannot be seen when the drawers are open.

103. *Dead or Alive?*

EFFECT: The performer asks the spectator to write a list of eight or ten names. All these names must be of living persons, except one, which must be of a dead person. The performer looks at the list, concentrates, and then reveals the name of the dead person.

PRESENTATION: Ask a spectator to write down on a piece of paper a list of numbers from 1 to 8 or 10. Then tell him to write the name of a person next to each number. Tell him that all these names must be names of living people, except one. He is to decide beforehand at what number he is to place the name of the deceased. Also, tell him to use names of persons whom you (the performer) are not acquainted with. As he does all this, he is prone to hesitate before writing each name. When he comes to the name of the dead person, there will be barely any hesitation, as he has already predetermined this name. When he has completed this list, scan it with some concentration, and then reveal the dead person's name.

104. *From the Spirit World*

EFFECT: A piece of blank cigarette paper is shown. A spectator calls out the name of any famous dead person. The blank cigarette paper is rolled into a small pellet and thrown into an empty glass. After a moment of "spiritualistic meditation," the pellet is removed by the spectator and opened up. On it is written the name of the dead person.

PREPARATION: Place a packet of cigarette paper in your right-hand trouser pocket, with the top sheet facing outward. Also, in the same pocket, have a very small pencil.

PRESENTATION: Say to the audience, "If everyone remains quiet I will try an experiment with the spirit world. However, perfect decorum must be observed, otherwise the spirit, or spirits, will not respond and the experiment will be a failure." Hold up a blank sheet of cigarette paper, which you may pass out for examination. When everyone is perfectly satisfied that it is blank on both sides, tell one of the spectators to hold it. At this time ask anyone in the audience to call out the name of a famous dead person. If more than one name is called out, allow the spectators to decide among themselves which one they wish to use.

When the name that has been decided upon has been called out, go into an attitude of deep concentration, as if you are invoking the spirit of this dead person. While you are doing this, your right hand is in your right trouser pocket. With the small pencil therein, write the name of the dead person on the top sheet of the packet of cigarette papers. After you have written this, roll the cigarette paper into a small pellet and place it between the tips of the first and second fingers, so that when you remove your hand from the pocket it cannot be seen. Now ask the spectator who is holding the blank cigarette paper to roll it into a pellet. Take the pellet from him with the tips of your right thumb and forefinger, and make as if to throw it into an empty glass. But instead release the hidden pellet between your first and second fingers. This should look perfectly innocent to the audience, exactly as if you threw in the pellet which was handed you.

Go into another attitude of concentration, invoking the spirit of the dead person. At this time you may very easily get rid of the other pellet by dropping it into a pocket. Now ask a spectator to take the pellet out of the glass, unroll it, and read the name written on it. This, of course, is the name of the dead person. This effect is so strong you may end up with several converts to spiritualism in the audience.

105. *For a Change*

EFFECT: The age of a spectator and the amount of change in his pocket are unknown to the performer. Yet, by means of a bit of arithmetic, the performer divines both the spectator's age and the amount of change in his pocket.

PRESENTATION: For this example let us assume that the spectator is forty-two years of age and has fifty-one cents in loose change in his pocket. Tell the spectator to multiply his age by 2, and then add 5 to the result. He is to multiply the answer by 50, and then subtract from this result the number of days in a year (365). To the result so obtained tell him to add the total amount of loose change in his pocket. Now he is to announce the final result. Of course, all this time the performer is not aware of the spectator's age or the amount of change in his pocket. The arithmetic will look as follows:

```
AGE————————42
MULTIPLY BY 2————84
ADD 5———————89
MULTIPLY BY 50——4450
SUBTRACT   365——4085
ADD CHANGE (51)——4136
```

As is seen, the final result is 4136. The performer now adds, mentally or on paper, the number 115 to this result. This gives us the total 4251. The first two digits of this result represent the spectator's age. The last two digits represent the loose change in his pocket.

106. *Finger Waves*

EFFECT: The performer asks any two spectators to hold out, at the same time, any number of fingers from one to five. Though the performer's back is turned, he announces the number of fingers each spectator holds out, when the sum of all the fingers is told him.

PRESENTATION: One of the two spectators chosen for this effect is a confederate of the performer's. The performer turns his back and tells the two spectators to hold out any number of fingers from one to five, in the same manner as boys sometimes do to choose first turn up in a game of baseball. Either spectator may hold out his fingers first. The total sum of the fingers held out is announced. After a bit of concentration, the performer calls out the number of fingers extended by each spectator. This can be repeated indefinitely.

EXPLANATION: The first time the fingers are extended, the confederate always holds out two. Thus, when the sum is announced, the performer is able to tell very easily the number of fingers extended by each spectator. When the action is repeated, the confederate holds out the same number of fingers as the other spectator held out previously. Knowing this, the performer is again able, very easily, to announce the number of fingers held out by each spectator. This may be repeated ad infinitum. You may repeat this stunt with another victim, using any other formula agreed upon beforehand with the confederate.

107. *Slate Telepathy*

EFFECT: While the performer's back is turned, a spectator writes a word and a number on a slate. He also draws any design or picture. He shows all this to the audience, and then erases it completely. The performer now takes the slate and writes on it the word and number, and draws the design.

PREPARATION: Clean the two surfaces of the slate with ammonia water, and allow it to dry. This cleans all oil off the surfaces. Soak a piece of chalk for a short while in 3 in 1 Oil. Remove the chalk and dry it thoroughly so that it does not feel oily. Anything written on the slate with this chalk, and then erased, will show up in light oily strokes, when the surface of the slate is held at any angle under the light. Though the performer can see this, the slate looks thoroughly blank to the spectators.

PRESENTATION: Hand the slate and chalk to a spectator, and tell him that while you are at the far end of the room, and your back is turned so that you cannot possibly see, he is to write a word and a number on the slate. Then he is to draw any simple picture or design on the same side. When he has completed this, he is to turn the slate toward the audience so they can verify what he has written and drawn. He is then to erase, with a

soft dry cotton cloth, everything that he put on the slate.

The performer now turns around, takes the chalk and slate, and faces the audience. He tells them to concentrate on the word. He hesitates a moment and then writes the word on the slate. He turns this to the audience, and their applause confirms its correctness. He repeats this with the number and the picture. Of course, all this time the light oily lines of the word, number, and design are visible to him only. This effect appears to be real telepathy, and the audience will be very much impressed.

108. *Arithmetical Matches*

EFFECT: The performer hands a full packet of matches to a spectator. The spectator is told to remove some matches, place some in his pocket and hold the remainder in his hand. The number in each case is unknown to the performer, and yet he announces the number of matches that is held in the spectator's hand.

PRESENTATION: The performer hands a full packet of twenty matches to

YOU HAVE FOUR MATCHES IN YOUR HAND!

a spectator. He is told to turn around so that the performer is unable to see what he is doing. The performer tells him to remove several matches from the packet and place them in his pocket. He is to count the remaining matches, add the digits of the result, and is then to remove as many matches more as the result designates. For instance, if fourteen matches are left, he removes five $(1 + 4 = 5)$. He places these also in his pocket. All this time the performer is unaware of the total number of matches removed. Now he tells the spectator to remove any number of matches he wishes and to hold them in his closed hand. The spectator is asked to turn around and hand the packet back to the performer.

At this time, while in the act of nonchalantly setting the matches aside, the performer takes a quick look and counts the remaining matches. He merely subtracts this number from nine, and this will give him the number of matches held by the spectator in his hand. When the first two actions are followed through by the spectator, according to the instructions, nine matches will always be left. So, in order to tell how many matches are held in the spectator's hand, all the performer need do is subtract the number of matches left in the packet from nine. When the performer announces the number of matches held by the spectator, it appears to be quite a baffling feat.

109. Gravity Defied

EFFECT: The performer holds a ruler in his right hand, held between the thumb and fingers, palm facing the audience. Most of the ruler is below the hand. Upon command, the ruler slowly begins to rise, or jumps up suddenly, without any visible means of motivation.

PREPARATION: Secure a twelve-inch thick ruler and prepare as follows. Get a small screw whose head has a small circular opening, the type used for picture-frame hanging. Screw it in the back of the ruler about one inch from the bottom edge, but do not screw it all the way through as it should not be seen from the front. Place the same type screw about one inch from the top end of the ruler, also. Secure a string of elastic about ten inches long that will stretch almost twice this length. Attach a button to one end of the elastic, the button being slightly larger than the hole in the screw head. Run the free end of the elastic through the top screw and attach it to the head of the bottom screw (Fig. 1).

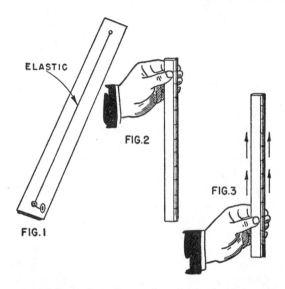

ELASTIC

FIG.2

FIG.3

FIG.1

PRESENTATION: Pick up the ruler so that the back of the ruler is hidden from the spectator's view, and place in the palm of the left hand, with the button at the bottom end. Grasp the button between your second and third fingers, and hold it firmly. Grasp the bottom end of the ruler with the right hand and pull it, causing the button to go to the opposite end of the ruler, by stretching the elastic which is hidden from view (Fig. 2). Now the left hand is near the top of the ruler, still grasping the button between the fingers and holding the ruler firmly. Command it to rise. Slightly release the pressure of the fingers around the ruler, and the tension of the elastic will cause it to rise slowly (Fig. 3). You may tell it to stop at any time. Stop it at will by contracting your fingers again. After this demonstration, push the ruler down again and command the ruler to jump. Release the grip on the ruler and it will jump into the air. Naturally, the ruler cannot be passed around for examination.

110. *Watch-It*

EFFECT: Two numbers on the face of a watch are added together by a spectator. From the sum, the performer, with only a moment's concentration, announces the two numbers. In the same way, the smaller of the two numbers is subtracted from the larger, and the performer announces the result.

PRESENTATION: Ask a spectator to remove his watch, look at its face and mentally add any two opposite numbers together. Ask him to announce the result. Concentrate a moment and then announce the two numbers he added. Immediately ask him to repeat this and mentally to add any other two opposite numbers, and again announce the result. You again immediately tell him the numbers he added. Now, without allowing time for anyone to analyze this procedure, ask a spectator to subtract mentally two opposite numbers, the smaller from the larger, but not to announce the result, just to concentrate on it. Almost immediately you tell him the correct figure.

EXPLANATION: This effect is very simple, and some people in the audience may catch wise. However, if presented correctly and followed immediately by another effect, many in the audience will remain mystified. When the opposite numbers on the face of a watch are added there are only six possible sums, 8-10-12-14-16-18. As you can see, this is a simple arithmetical progression, and is very easily remembered. Thus, when any of the above numbers are announced as a resulting sum, it is quite easy to break it up into its component, opposite numbers.

It is important that you have the spectator do two such additions to impress psychologically upon his mind the fact that the results are always different. Now, when you ask him to subtract one opposite number from another, he will assume that the results will also be different, depending upon the numbers chosen. Actually, the result is always six, no matter which opposite numbers are chosen. Do not give the spectator, or spectators, a chance to think this over, but immediately proceed to another effect.

111. *Divination of a Sum*

Most people who have had a smattering of education in mathematics know the principle of the number 9, and its many peculiar antics. A favorite effect for many years was the writing of a column of figures, and by use of the nine principles, the predestination of the result of their addition. However, too many spectators know of this principle, and therefore it cannot be used too often. However, the following effect, though still using this principle in a disguised form, may be done, and at the same time the method used will fool the experts completely.

In order to better understand the secret, and for those who are not acquainted with the principle, the old method is reviewed, as follows.

Three spectators would write three numbers, one under the other, and the performer would write two more numbers right under these. It would finally look like this:

1)	84219
2)	67310
3)	40019
4)	15780
5)	32689

If you examine the first and fourth row of figures you will find that each pair of digits, vertically, totals nine. The same thing happens with the second and fifth numbers. In order to predict the sum, you took row 3, subtracted 2 from the last digit and placed a 2 in front of the result. Therefore, the third or middle number being 40019, the predicted result would be 240017.

The following effect disguises the principle quite cleverly.

PRESENTATION: Have a pad and pencil in your hand. Ask any spectator to call out a five-digit number. Write it at the top of the pad. At this point remind yourself that you wished to make a prediction, and on a separate piece of paper write this prediction.

Let us say the first number called out was 84219. Your prediction of the final sum will be (following the above rule) 284217. Fold the piece of paper with this prediction on it, and hand it to a spectator to hold.

You have on the pad the first number called out by a spectator. Hand the pad and pencil to another spectator for him to write a second five-digit number under the first. Repeat this again with another spectator. You should now have three five-digit numbers, written one under another, and freely chosen. Take the pad and pencil, quickly add two more five-digit numbers, and immediately hand the pad to someone and tell him to total the figures. Have someone read aloud the prediction made previously by you, and the audience will think that you are either clairvoyant or are a mathematical wizard, because the actual total and the predicted total correspond.

EXPLANATION: The nine principle is used, but in a completely disguised form. Let us say the figures written are as follows:

1)	84219—Spectator	4)	35878—Performer
2)	67310—Spectator	5)	56791—Performer
3)	40019—Spectator		

The numbers on lines 1, 2 and 3 are freely chosen by the spectators. The numbers on lines 4 and 5 are selected by the performer on the following basis: he subtracts the sum of the *vertical* digits in lines 2 and 3 from 18, and makes the *vertical* digits in lines 4 and 5 equal the difference. In other words, if you look at lines 2 and 3 and add the last digits vertically, you get 9. Subtract this from 18, which leaves 9. When you now begin writing your numbers, begin writing from right to left any two digits whose sum is 9. In this case, 8 and 1. Move to the left in lines 2 and 3. Add the next two vertical digits, 1 and 1 which equal two. Subtract this from 18. This leaves 16. Now to your first two digits, and to the left of them, add two digits whose sum will be 16. In this case 7 and 9. Keep this up until you have two five-digit numbers written. When all the five-digit numbers are totaled, it will be the same as the predicted total. No matter how closely anyone may look, he is unable to find the principle of 9, but it is there, very cleverly hidden. Though this sounds involved, it is very simple and can be done quite quickly.

112. *Burning Sugar*

EFFECT: The performer challenges the spectators to light a piece of sugar so that it burns with a flame. They are unsuccessful, but the performer displays his magical powers by effecting this feat.

PRESENTATION: Before you do this effect, have in front of you, on the table, a very small amount of cigarette or cigar ash. This will be unnoticed by the audience, especially if you pay no attention to it. Pass out several lumps of sugar to some spectators in the audience, and say, "This sugar is not for eating purposes, but is part of an experiment to prove my magical powers. I now challange anyone with a piece of sugar to light it with a match, and cause it to burn with a flame." The spectators now try this and they are completely unsuccessful, for the sugar will melt as it burns, but there will be no flame.

ASHES ON
EDGE OF
SUGAR

When they have fully satisfied themselves that it cannot be done, say to them, "Now that you are satisfied that it cannot be done by ordinary means, will someone please hand me any one of the lumps of sugar." When you get a lump of sugar, place it on the table with one end on the small pile of ashes, while you continue to say, "I am able to do this because of my magical powers." Remove a packet of matches from your pocket, or borrow some. Light a match, hold it in your right hand, and with your left hand pick up the lump of sugar from the table. As you do so, press the sugar down on the ashes to make sure that some of the ash adheres. Bring the lighted match to that part of the sugar which has the ash on it, and the sugar will begin to burn with a flame. The ashes act as a catalytic agent, which makes the sugar burn, thus proving your magical powers.

113. *Telephone Mind Reading Experiment*

The following effect cannot be done on the spur of the moment, but it is so effective that it is worth the trouble of previous preparation. It will definitely convince your victim that you have telepathic powers.

EFFECT: The performer calls a friend on the telephone. He asks him to take in his hand any magazine that is available to him. He is to open to any page and concentrate on the first word or passage. After a moment, the performer tells him the name of the magazine and the word or passage he is concentrating on.

PREPARATION: Next time you go visiting, observe the magazines that are lying around your friend's home, and make a list of them, preferably of recent issues. Obtain duplicates of these magazines and keep them available at home. Next to each one on the list, place the number of pages in each magazine.

PRESENTATION: Call up your friend and tell him you wish to try an experiment in telepathy. Tell him to pick up any magazine, of recent vintage, he has available at home. Then tell him to open to a page from 1 to —. At this time you hesitate and ask him how many pages the magazine has. If he says 150, you complete the instructions—"from 1 to 150." The number of pages in the magazine will give you a clue as to which magazine is being used, since it is unlikely that any two magazines will have the same number of pages. When he has selected a page and told you the page number, tell him to concentrate on the first word or, preferably, passage on that page. Take your duplicate magazine and turn to the designated page. After a moment of concentration, read the word, or passage, to him. He certainly will be flabbergasted—and convinced that you are a genuine telepathist.

114. *The Twice-Lit Match*

EFFECT: A match is lit by striking it against the side of a match box. The flame is blown out. The burnt match is struck again on the other side of the box, and mysteriously lights again.

PREPARATION: Take a wooden match and dip its head into a bottle of ink, blackening the head and part of the stick, so that it looks like a used match. Allow it to dry. Stick it lengthwise, with a bit of wax, to the under side of the match box and place the entire thing in your pocket.

PRESENTATION: Say to the audience, "There is a peculiar thing about some matches and match boxes. For instance, if I were to take a match from this match box and strike it on one side of the box, it will light." Take the prepared box out of your pocket, remove a match and proceed to demonstrate. Hold the lit match a moment, blow it out and let it lie in the palm of your hand. The box, which meanwhile is being held with the other hand, is placed on the palm, covering the match. With the same motion, reach under the box and removed the prepared match. This should look like a simple exchange of objects from one hand to another. Now say, "However, if we strike the same match on the opposite side of the box, it will also light." Proceed to do this, proving the peculiarities attached to some matches and match boxes.

115. *Knots That Are Not*

EFFECT: The performer causes knots in a rope to vanish and reappear on command.

PREPARATION: In a rope about five feet long, tie two regular knots about a foot from one end of the rope. Tie these knots close to each other, like a double knot. About four inches below this tie a slip knot. This is done by crossing the rope and drawing a loop through, pulling it tight so that it looks like a real knot (Fig. 1). Tie a second slip knot about four inches below the first. The rope should look as in Fig. 2. Hold the rope with the left fist, allowing it to hang down and enclosing the three upper knots in the fist, allowing only one slip knot to show. When held so, it looks as if it were a piece of rope with one knot in it (Fig. 3).

PRESENTATION: Call the attention of the audience to the knot. Enclose it in your right hand, and with a slight pull, release the knot. Remove your hand and make a throwing motion with it as if you removed the knot and are throwing it away. The knot has vanished, but with a brisk shake of the left hand you cause it to reappear, by dropping the second slip knot. This is done so fast that the movement of the knot dropping cannot be seen by the audience. You cause this one to vanish also. This time, when you make it reappear, drop both genuine knots. Hand the rope out for examination, and explain that the two knots that vanished have reappeared.

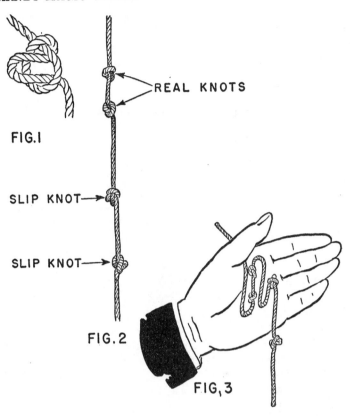

REAL KNOTS

FIG.I

SLIP KNOT→

SLIP KNOT→

FIG.2

FIG.3

116. *Pendulum of Fate*

EFFECT: A weight, tied onto the end of a string and held as a pendulum by a spectator, will respond to questions by swinging of its own volition in one of two different paths—a straight line or a circle.

PREPARATION: Obtain a brightly colored stone, about the size of a marble, and tie this to one end of a string about ten inches long.

PRESENTATION: Tell the audience a story about having obtained, with a great deal of difficulty, from a friend in ancient Tibet, a peculiar substance which has psychic powers. Show the colored stone tied to the string. Have a spectator volunteer, and have him hold the end of the string with the stone hanging downward like a pendulum. Tell him to hold it extended from his body, and as steady as possible. Request that he ask any questions that require the answer "Yes" or "No." Explain that if the stone swings in the path of a straight line, the answer will be "Yes." If it swings in a circular path, the answer is "No." After a moment or so, no matter how steadily the spectator tries to hold it, the stone will mysteriously begin to move—either in a straight path or a circular path (see illustration).

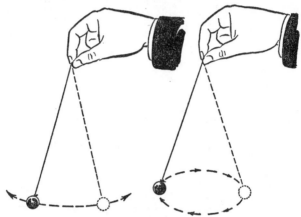

The explanation for this is rather uncertain. However, the most logical explanation is that there is a very slight muscular movement of the spectator's hand, according to whether he wishes the answer to be "Yes" or "No." The spectator is completely unconscious of this action. No matter what the explanation is, it will definitely work. Try it yourself and see. You may repeat the experiment as often as you wish.

117. *Melting Coin*

EFFECT: A coin is dropped into a glass of water, under cover of a handkerchief. The handkerchief is removed and the coin is seen in the glass. The glass is again covered with the handkerchief for a moment. When the handkerchief is removed this time, the coin has vanished.

PRESENTATION: In your left hand hold a glass about half full of water. Allow the glass to rest on your flat palm. Have someone place a coin in the center of a handkerchief. Have him pick up the coin through the handkerchief. Then he is to drape the handkerchief over the glass and to drop the coin into it. As the spectator does this, tip the glass toward you, so that when the coin drops it will hit the side of the glass and then fall into your hand. The tinkling sound will convince the audience that the coin went into the glass. Have the spectator let go of the hand-

kerchief so that it will rest on the glass. With your right hand, grasp
the rim of the glass through the handkerchief, and place it (the glass)
directly over the coin. Remove the handkerchief and allow the spectator

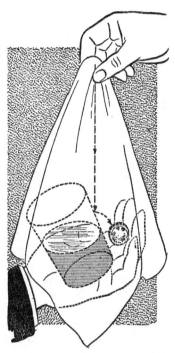

to look into the glass to verify that the coin is still there. The refraction
of light through the bottom of the glass will make it appear so. Cover
the glass with the handkerchief again and move the covered glass to
your right hand. Conceal the coin in your left hand, which now removes
the handkerchief to show that the coin has vanished.

118. *Hopping Rubber Band*

EFFECT: The performer places a rubber band around two fingers of his
hand. At his command the band seems to jump from one pair of fingers
to another, without any visible means of propulsion.

PRESENTATION: Place a rubber band around the first and second fingers
of the left hand. Hold the hand up with its back toward the audience,
the fingers extending upward. The rubber band should be loose enough
for a small part of it to hang down on the palm side (Fig. 1). With the

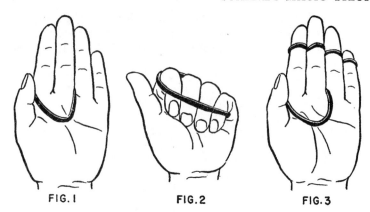

FIG. I   FIG. 2   FIG. 3

right hand, snap the palm side of the rubber band once or twice. When you are about to snap it again, pull the band out and curl the fingers toward the palm, so that they are all within the rubber band (Fig. 2). Snap the band and, at the same time, straighten your fingers again. The band will automatically release itself from the first two fingers and suddenly appear around the third and fourth fingers.

Repeat the above procedure and the rubber band will reappear on the first and second fingers. From the front this appears to be quite tricky. To make it look even more mysterious and puzzling, you may add the following twist. While the band is around the first and second fingers, loop another rubber band around the tips of the fingers so that it ties the fingers together (Fig. 3). Now it certainly appears as if it were impossible for the band to jump from one side to the other. However, you will find that it will work exactly as before. The above routine may require a slight bit of practice in order to do it smoothly.

119. *The Literary Glasses*

EFFECT: The performer wraps a small book in a handkerchief. He places two glasses next to each other on one surface of the wrapped book. When he inverts the entire thing, the glasses do not fall, but mysteriously cling to the book.

PREPARATION: Tie two beads together by a bit of cord, so that there is a little less than an inch between them (Fig. 1). Sew this into the hem of a handkerchief so that it is situated equidistant from both corners (Fig. 2).

PRESENTATION: Explain that with your magical powers, you will attempt

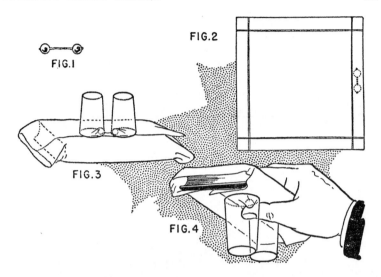

FIG.1

FIG.2

FIG.3

FIG.4

to overcome the law of gravity. Take a small book about four or five by six inches, and wrap the handkerchief around it. Wrap it so that the beads end up outside and on the center of one of the surfaces of the book (Fig. 3). Place two inverted glasses on the center of this surface, so that a bead lies within each of the glasses (Fig. 3). Now, if you place your thumb between the two glasses, and force it to the surface of the book, the tension so obtained between the beads and the thumb will hold the glasses firmly to the book. Slowly invert the entire thing and the glasses will hang to the book without falling (Fig. 4). Turn it upright again and remove the glasses. Place the handkerchief in your pocket and hand around the book and the glasses for examination.

120. *The Chameleon Handkerchief*

EFFECT: The performer shows a red handkerchief. He draws the hand-kerchief through his closed fist, and it changes from red to green.

PREPARATION: On one side of a white silk handkerchief sew a square piece of red silk, and center it so that a white border of about three-quarters of an inch is left. On the other side of the handkerchief sew a piece of green silk so that a white border of the same size shows. The two pieces of colored silk should be the same size.

PRESENTATION: Hold the prepared handkerchief by two corners, so that only the red side faces the audience. Drape the handkerchief over the left fist, red side up. The fingers of the fist are in a horizontal position. Make sure that in doing this the audience does not see the reverse side of the handkerchief. With the index finger of the right hand, poke the center of the silk down through the fist, and then grasp it as it comes through at the bottom. Pull it through quickly and then immediately grasp the corners so that the green side faces the audience. Do everything quickly and snappily, so that later the members of the audience will swear that they saw both sides of the handkerchief. With proper presentation, this becomes a very mysterious color change.

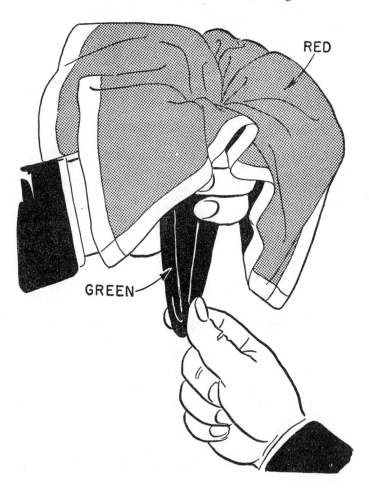

RED

GREEN

121. *Impossible Escape*

EFFECT: Three or four small pills are placed in a small vial or bottle which is full of water. This is then corked. The performer places this behind his back, and in a moment brings it forward. The vial, still full of water and tightly corked, is in one hand, but the pills are in the other hand.

PREPARATION: Obtain a small vial or bottle.. The opening of this vial, or bottle, should be small enough so that none of the fingers could enter it. Supply it with a tight-fitting cork. Just below the top surface of the cork, insert a small piece of Alnico magnet. Make sure that this is not too noticeable. Obtain three or four small steel bearings and paint these a solid white. They will now look like small pills.

PRESENTATION: Show the open vial full of water to the audience. Drop the "pills" into it, one by one. Cork the vial tightly. Show it around so that everyone is satisfied with the conditions. Bring the vial behind you so that the audience may not see what transpires. Remove the cork, holding the vial upright. Place the upper surface of the cork against the bottom of the vial. The magnet in the cork will attract the "pills" through the surface of the glass. Carefully running the cork along the surface to the opening of the vial, it will bring the "pills" with it. As you release the cork from the mouth of the glass, the "pills" will cling to it. Remove the "pills" and hold them in your right hand. Cork the bottle tightly again and bring your hands forward, showing that you have accomplished the impossible.

122. *The Traveling Signature*

EFFECT: A spectator writes his signature on one of three oblong pieces of paper. The three pieces of paper are then placed together and rolled up into the shape of a tube. The spectator is now asked to point out the paper on which his signature appears, but no matter what he announces, he is always wrong.

PRESENTATION: For this demonstration you will need three oblong pieces of paper of the same size (about six by two and a half inches will do). Ask a spectator to place his signature across one of the pieces of paper. Place this piece of signed paper between the other two, and then place the three sheets together and overlapped flat on the table (Fig. 1). Start rolling the three sheets together in the shape of a tube. Start with the corners facing you, and roll them forward, away from you (Fig. 2). When

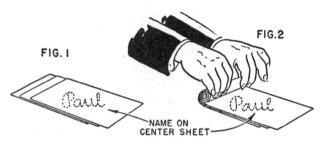

FIG. 1 FIG.2

NAME ON
CENTER SHEET

you have completed the roll, continue until the corners you started with begin to fall flat on the table. You will notice that they fall one at a time, due to the fact that they were originally overlapped. The position of the center sheet, with the signature, will depend on how many corners you allow to drop before you begin unrolling. For instance, if you allow just one corner to drop, the signature will appear on the bottom sheet when the papers are unrolled. If you allow two corners to drop, the signature will appear on the top sheet when the papers are unrolled. If you allow the three corners to drop, the signature will appear on the middle sheet, in its original starting place.

After you have completed the roll the first time, allow the three corners to drop to the table. Then ask the spectator on which sheet the signature was put. He undoubtedly will say it is the middle one. Unroll the sheets and show him that he is correct. Roll the sheets up again, but before you allow any corners to drop, ask the spectator where he thinks the signature is now. No matter what he answers, drop the appropriate number of corners to prove that he is wrong. This may be repeated several times.

This trick may also be performed by making use of two one-dollar bills and a five-dollar bill. The five-dollar bill is handled in the same manner as the piece of paper with the spectator's signature on it. Great as an impromptu stunt when paper is not available.

123. *Sour Dollar*

EFFECT: The performer borrows a dollar bill from a spectator in the audience. The serial number is recorded for identification. The performer makes the dollar bill vanish, and it is subsequently found in a lemon.

PREPARATION: Go to your neighborhood bank and exchange a ten-dollar bill for ten new singles. You will find, usually, that the numbers on these single bills run in consecutive order. You will need only two of these consecutive bills. Change the last digit of one of the serial numbers to match the other bill. For instance, if you have two bills, the serial numbers of which end in 3 and 8, it is quite easy to make an 8 out of the 3 with blue ink. With a bit of good printing you can make the two bills look exactly alike, even under fairly close observation. After you have done this, take a lemon and remove its end pip. Do not discard this. By running a thin pencil through the length of the lemon, up to its other end, you will create a space large enough to conceal a rolled-up dollar bill. Roll one of the prepared bills into a small packet and insert it into

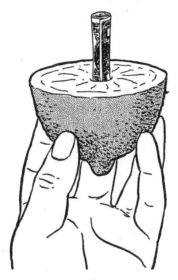

the space. Cover the entrance to this space with the pip you originally removed, and cement it on with any good glue or cement. To all appearances the lemon looks perfectly natural, and may even be examined fairly closely. Place this lemon in a saucer, together with two other unprepared lemons. Have them ready on the table. Place the other dollar bill in your side pocket. Prepare a handkerchief by sewing a piece of paper the size of a dollar bill rolled up into a small packet into its hem at a corner. Have this prepared handkerchief in your pocket.

PRESENTATION: Borrow a dollar bill from a spectator in the audience. Accept only a fairly new bill, since it has to match as closely as possible the prepared bills. Look at the spectator who gave you the bill and say, "Did you *give* me this bill? Thank you." Place the borrowed bill in the same pocket that has the concealed bill; then remark that you were only fooling and remove the hidden bill from your pocket, leaving the borrowed bill in its place. Tell someone to copy the serial number of the bill for future reference.

Pick up the saucer with the three lemons, and by using the "magician's choice," have the prepared lemon selected. This is done as follows. Have a spectator remove any two lemons. If he leaves the prepared lemon in the saucer, say, "This is the one you wish me to use." Hand it to another spectator to hold. If the spectator removes the prepared lemon and another one, ask him to return one to you. If he hands you the prepared lemon, repeat above statement and action. If he keeps the prepared lemon, tell him to hold it, as it is the lemon he wishes to use.

Now roll up the bill into a small packet and hold it in your right hand. With your left hand remove the prepared handkerchief from your pocket. Use this handkerchief as described in the trick, "Two Minus Two Equals Two," page 67, in order to make the bill vanish. When this has been accomplished, hand a knife to the spectator who is holding the lemon, and tell him to cut it. Tell him to cut all around to the center of the lemon, and then separate the halves. He will find a dollar bill jutting out of one of the halves. Tell him to remove it, unroll it and check its serial number with the recorded one for identification. The bill of course matches. If you wish you may have someone cut the other lemons in half to verify the absence of any bills.

124. *Obedient Handkerchief*

EFFECT No. 1: The performer balances a handkerchief on the tips of his fingers. The handkerchief rises or falls at a command.

PREPARATION: Obtain a waxed drinking straw and flatten it along its length. Sew this into the hem of a handkerchief with one of its ends at a corner (Fig. 1, B). Place this handkerchief, folded up, in your breast pocket without bending the straw.

PRESENTATION: Remove the handkerchief from your pocket, and grasp it with the fingers by the corner (Fig. 1, A), allowing it to hang down. Tie a knot at this corner. Holding the knot with one hand, stroke the handkerchief downward with the other, two or three times. Still holding it by the knot, bring the other hand down, and extend the fingers as if you are about to balance the handkerchief on them. With the tips of the forefinger and thumb at the lower end of the straw, close your fingers around the lower part of the handkerchief. Release your hold on the knot, and it will look as if the handkerchief is balanced upright.

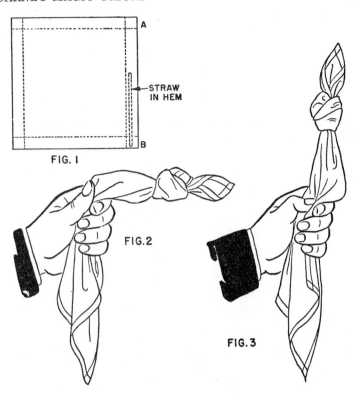

Make this action look deliberate and difficult, as if you are really trying to balance something. Hold it in this position for a moment, and then command, "Down Rover." By a sliding movement of the forefinger and thumb, allow the handkerchief to recline slowly. Now say, "Up Rover." By a reverse movement of the fingers, cause it to stand up again. After you have done this several times, throw the handkerchief up into the air, catch it, crumple it up and replace it in your pocket. This effect, done correctly, is not only very mysterious but very funny.

EFFECT No. 2: The performer causes an end of a handkerchief to rise and fall at will by merely waving his hand over the handkerchief.

PREPARATION AND PRESENTATION: The performer ties one end of the handkerchief into a knot about two inches from the end. The handkerchief is placed into the cupped left hand as shown in Fig. 2. Merely by moving the thumb back and forward, the tied end of the handkerchief will rise and fall on command (Fig. 3). To make the effect more startling, it is suggested that the performer wave the right hand over the handkerchief while it is rising and falling.

125. *The Elusive Marble*

EFFECT: The performer places a marble on the table and covers it with a handkerchief. He whisks the handkerchief away and the marble is no longer there. It is then found in the performer's mouth.

PREPARATION: Get two marbles exactly alike in color and size, a small rubber band (or one can be made by cutting off the end of a fountain pen tube), and a handkerchief.

At the start of the trick, you secretly place one of the marbles in your mouth, under your tongue so that you will be able to talk. The small rubber band is in your left-hand coat pocket, and the duplicate marble is in your right-hand coat pocket.

PRESENTATION: Remove a handkerchief from your pocket and spread it out on the table. Reach into both of your coat pockets, take out the marble with your right hand and place it on the center of the handkerchief. At the same time, remove the rubber band from your left-hand coat pocket by having it around the thumb and first and second fingers of your left hand. This is not to be seen by the audience. Immediately place your left hand holding the rubber band under the handkerchief, and with the right hand, bring the lower right-hand corner of the handkerchief over the marble (Fig. 1).

As you place the corner down, allow the rubber band to slip off the fingers and around the marble, so that the marble will be enclosed by the center of the handkerchief and held there by the rubber band. At the same time, with the left hand bring the lower left-hand corner of the

FIG. 1   FIG. 2

handkerchief up and over the other corner. These corners should cover the marble. Bring the other two upper corners down the same way. Now you will have the four corners of the handkerchief covering the marble and the center of the handkerchief. Pause a moment, grasp one of the corners, and with a sudden move, whisk the handkerchief into the air, keeping it in motion and showing that the marble has vanished. Crumple the handkerchief and place it in your pocket. Bend your head over the table, and slowly allow the concealed marble to protrude between your lips and then drop to the table (Fig. 2).

126. *Color Discernment*

EFFECT: Three squares of cardboard, colored differently on each side, are placed before a spectator. While the performer's back is turned, the spectator turns these cards over (opposite side up), each one as many times as he wishes. Then he covers one of them with his hand. When the performer turns around he divines the color that is covered.

PREPARATION: Prepare three small cards (about two by two inches) as follows: With crayon, color one of them red on one side, green on the other side. The second, color white on one side, black on the other. The third, color blue on one side, yellow on the other. (You may, if you wish, merely write the names of these colors on each side of the cardboard.) Mentally note a numerical value of one for each of the colors red, white, and blue; a value of zero for green, black and yellow.

PRESENTATION: Hand the three cards to a spectator and tell him to place them in a row in front of him on a table. Note which colors are up and mentally add their numerical values. Turn your back and instruct the spectator to do the following. He is to turn the cards around to their other sides as many times as he wishes, but is to turn only one card at a time. As he makes each turn, he is to say, "Turn." When he is satisfied,

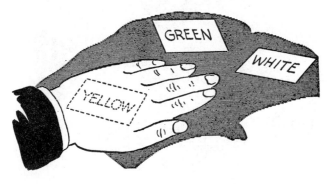

he is to cover one of the cards completely with his hand, so that you (the performer) will not be able to see it. When he has done this, turn around, concentrate a moment, and then tell him the color of the top surface of the card he is covering. This is the way it is done.

While your back is turned, mentally add one to your previous total for each time the spectator says, "Turn." When the spectator is through, if your total is odd, there will be one or three of the colors valued at 1 turned up. If the result is even, there will be two or none of the colors valued at 1 turned up. From this information it is easy for the performer to divine the color under the spectator's hand.

For example, should the colors red, white and blue be face up at the start, the performer starts his count at three and continues adding one to this total each time the spectator says, "Turn." When the spectator is through, should the performer's total count be an odd number, for example, 11, and the two visible cards are white and blue, the performer knows that the face-up color hidden by the spectator is red. By making use of this formula, it is possible to calculate the face-up color of the hidden card.

127. *Under the Table*

EFFECT: One of three paper matches is marked by penciling a line on it. The performer and spectator sit at a table opposite each other. The spectator passes any one of the three matches under the table to the performer, who, without looking, tells the spectator whether it is the marked one or not.

PREPARATION: The performer secretly removes a packet of matches from his pocket and prepares it, as follows. Hold the end match by the head

with one hand and the match case with the other. Then twist the match back and forth to loosen its fibers. Put the packet back into the pocket.

PRESENTATION: Tear out three matches from the match packet, making certain that one of the matches is the prepared one. With a pencil, mark a line on both sides of this match. Announce that you are about to demonstrate the extreme sensitivity of your finger tips. Hand the spectator, who is sitting opposite you at a table, the three matches. Tell him to pass any one of the matches to you under the table and you will tell him, without looking, whether it is the marked one or not. In order for you to do this, just twist the ends of the match. If it feels loose, it is the marked match. If it feels stiff, it is one of the unmarked ones.

128. Shirt Off

EFFECT: The performer, after unbuttoning several buttons of a spectator's shirt, takes hold of the shirt by the collar and pulls hard. Behold! the spectator's shirt is held by the performer. The spectator is shirtless but still has his coat on.

PRESENTATION: The following trick is not only mystifying but is a great laugh provoker. A confederate is used, but he is trained by the performer to act innocently, so that no one would ever guess that he is in on the trick.

Prepare him by asking him to remove his coat, then his shirt and tie. Drape the shirt over his back. Bring the collar, as usual, around his neck and button it. Put his tie on in a normal fashion. Bring the sleeves of the shirt down alongside his arms, and button the cuffs on his wrists (Fig. 1) also in the usual way. Tell him to replace his vest, if he has one, and then his coat. To all outward appearances he is dressed normally (Fig. 2). Have him sit in the audience.

During your program, or before you proceed to do the effect, call for a volunteer assistant from the audience. Your confederate comes up, and once he is in front of the audience, he becomes bashful and nervous. You tell him to relax by removing his tie and unbuttoning his collar. You then unbutton his cuffs. Ask him if he feels better, now that you have unloosened his clothing a bit. He shakes his head doubtfully. Reach behind him and grasp the back of the collar of his shirt (Fig. 3). With a sudden upward sweep of the arm, pull the shirt completely off. It will come off easily, since there is nothing restraining it. Tell him that, now, he should feel much better. The audience, meanwhile, will be convulsed with laughter.

129. *The Self-Tying Handkerchief*

EFFECT: The performer holds a handkerchief by a corner, letting it hang down. He lifts up the opposite corner with the other hand. He gives the

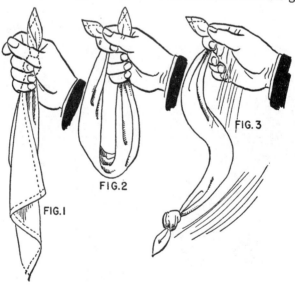

FIG.3

FIG.2

FIG.1

handkerchief a sudden snap and a knot suddenly appears in it.

PREPARATION: Tie a knot near one corner of the handkerchief.

PRESENTATION: Pick up the handkerchief by the corner that has the knot tied in it. Hold your hand cupped around it so that the knot is hidden in the hand (Fig. 1). With the other hand, bring the opposite corner of the handkerchief up (Fig. 2) and snap it. Do this once or twice, as if you have failed. The third time, when you bring the corner up, switch grips so that when you snap the handkerchief this time, the knotted end will come down. The sudden movement will cover this switch and it will appear as if the handkerchief knotted itself (Fig. 3). This sounds very simple, but try it and you will see the marvelous effect it has on an audience.

130. Magnetic Bottle

EFFECT: The performer places the end of a rope inside an empty bottle. Turning the bottle upside down, the rope does not fall out. Grasping the other end of the rope, the bottle does not fall off. The performer may even swing the bottle back and forth.

PREPARATION: For this effect you should use a bottle with a narrow neck and made of very dark glass. Place a small soft rubber ball in this bottle. The circumference of the ball plus the circumference of the rope you will use should be slightly larger than the neck of the bottle. Have the bottle standing on the table, and near it, about two feet of rope.

PRESENTATION: Talk about the ability that certain Hindu magicians have in endowing inanimate objects with peculiar powers. Tell the audience that in your travels through India, you learned the secret of this power through an Indian magician with whom you became very friendly. Proceed to demonstrate.

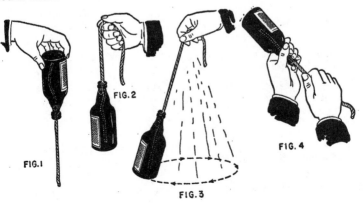

FIG. 1

FIG. 2

FIG. 3

FIG. 4

Pick up one end of the rope and allow the hanging end to enter the bottle. While holding the rope with the right hand, pick the bottle up with the left hand and turn the entire thing over slowly, so that the bottle will be upside down and the rope below it (Fig. 1). In doing this the small rubber ball will fall against the rope at the neck of the bottle. A slight tug on the rope will carry the ball into the neck, and the pressure will hold the rope in place. Let go of the rope and show that it hangs there mysteriously without any visible means of support (Fig. 1). Grasp the end of the rope again and allow the bottle to swing free (Fig. 2). The grip is pretty strong, and you may even swing the bottle in all directions (Fig. 3). When you have completed your demonstration, hold the bottle at the neck (Fig. 4) and gently pull the rope with steady pressure. This will bring the rubber ball out of the bottle, with the rope, and it will fall into the palm of your hand. You may now pass the bottle and rope out for examination.

131. *Mind Reading De Luxe*

EFFECT: Pieces of paper, upon which questions have been written by members of the audience, are folded and dropped into a hat. The performer removes these folded papers, one at a time, and holding them to his forehead, "telepathically" answers the questions written thereon.

PRESENTATION: Have several members of the audience write on pieces of paper any question they wish to have answered. Instruct them that these questions must make sense, and should not be too confusing, since you will answer them telepathically; for this purpose, it is important that they be clear. When they have written the questions, instruct them to fold the papers into small packets and drop them into a hat, which is held by a spectator. When these preliminary instructions have been completed, you are ready to proceed, as follows.

Reach into the hat and remove one of the folded papers. Immediately bring it, as it is, to your forehead, and assume a pose of deep concentration. You seem to be having difficulty, and are unable to read the question. A bit of good acting is required at this point. Finally you give up, unfold the paper, and look at the writing. Look pleasantly surprised, and say, "It isn't any wonder that I could not 'telepathize' this question, as it is written either in a foreign language that I am not acquainted with or it is just an illegible scrawl." Crumple the paper up in disgust, and place it in your pocket.

Meanwhile, of course, you have actually glimpsed the question written on the paper, the entire "act" having been a subterfuge to enable you to do so. Having glanced at the first question, it now becomes quite easy to read the others. Take a second folded paper out of the hat, hold it to your forehead, and actually answer the first question which you have already seen. Unfold the paper, look at it to "verify" that you have answered the "correct" question. Meanwhile, of course, you are looking at a second brand new question. Lay this paper aside and proceed with a third paper from the hat. In this way you are always one question ahead of the answer. If you put a bit of good patter and acting into this effect, you will either puzzle your audience immensely, or will convince them that you are telepathic.

In answering the questions, it is good showmanship not to be too exact; be a bit vague on certain points. This is very convincing.

132. *Pencil and Loop*

EFFECT: The performer takes a long pencil, through one end of which a loop of cord is attached, and loops it through the buttonhole of a spectator's coat. He challenges the spectator to remove the pencil and loop, without in any way injuring the cord, pencil, or coat.

PREPARATION: Through one end of the pencil bore a small hole, large enough for a piece of cord to pass through. Tie the ends of the cord, mak-

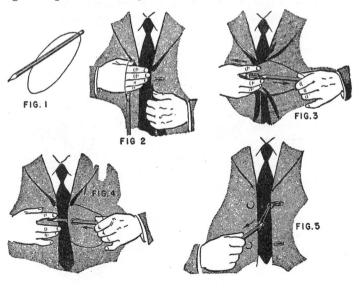

FIG. I

FIG 2

FIG.3

FIG.4

FIG.5

ing an endless loop. This loop should not be large enough for the pencil to swing through (Fig. 1).

PRESENTATION: Loop the cord over the hand so that it hangs loosely on the thumb and fingers of your right hand (Fig. 2). Grasp the cloth around a buttonhole of the coat, and pull the loop of cord over this, at the same time pulling more cloth through it. When you have pulled enough cloth through, so that the unlooped end of the pencil reaches the opening of the buttonhole, pass this end of the pencil through (Figs. 3 and 4). Pull the pencil downward, tightening the loop (Fig. 5). With a slight amount of practice you may do this very quickly.

Now, challenge the spectator to remove this without injuring the cord, pencil, or coat. Not only will the spectator become exasperated while trying, but it will provoke a great deal of laughter. After the spectator gives up, you proceed to remove it very quickly. This is done by reversing all the motions.

133. *Sympathetic Twins*

EFFECT: One of two bananas, attached to a single stalk, is cut in half. When the other banana is peeled, it, too, is found to be cut in half.

PREPARATION: Obtain two bananas that are attached to a single stalk. These bananas should be as much alike as possible. Prepare one of the bananas, as follows. Run a threaded needle through the skin, perpendicular to the length of the banana, at about the middle of its body (Fig. 1). Do not pull the thread all the way through, but allow for suffi-

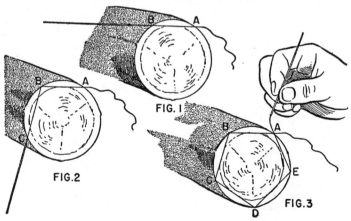

CROSSECTION OF BANANA
Showing thread drawn through with needle

FIG. I

FIG.2

FIG.3

cent length, so that about two or three inches of thread remain at puncture A. Now run the needle and thread through again, starting at the second puncture, B, and ending at a new puncture, C (Fig. 2). Keep going around the banana, to D and E, until you complete a polygon of thread (Fig. 3) and the thread exits from puncture A. If you pull both ends of the thread at this puncture, it will come through and at the same time will cut the banana in half at this point without cutting the skin. The holes formed in the skin of the banana by the needle will barely be noticed. You are now ready to proceed.

PRESENTATION: Tell the audience of the weird affinity that exists between twins. For instance, there have been cases of one twin developing a toothache at the same time that the other twin develops a toothache. There have been authenticated cases of twins who though thousands of miles apart have the same accident occur to them—such as both breaking their arms in the same way at the same time. Cite several other similar incidents.

Now show the bananas and emphasize that they are twins, since they are borne on the same stalk. According to the above rules, anything that may happen to one will happen to the other. Proceed now to demonstrate this fact by cutting the unprepared banana in half. Have a spectator peel the other banana, and behold! this banana is cut in half also, proving the sympathetic tie that exists between twins.

134. Hypno-Magnetism

EFFECT: The tip of a cane is placed on the horizontally opened palm of the performer. It is held at the other end by a spectator. The cane may not be lifted by the spectator, except by the will of the performer, no matter how much force he applies.

PREPARATION: Tie the end of a strong thin black thread into a loop about twice the circumference of the base of the middle finger of the left hand. Cut the other end of the thread so that about two inches of free thread remain. Tie this end to a piece of thin but strong elastic. Pin the other end of the elastic on the inside of the sleeve of your coat at shoulder height. When the loop hangs free inside the sleeve, it should reach just to the edge of the sleeve, and should not be seen when the arm is in any natural attitude. You may clip the loop to the edge of the sleeve in order to avoid tangling and to make it easily accessible. Have a cane handy. Just before you begin the effect, pull the loop of thread over the middle finger of your left hand so that the elastic and thread run along the back

of your hand. In this way, when your hand is held palm up, it looks perfectly innocent.

PRESENTATION: Explain to the audience the power that suggestion sometimes has over the mind of some individuals. Call a spectator up from the audience to assist you. Pick up the cane, and holding it with the left hand by the ferrule end, hand the other end to the spectator and have him hold it. Tell him that you are about to try an experiment, in which he will or will not be able to lift the tip of the cane from your hand, according to your command or will. While you are explaining this to him, it becomes easy for you to slip the ferrule into the loop around your finger, even if it is necessary to use the right hand to assist you. This should not be noticed. The thread will not be broken by the force applied to the other end of the cane, no matter how strong it is.

Hold your left hand, palm up, with the tip of the cane resting in it (it is now in the loop). Tell him that no matter how much force he applies to his end of the cane, he will not be able to lift the other end off your open palm. When the spectator tries this, he is astounded, because even with all his strength he cannot lift it. After he has tried this a few times, stop him, and then tell him that now he may lift it. (At this time you allow the ferrule to slip out of the loop.) The spectator tries to lift it now and finds that it is quite easy.

To get rid of the loop of thread, you may slip it off your finger immediately after he lifts the cane, or you may even break the loop and allow the thread to be pulled into your sleeve. Now you may show that your hands are absolutely empty, and pass the cane out for examination.

135. *Runaway Loop*

EFFECT: The performer twirls a loop between his first two fingers, then stops and locks it between his thumb and first finger. The loop then drops without separating the fingers.

PRESENTATION: A small rubber band is used. If a rubber band is not available, tie a string into a loop, or use a lady's bracelet. Place the loop over your two fingers, as shown in Fig. 1. Notice that the backs of both first fingers are away from the body. Twirl the loop around your fingers but always keep the back of your fingers away from your body. After you have finished twirling the loop, lock the loop between the first finger and thumb of each hand (Fig. 2). Now bring your hands together and push each first finger tightly against the thumb of the other hand (Fig. 3). Now spread your fingers apart (Fig. 4), and the loop drops. Do this trick for a friend and have him try it. You will have plenty of laughs seeing him fail.

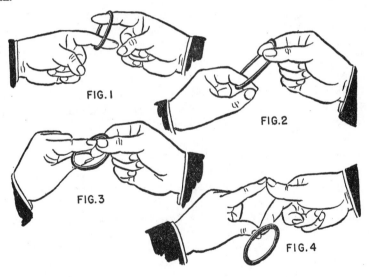

FIG. 1

FIG. 2

FIG. 3

FIG. 4

136. *Shifty Number*

EFFECT: A spectator multiplies a six-digit number by any other digit between 1 and 7. The performer has previously divined the result so obtained.

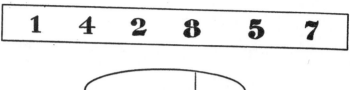

PREPARATION: On a strip of paper write the number 142857, neatly spaced so that when you glue the two ends of the strip of paper together, you will have a ring of paper upon which the number will appear in a continuous circle on the surface of the ring (see illustration). Hold this, flattened, in your hand.

PRESENTATION: Have a spectator ready with a pencil and a piece of paper. Assume a thoughtful attitude, and then say, "My Social Security number is 142857. We will use this number for the effect." Ask anyone to call out a number between 1 and 7. Then tell the spectator to multiply 142857 by this number.

It so happens that when any number between 1 and 7 is used to multiply 142857, the digits in the result do not change. The numbers are transposed in a regular fashion. For instance, if it is multiplied by the following numbers, the results will be as follows:

2	285714	5	714285
3	428571	6	857142
4	571428		

All you do is memorize the first digits of these results in relationship to the digit called by the spectator. When you know the first number, the result is just a succession of each digit of the number 142857, in the same rotation. Therefore, when a number between 1 and 7 is called out, all you have to do is look at the piece of paper in your hand, tear the ring at the proper number, and hand it to another spectator. When the result of the multiplication is announced, it matches your "prognostication."

Note: To make the use of the number 142857 less suspicious, it is suggested that you have it printed on a card you carry, and noted as your Social Security number.

137. *Coin Through Elbow*

EFFECT: The performer rubs a coin on his elbow, and it vanishes instantly.

PRESENTATION: Spin a coin on the table, and announce that it is a magical coin and you are going to rub it into your elbow. Spin the coin on the table, pick it up with your left hand, and rub it on the elbow of your right arm. Rub for a while, then let it fall to the table, remarking that you probably didn't rub hard enough. Now, pick the coin up with your right hand and pretend to put it into your left hand. Lift your right arm so that your left hand can get to your elbow and calmly insert the coin in your collar. Meanwhile, rub with your left hand and go through a line of patter about the magic of the coin and elbow.

While the rubbing is going on and the coin is neatly tucked in your collar, remove your right hand from your collar to avoid suspicion. Then slowly show your left hand. The coin has vanished. By reversing the above procedure, the coin can be made to reappear from the elbow.

138. *Mysterious Dollars*

EFFECT: The performer shows that both his hands are empty, mumbles a few magic words, places his hands together, and behold! he produces a number of one-dollar bills from his bare hands.

PREPARATION: Roll a number of one-dollar bills tightly together. Tie them with a piece of thread to prevent them from unrolling. Now tuck this roll of bills into the crotch of your left arm, pulling part of the cloth

ROLL OF BILLS
←UNDER FOLD
OF SLEEVE

of your coat sleeve over the bills so that they are concealed from view. PRESENTATION: Show your empty hands, but keep your left arm slightly bent to prevent the hidden bills from being seen or falling from their hidden position. Remark that you once saw a magician who not only showed that his hands were empty, but, to further assure the audience that nothing was up his sleeve, pulled it up a little. Now you do exactly that. First pull up your right sleeve with your left hand, then pull up your left sleeve with your right hand. While doing this, grab the roll of bills with your right hand from the crotch of your left arm and bring both hands together. This move is quite easy to do and very deceptive.

Now, break the thread, and with an up and down movement with both hands, slowly unroll and spread out the bills, remarking that the magician you saw produced an endless number of dollar bills. Act surprised when you see the bills appear in your hand, and remark that the magician you saw do this trick gave you the secret. A really startling trick if properly presented.

139. *The Ventilated Hand*

EFFECT: A spectator is given seven pennies, and told to hold them tightly in his hand. The magician causes one of the pennies to penetrate through the spectator's hand. If pennies are not available, nickels or dimes may be used.

PRESENTATION: Reach into your pocket and produce seven pennies, or borrow them if need be. Hold them in your cupped left hand. Have a spectator cup his hand, and pour the pennies into it. Have the spectator return the pennies to your left hand, counting them as he does. This little bit of by-play is necessary to impress upon the audience that seven coins are used. Have the spectator hold out his left hand in cupped fashion and tell him that now you are going to count the pennies into his hand. Instruct him that when you drop the seventh penny into his hand, he is to clench his fist quickly.

Using your right hand, take a penny from your left and place it in the spectator's cupped hand. Make sure that each succeeding penny clicks against those in the spectator's hand. After you have counted and dropped five pennies into the spectator's hand and clicked the last four, his eyes and ears are ready for the sixth penny. You then pick up the sixth penny with the thumb and forefinger and click it against the pennies in the spectator's hand. Immediately after the click, come right out with it again and count seven, and presumably throw the last penny from your left hand. The spectator closes his fist; you grasp the back of his hand with your right hand (this hand contains the hidden penny). The

spectator's clenched hand contains the six pennies; the back of his hand is to the floor. Your right hand is cupped slightly and holds his fist from below. The cupping is to prevent the penny from touching the spectator's hand.

From now on the rest is up to you. Give out with a bit of patter about the difficulty of making a coin penetrate through solid flesh, or any comment that fits your personality. Slowly bring your coin into contact with the back of his hand and say that the coin has penetrated his fist.

140. *The Money Tie*

EFFECT: The performer borrows a handkerchief and a half dollar. Placing the half dollar under the handkerchief, he causes the coin to vanish.

PREPARATION: Prepare a necktie in which a half dollar is sewn at the extreme tip of the tie, nearest to the trousers.

PRESENTATION: Borrow a handkerchief and a half dollar from a spectator. Drape the handkerchief over your right hand. Your hand should be about on a level with your chin, not too far away from the body. With the left hand take the half dollar from its owner and place it under the handkerchief; as you lift your hand, seize the end of the tie that has the half dollar in it. Your right hand now grasps the tie through the cloth so that the spectators see the shape of the half dollar through the handkerchief.

Your left hand, with the half dollar hidden in it, goes to your pocket for a pencil, and you secretly drop the half dollar there. Tap the handkerchief with the pencil. The spectators hear the metallic or solid ring of the half dollar. This convinces them the borrowed coin is still under the handkerchief.

To effect the vanish, merely shake out the handkerchief. The tie falls back into place and you hold only a pencil and a handkerchief. Practice this trick before a mirror and you will see how perfect the illusion is.

141. *The Diving Doll*

EFFECT: A miniature doll, placed in a pint-size whiskey bottle that is securely corked, is commanded to rise and fall at will by the performer.

PREPARATION: Purchase a small celluloid doll about an inch in height and about a half inch wide, one that will fit into a pint-size whiskey bottle. The doll can be purchased at a five and ten cent store. If a doll is not obtainable, any small celluloid animal or object will do. Puncture the bottom of the celluloid doll with a knife and insert a little steel weight—one or two B.B. shots will do the trick. This is done to give the doll a little weight so that it will sink to the bottom of the bottle. Fill the whiskey bottle to the top with water. Drop the doll into the bottle. The doll must have just enough weight in it to allow it to float. Put a new cork into the top of the bottle. Put it on tight and the doll will sink to the bottom. Experiment with the cork till you find that the floating doll will sink when a slight downward pressure is put on the cork. You now have made all the necessary preparations to perform this remarkable trick.

PRESENTATION: As you show the bottle to the spectators, the doll will be floating and touching the bottom of the cork. Grip the bottle, as shown

in the illustration, thumb on one side and four fingers on the other. Merely apply pressure on the bottle (as though trying to squeeze the bottle) and the doll will sink to the bottom. Release the pressure and the doll will float to the top again. After several demonstrations, cause the doll to sink to the bottom and hand the bottle to a spectator, at the same time pressing the cork in real tight. Pressure or no pressure, no matter what the spectator does, he will not be able to have the doll float up to the top.

It is suggested that after performing this trick the doll should be removed from the bottle, because it will fill up with water and won't work. Take it out, shake it well to get all the water out, then put it back in when ready to do the trick again.

142. *Scarne's Egyptian Bead Mystery*

EFFECT: The performer pours a number of loose beads into a glass, sets fire to a piece of thread, throws the burning thread into the glass, and behold! the beads are magically strung together. (Created by the author.)

PREPARATION: Buy two identical magazines, two identical necklaces which can be purchased from your local five and ten cent store, and a spool of thread the same color as the beads.

Tear off the front cover of a magazine and cut it in half. Paste this half cover on the front of the other magazine on three sides, thereby forming a pocket on the front of the magazine (Fig. 1). Glue together half of the inside pages of the magazine. With a razor blade cut out a space in the center of the glued pages (Fig. 2), leaving the opening facing opposite the opening of the pocket on the cover of the magazine. Remove the beads from one of the necklaces and thread them together with the matching colored thread. Now place these beads into the cut-out space of the glued pages and close the magazine. Remove the beads from the other necklace and drop them into a glass. You are now ready to perform this Egyptian mystery.

PRESENTATION: Pick up the magazine with your left hand, holding the cut side with the opening toward your body. Curve the magazine slightly and pour the beads from the glass onto the magazine. Pour them back into the glass again. Now reverse the position of the magazine in your hand, so that the opening that conceals the beads is away from your body, and curve the magazine on the end nearest the body, so that the pocket on the front of the magazine opens. Pour the beads from the glass onto the magazine, so that they will fall into the pocket.

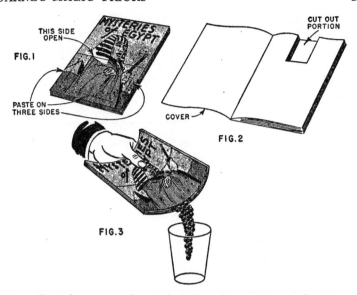

THIS SIDE OPEN

FIG.I

PASTE ON THREE SIDES

COVER

CUT OUT PORTION

FIG.2

FIG.3

Now, place the empty glass right below the opening in the magazine and tip it rapidly, allowing the set of strung beads to fall into the glass (Fig. 3). The loose beads are hidden in the pocket of the magazine. Put the magazine down. Tear a piece of thread off the spool and apply a lighted match to it. While the string is burning, drop it into the glass. Utter the Egyptian magical words of "Gulli Gulli," or any patter you desire. After the thread has burned, reach into the glass, pick up an end of the beads, and pull them out slowly. Your audience will be amazed to see that the beads are strung together.

143. *Scarne's Magic Ball of Yarn*

EFFECT: The performer spins a coin on the table, covers it with a hat, lifts up the hat, and a large ball of yarn appears magically. (Created by the author.)

PREPARATION: Secure a large ball of yarn, as large as the inside of a hat (when ball is expanded). Secretly place the ball of yarn inside your coat under your left armpit. A slight pressure of your arm against your body will hide it comfortably for a long period of time, since the ball of yarn will flatten out.

PRESENTATION: Borrow a hat and a coin. State that you have a new guessing game you would like to demonstrate. Hold the hat in your left hand,

and spin the coin with your right. Cover the spinning coin with the hat, holding it at its top with the fingers and thumb of your right hand. Ask a spectator to guess whether the coin is heads or tails up after it has stopped spinning. Should the spectator call the turn correctly, remark that he is lucky. Should he fail to call the turn, say, "This is one game that you can't beat me at."

After two or more spins, pick up the hat by its top with your left hand. Bring the hat close to your body. This time ask a spectator to spin the coin. At the same time, reach under your coat, grab the ball of yarn, and push it into the inside of the hat (Fig. 1). Immediately apply pressure with your left hand on the outside tip of the hat, holding the ball of yarn on the inside (Fig. 2). Remove your right hand and spin the coin

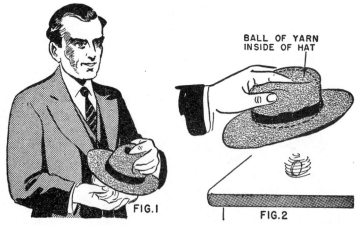

BALL OF YARN
INSIDE OF HAT

FIG. I   FIG. 2

yourself, saying to the spectator, "You seem to be an experienced hand at spinning coins." Immediately cover the spinning coin with the hat, and ask a spectator to call heads or tails. Lift the hat up, and watch the expression on the spectators' faces when the big ball of yarn appears from under the hat. The surprise ending will cause the spectators to forget about the coin for a moment. During the confusion, try to slip the coin away. If it's seen, it doesn't matter.

Practice this trick several times just to get the proper timing and misdirection.

144. *Loop the Loop*

EFFECT: A band of cloth is torn into two separate bands. One of these bands is again torn the same way, but the result is two bands linked together. The second band is then torn like the first, but the result this time is one long continuous band.

PREPARATION: This effect, when prepared and presented properly, becomes a very mystifying and entertaining routine. Take a piece of cloth (preferably colored) about four inches wide and about thirty inches long. At one end cut a slit along the middle, about one inch long. At the other end cut another slit, also along the middle, and about two or three inches long (Fig. 1). Bring the two ends together, forming a band. Using the longer flaps formed by the longer slit, give one of them a half twist and glue it to its mate at the other end of the band (Fig. 2). Give the other longer flap a full twist, and glue this to its mate at the other end of the

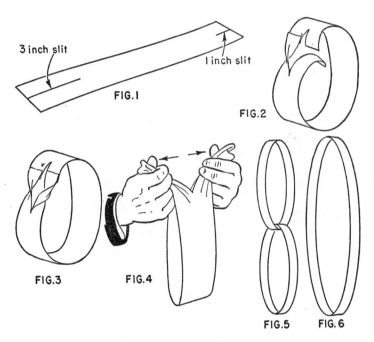

band (Fig. 3). When the glue has dried, flatten the prepared side so that it does not curl too much.

PRESENTATION: Hold the band so that the prepared side is toward you most of the time. Also, keep it in motion. This must be done so that the audience will have less chance to see anything on the band. Tear the band in two (Fig. 4), at the same time saying, "Naturally, when we tear a band of paper in two it becomes two bands." Show the two bands and place the one with the half twist over your arm. Proceed to tear the other band, and say, "However, if we use a bit of magical concentration, when we tear this band, we find that we also end up with two bands, but they are linked together" (Fig. 5). You may throw this out to the audience and proceed to tear the other band, saying, "This time when we tear the band, our mind concentrates on but a single thought, and so we end up with a single band" (Fig. 6). Show the single, but larger, band and throw this out to the audience.

145. *Clipped*

EFFECT: A piece of paper is folded and then cut in two by the performer. When unfolded, the paper is seen to be restored. When a spectator tries the same thing, the paper is always found to be cut through.

PREPARATION: Cut a column of printed matter, about two feet long, from a newspaper. Coat one side of this very lightly with a good rubber cement, and allow it to dry. When it has dried, in order to eliminate any tell-tale gloss, sprinkle talcum powder over the prepared side and smooth it over the surface with your fingers.

PRESENTATION: Fold the strip of paper into two equal lengths, making sure that the prepared sides are inside the fold. Say to the audience that you are about to demonstrate the unusual power you possess as a magician. With a pair of scissors cut the folded end off, cutting the strip into two pieces (Fig. 1). Grasp one of the uncut ends, and allowing the strip

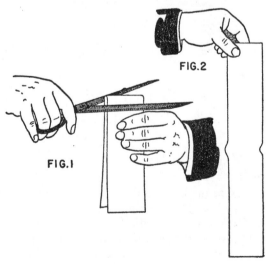

to unfold, show the audience that it is not really cut at all (Fig. 2).

Now fold the strip again (at the cut edges), but this time fold it the opposite way, bringing the prepared surfaces to the outside. Give the scissors to a spectator and tell him to cut the strip. At the same time, tell the audience that this is to prove that only a magician possesses these unusual powers. After the spectator has cut the strip, separate the two pieces to show that they have actually been cut, and that the restorative power is absent. Place the two pieces together, prepared sides on the inside, and cut it yourself again. Proceeding as above, you then show that you have restored the strip. You may repeat this as long as you wish, remembering that the strip will be restored only when the prepared sides face each other on the inside.

146. *Jack's Beanstalk*

One of the prettiest and most entertaining effects is the construction, with paper, of a tree or beanstalk. You may patter along the following lines: "If you remember the story of *Jack and the Beanstalk*, you will recall that it took all night for Jack's beanstalk to grow to its full height. I am going to show you a method whereby the same thing may be accomplished in a few moments."

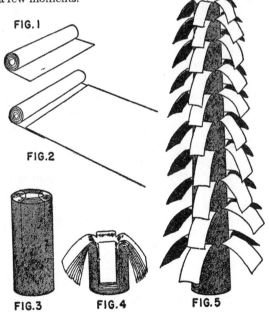

FIG. 1

FIG. 2

FIG. 3   FIG. 4   FIG. 5

METHOD: Roll a spread-out double sheet of newspaper (tabloid size) into a tube, allowing one end to extend freely for about three to four inches (Fig. 1). Place the end of a second sheet on this free end (Fig. 2) and keep rolling, until again about three or four inches of an end remain. Repeat this process with about eight to ten sheets, until you have a pretty thick tube of paper. Flatten one end of the tube and tear twice, making four separate tears, as shown by dotted lines in Fig. 3. Make the tears down to about the middle of the tube. Separate the torn portions and flatten them down alongside the remaining portion of the tube (Fig. 4). Holding the untorn portion of the tube in the left hand, insert the index finger of the right hand into the opening, and pull the inside of the tube up and out. Keep pulling, and you will obtain a tree as long as ten feet (Fig. 5). If you wish to obtain a startling and very pretty effect, you may use sheets of varicolored papers instead of newspapers.

147. *Paper Tears*

Paper tearing, though not actually "trickery," is a "demonstration" of great skill, and may be very entertaining if presented properly. You will be able to make the audience believe that you have put in years of practice in order to become so adept. You must remember, that when presenting any paper-tearing effect, you must keep talking and chattering about any interesting or humorous topics, or even tell a story pertaining to the subject at hand. This is necessary because the actual process of paper-tearing can become boring to the audience; so in order not to lose their attention, you must present it with interesting patter.

PAPER TEAR No. 1: To produce a string of dangling skeletons.

METHOD: Take a double sheet of newspaper and fold it, in accordion fashion, into eight equal parts (Fig. 1). The center fold of the newspaper should remain as the center fold of this arrangement. Fold the entire thing flat, and on one side outline in pencil, very lightly, a half skeleton, as shown in Fig. 2. Make sure the pencil marks are light, so that they will not be seen by any spectator. The shaded portion in Fig. 2 is what you tear, or cut, away. When you have done this, separate or unfold the remainder, and you will have a set of dangling skeletons. After doing this several times, you will find that it will not be necessary to draw the outline, and you may perform this effect in impromptu fashion at any time.

PAPER TEAR No. 2: To produce a string of dolls.

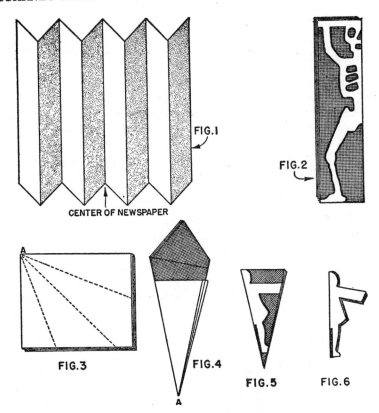

FIG.1

CENTER OF NEWSPAPER

FIG.2

FIG.3

FIG.4

A

FIG.5

FIG.6

METHOD: Take the double sheet of a large newspaper and fold it along its center. Then fold this in half, at point A, as in Fig. 3. Fold it now in the form of a cone, using A as its apex. Fold along dotted lines, as shown in Fig. 3. You will now produce a cone that you can flatten so that the edges are aligned (Fig. 4). Tear off the shaded portion and discard this piece. Now, lightly draw in, with pencil, the half figure of a doll (Fig. 5). Tear away the shaded portion.

After trying this once or twice, you will find that you do not need the marked outline, as it is very easy to do from memory. When you have finished tearing the paper, carefully unfold it and you will have a pretty wheel of dolls. Refold the paper again, and tear out the shaded portion (Fig. 6). Tear apart one set of arms. Now when you unfold the paper, you will have a long string of dolls.

148. *The Stretching Finger*

EFFECT: The performer succeeds in stretching his little finger until it is the same length as his forefinger.

PRESENTATION: Show your left hand by turning it over several times, meanwhile remarking that your little finger is quite different from your other fingers. Extend your left hand forward, palm away from you and toward the spectator. Point to the length of your little finger, which is, naturally, the smallest of the four. Mention that your first, second and third fingers are much longer than your little finger. To show the difference in length, place the forefinger of your right hand across the palm of your left hand slightly below the tip of the little finger (Fig. 1). This position accentuates the shortness of the little finger in comparison with the other fingers. Now point to your first finger and explain that it is much longer than your little finger and that you intend to stretch the little finger so that it will be as long as your forefinger.

Move your left hand to the right so that it will be on the same level with your elbow, directly in front of your body. Pull the little finger with your right hand several times, pretending that you are trying to stretch it

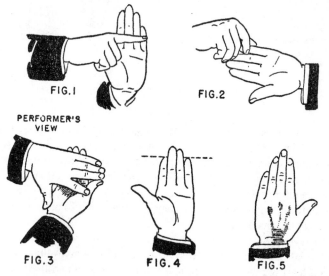

FIG. 1

PERFORMER'S VIEW

FIG. 2

FIG. 3

FIG. 4

FIG. 5

(Fig. 2). With your left hand in the same position, place the thumb of your right hand directly under the tip side of the second finger of your left hand. The fingers of your right facing upward are against the fingers of your left hand (Fig. 3 shows the position of hand from your view). Now push your left hand upward to its original position, applying pressure with your right thumb on the second finger of your left hand and moving your elbow as little as possible. Hold the four fingers of the left hand close together and remove your right hand. The spectators will be astonished to see that your little finger is the same length as your first finger (Fig. 4).

Do not hold this position too long because of the strain on your fingers and wrist due to their awkward position. Quickly turn the back of your hand toward the spectators, relaxing your hand at the same time. Now your little finger will be back to its normal position (Fig. 5).

149. Scarne's Indestructible Handkerchief

Created by the author, and one of his favorite impromptu tricks.

EFFECT: The performer borrows a gentleman's handkerchief and spreads it over his (the performer's) left fist. With his thumb, he pushes the center of the handkerchief down into his left fist, thereby forming a well in the handkerchief. A long pencil is pushed down into the well. The performer moves it up and down several times, and finally the right hand goes below the handkerchief and pulls the pencil through the bottom. It looks to the audience as though the pencil passed right through the handkerchief. Upon examination, the handkerchief is found to be unharmed.

PRESENTATION: With your left elbow resting against your body, extend your left hand forward. Draw attention to this hand, close it and form a fist (Fig. 1). Borrow a man's handkerchief and place it over the closed fist. Under cover of the handkerchief, open the left hand so that it forms a cup (Fig. 2). Now move your right hand toward your left, with your right thumb facing downward. Bring the right thumb against the handkerchief into the cupped left hand (Fig. 3). Close the left hand around the right thumb, and at the same time swing both hands toward the body so that the thumb of each hand is facing your body. Upon completion of this motion, immediately withdraw your right thumb, leaving your left hand in the same position. This action has caused a ditch to be made on the outside of the handkerchief, but it appears to the spectators as if you were merely forming a well by tucking the center of the handkerchief into the closed fist.

Now, with the forefinger of your right hand, tuck into the ditch any

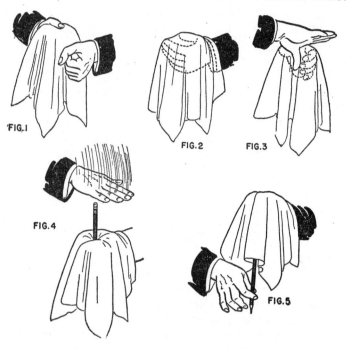

FIG. 1 FIG. 2 FIG. 3 FIG. 4 FIG. 5

part of the handkerchief that protrudes too high above the opening of the ditch. This action, when done smoothly, defies detection. Take a sharp pencil and push the eraser end into the ditch. Push it up and down several times about one third the length of the pencil. Now turn the pencil over and push the pointed side into the ditch, remarking that it will be much easier to push this end through the handkerchief. Pretend that you are having a little difficulty passing it through the handkerchief. When you have the pencil halfway down into the ditch, hit the top of the pencil with your right hand, driving the pencil down into the ditch (Fig. 4). Reach under the handkerchief with your right hand and pull the pencil through (Fig. 5). It appears as if the pencil went through the handkerchief. Now open your fist under the handkerchief and turn the palm of your left hand upward. This action completely loses the ditch which was made on the outside of the handkerchief. Show that the handkerchief is unharmed.

Note: If you are seated at a dinner table, you may perform this trick with a linen napkin and table knife instead of a pencil and handkerchief.

150. *The Magic Birthday Square*

EFFECT: Using only the numbers appearing in the date of a spectator's birthday, the performer constructs a perfect magic square.

PRESENTATION: In order to prepare the audience, so that it will understand what you are about to do, explain, as follows.

"From obscure ancient times to the present day, many people have believed in the influence of cabalistic signs and numbers upon the lives of individuals. One of the oldest and most mystic of these signs has been the magic square. Discarded by the mathematician and scientist as a mathematical curiosity, it has been adapted by the mystical fraternity as a formula of great significance. One of the simplest of the magic squares is the one composed of nine units. Using numbers one to nine, and placing each number in one of the squares—the sum of any three numbers in a straight line, in any direction, up or down or diagonally, will be fifteen. For instance . . ."

Draw on a blackboard, or piece of paper, a simple magic square (Fig. 1). It is easy to memorize this so that you are able to write it down without hesitation. This will impress the audience. Now that they understand what a magic square is, continue your patter, as follows.

"I will now proceed to show you how the magic square plays an important part in the life of an individual, by constructing one and using only the numbers appearing in that individual's birth date."

Point to a spectator, preferably one unknown to you, and request him to state his birth date. Let us suppose it is March 17, 1898. Draw a magic square of nine units, and place the date in the form of numbers (3-17-98) over it (Fig. 2). It will be necessary for you to have memorized previously the squares designated by numbers, which signify the order of the squares according to their use (Fig. 3). Remember that these numbers signify the order in which each square is to be used, but they are not to be written into the squares. These numbers and their positions must be memorized by you. Only the square and date (as shown in Fig. 2) are to appear on the blackboard or paper. Now place the year number in square number 1. Ask anyone in the audience which number he wants you to use, the 3 or 17. After a choice has been made, ask whether the number selected should be added or subtracted.

(*Note:* If the birth date being used falls in the nineteenth century, such as the example we are using, the above procedure may be followed safely.

3 - 17 - 98

FIG. 1

8	1	6
3	5	7
4	9	2

FIG. 2 (empty square)

FIG. 3 — TO BE MEMORIZED

8	1	7
5	6	3
2	9	4

KEY NUMBERS — FIG. 4

	98	
		64
8		

COMPLETED SQUARE — FIG. 5

61	98	75
92	78	64
81	58	95

However, if the birth date falls in the twentieth century, the choice of subtraction in most cases must be eliminated, as you may obtain negative numbers, which will not work. Therefore, when you write the birth date, with a quick glance you can tell whether you are able to use the process of subtraction with either number designating the month or day. If you are able to use one of them, as above, do so. If you are unable to subtract one or both of them, explain to the audience that you must use addition, as negative numbers are not suitable for this experiment.)

Now let us assume that number 17 has been chosen, and subtraction has been designated. Subtract 17 from 98 and place the result, 81, in square number 2. Now subtract 17 again from 81, and place this result, 64, in square number 3 (Fig. 4). These three numbers, 98, 81, and 64, now become the key numbers. You are through using number 17, so now you proceed to use number 3. Let us say that subtraction again is selected. Subtract the number 3 from the first key number, 98. Place the result, 95, in square number 4. Then subtract number 3 from 95, and place the result, 92, in square number 5. Proceed to the second key number, 81, and repeat the same subtraction process with number 3, placing the first result, 78, in square number 6, and the second result, 75, in square number 7. Now complete this process with the third key number, 64. Place the first result, 61, in square number 8, and the second result, 58, in square number 9 (Fig. 5).

You have now constructed a perfect magic square, whose squares total, in any direction, the sum of 234.

Remember that either 3 or 17 could have been used first, and could have been either subtracted or added. The final total would have been different, but the effect would have remained the same.

151. *Under Two Hats*

EFFECT: The performer passes four paper balls from under the table to above the table, making them appear singly under a hat resting on the table.

PREPARATION: Secure four sheets of paper six by six, or you may tear four pieces approximately six by six from a newspaper. Roll each piece of paper into a ball, making four balls in all. If you prefer, you may wind a small rubber band around each paper ball to help hold its roundness. Borrow two men's hats. These preparations may be made while the spectators are watching.

PRESENTATION: Place the four paper balls on a table, forming a square, each ball about eighteen inches from the other. For clarification, the paper ball in the upper left-hand corner shall be referred to as A; upper right-hand corner as B; lower left-hand corner as C; and the lower right-hand corner as D (Fig. 1). Take the two hats, and hold one in each hand by the brim so that the thumb is on the outside of the brim and the four fingers are inside the crown. With the hats held in this position, cover balls C and D. Call attention to the fact that you can cover any two balls and leave any two visible. While pattering along these lines, move the two hats forward to cover balls A and B. As you cover ball B, the second and third fingers of your right hand clip the ball by its side, as shown in Fig. 2. Now move the hat covering ball A to the right, and just when it clears the hat covering ball B, the right hand comes out from

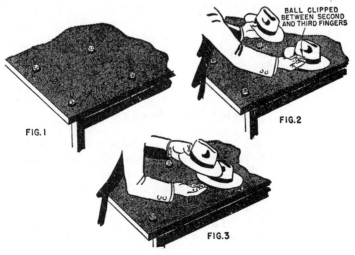

BALL CLIPPED
BETWEEN SECOND
AND THIRD FINGERS

FIG. 1

FIG. 2

FIG. 3

under it with the clipped ball, and is immediately covered by taking the hat from your left hand (Fig. 3).

Holding the hat and concealed ball with your right hand momentarily, the left hand occupies itself by apparently arranging the three visible balls. Now drop the hat with the concealed ball B on top of ball D, which is nearest to the lower right-hand corner of the table. The fingers of the right hand are spread apart, releasing ball B. At this stage you have balls B and D under the hat at the lower right-hand corner of the table. Nothing is under the hat at the upper right-hand corner of the table and there are two visible balls on the table. To the spectators it would seem that there are two visible balls and one ball under each hat. Pick up ball A with your right hand, bring your right hand under the table at the same spot where the hat that hides the two balls is resting. While your right hand is under the table, clip the ball between the second and third fingers. Now state that you are going to pass this paper ball through the table.

At this time, a bit of acting on your part will help. Say, "Go," and lift up the hat, revealing the two balls. (The hat is picked up by its top with your left hand.) At the same time you move the hat near the edge of the table. As the hat clears the edge of the table, the right hand with the clipped ball takes the hat by its brim (Fig. 2). The spectators are surprised to see two balls. Drop the hat over these two balls, releasing the concealed ball. You now have three balls under the hat. Follow the same procedure with ball C as you did with ball A. You now have four balls under the hat. But the spectators believe you have three under one hat and one under the other hat. Now, with a bit of acting, state that you are going to make the fourth ball join by saying, "Go." You say "Go," and instruct the spectator to lift up the hat which was supposed to be concealing the single ball. Naturally it is not there. Lift up the other hat and exhibit the four balls.

152. Scarne's Fire Trick

EFFECT: The performer bravely toasts his fingers in the bright flame of one or more matches, lights a cigarette, takes a few puffs, then holds the lighted cigarette between the thumb and forefinger, the lighted part of the cigarette resting against the forefinger. He endures the pain and jokes about it. This trick is a favorite of the author.

PREPARATION: The first part of the trick may be performed anywhere, but for the second part it is necessary to have a cold drink around, such as a cold glass of water or any cold liquid. Therefore the trick is best performed at a dinner table or at a party.

PRESENTATION: While seated at a table, place a cigarette in your mouth. Strike a match and pass the lighted match under the fingers of your left hand (Fig. 1). The trick is to keep the flame moving back and forth, passing over the middle part of the fingers; the fingers should be parted slightly to ventilate the hot tip of the flame. While performing this trick it is suggested that you keep the left hand in a relaxed position. By moving the flame back and forth, as described above, you will feel no burn whatever. It is suggested that you practice a bit so that you can get a bit of rhythm to your slow motion. If you want to appear to be a daredevil, strike several matches at the same time. As a matter of fact, it is easier to use several matches.

FIG.2

FIG.1

After this exhibition of toasting your fingers, light the cigarette you have in your mouth. Take a few puffs, and at the same time hold the cold glass for a minute or so with your left hand, pressing especially hard with your forefinger. This action chills the forefinger. Now take the burning cigarette out of your mouth and rest it between the thumb and forefinger of your left hand (Fig. 2). The burning cigarette will not burn the chilled finger. A bit of practice in private is necessary to perfect this trick.

153. *Scarne's Miracle Prediction*

EFFECT: The performer predicts the correct result of a mathematical problem involving the serial number on a one-dollar bill and a number mentally thought of by one of the spectators. Created by the author.

PREPARATION AND REQUIREMENTS: Go to your local bank and invest in ten new one-dollar bills. Note the serial numbers of these bills; you will find that the numbers are all alike with the exception of the last and, perhaps, the next to the last number. Secure nine standard visiting cards. On the back of one of these cards write down the first five figures of the serial numbers of these bills. On the second card mark down the answer of the first five numbers multiplied by 2. On the back of the third card, the answer of the first five numbers multiplied by 3. This procedure is followed with the remaining cards, multiplying by 4,5,6,7,8, and 9. Place these nine cards in their proper sequence in a small pocket in your wallet: the lowest figure will be first, the next highest number, arrived at by the multiplication of the serial number by the digit 2, will be second, etc. Place the wallet in your pocket. The gimmicked ten one-dollar bills are placed with some other bills in such a manner that they are easily accessible. Now, take nine one-dollar bills and place them in your right-hand coat pocket. These bills, naturally, will have different serial numbers. Armed with a pencil and an unprepared visiting card, you are ready to perform this remarkable trick.

PRESENTATION: While you are seated at a table, remark that you are going to attempt to perform an experiment that makes use of a number of bills. "I would like to borrow about ten bills—fives, tens or twenties." But, you say, the last time you borrowed some bills, it cost you ten dollars because one of the spectators claimed one of your bills. So you announce: "To prevent a recurrence, I am going to use my own money." Reach into your pocket and remove the ten gimmicked one-dollar bills from among the other bills. Place the other bills back in your pocket. Straighten out the bills by turning the serial numbers of all the bills downward. Turn the bills over rapidly to prevent any observant spectator from noting the serial numbers. Spread the bills face down on the table, look a spectator in the eye and say, "Think of a number from one to nine." Then ask what number the spectator is thinking of. In this case, let's say he says five. Reach into your pocket and produce a visiting card whose back has no writing on it. Hand it to the spectator and have him write the figure 5 on its back. You now state that you are going to write a prediction on the back of another visiting card and that you don't want anyone to see what you are writing.

Take a pencil in your right hand. Take the group of nine visiting cards, with the numbers face down, and place the cards and pencil under the table, pretending that you are writing something on the back of a card. Instead, you count down to the fifth card. Remove that card. The mere counting of cards under the table appears to the spectators as if the performer is writing. Place this card face down on the table and request a spectator to put his hand on it to prevent any switching. While this has been going on, the one-dollar bills are still spread on the table. Now request a spectator to select any bill he desires. This being done, have the spectator copy the first five numbers of the bill on a piece of paper. In the meantime, gather up the remaining nine bills and place them in the small-change pocket in your right-hand coat pocket. This is the same pocket that holds the other nine one-dollar bills. Hesitate for a moment, as though you changed your mind about leaving the bills in that pocket; bring your hand out, taking the bills which had been there all along and leaving the gimmicked bills safely disposed of. Now have the spectator multiply by five (his chosen number) the five-figure number he had written down on the card. When he has gotten his result, have him turn up the card with your prediction and ask him to compare the figures. Presto! Great trick!

154. *Magical Liquids*

EFFECT: The performer has before him several glasses and a clear glass pitcher full of ordinary water. He picks up each glass, wipes it out carefully, and then pours a different-colored drink into each glass—all from the same pitcher which is supposedly holding plain water. The performer drinks some of each to prove it is *not* a chemical trick. He patters that maybe someone in the audience would like to sample some of the drinks. He mixes all the liquids together by pouring the various drinks or parts of each into a large jar—and from this jar he pours out a glass of genuine soda or iced tea, the mixed drinks apparently having blended into the final complete drink that is now handed around in the audience.

PREPARATION: Purchase a package of food colorings; this may be obtained at any grocery store. This kit usually contains several colors, a small vial of each. Several hours before you expect to perform this trick, place a few drops of the coloring in each glass (a different color in each); these drops will dry and stick to the bottoms of the glasses. It is best to use small juice glasses. Now prepare a fairly large jar (such as an aluminum milk shaker) and place in it a tall glass tumbler, one that is small in diameter. Take a towel and force it down in the jar, all around the glass, so that when you tip the jar to pour, the glass will not fall out. Put some soda or iced tea in the glass; this is the final concoction that will be passed around to the audience (see illustration).

PRESENTATION: Show the pitcher of water, to prove there is nothing in it but plain water. Pick up each glass, cupping the bottom in your hand,

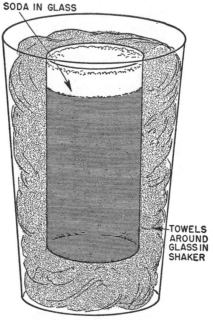

SODA IN GLASS

TOWELS AROUND GLASS IN SHAKER

and wipe it out, being sure that you do not disturb the dried spot of coloring. Now pour some water into the glasses—each of which will now contain a differently colored liquid—and sample some of each. When you "mix" these liquids, pour some of each into the jar, letting the liquid run down the inside edge so that the towel will absorb it. Then pour out the finished drink (the liquid from the glass that is in the jar). If you wish to use a bit of patter with this trick, the following is appropriate.

"The other night I went to a party and saw a magician put on an act which appealed to me greatly. He took a pitcher of plain water, and after wiping out some glasses, he poured water into them and got several different kinds of drinks—just as I am doing. I thought at the time it would be a good trick if he could change all those drinks into one nice tall drink and let me sample it, as I was getting very thirsty watching him drink all those pretty liquids. But he didn't do it. So when I arrived home, I decided to experiment. I mixed several different-colored liquids and poured them into a jar, just like this one. Then I muttered a few magic words—and, believe it or not, I poured out a nice tall cool drink, like this! My friends, tonight I am going to let you sample the result of my magical experiment!"

155. *Telepathy Par Excellence*

The use of telepathic experiments has become quite popular in entertainment. The following is a simple routine, but if you present it with the proper histrionic touch, it can be very convincing and dramatic. A bit of practice will help considerably.

EFFECT: On the center of a piece of paper, about three inches by four inches, draw a circle about half the size of the paper (Fig. 1). Hand this to a spectator and tell him that you are going to attempt to read his mind. Tell him to write any short message that he wishes within the circle (Fig. 2). Explain that this is necessary because you wish the message to be in a concentrated form. After he has done this, instruct him to fold the paper into four equal quarters, with the message within the fold so that you are unable to see it. The message, so folded, should be completely enclosed by the corner quarter of the folded packet. Have him

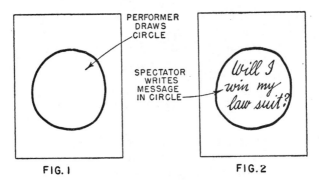

PERFORMER DRAWS CIRCLE

SPECTATOR WRITES MESSAGE IN CIRCLE

Will I win my law suit?

FIG. I   FIG. 2

PART OF TORN PAPER PERFORMER READS

Will I win my law suit?

FIG. 3

hand you this packet. Openly tear this into bits, as instructed below.

Tear the packet in half, placing the half, including the center piece, on the bottom. Tear this crosswise in half again, placing the center corner piece again at the bottom. Slide the corner piece into the palm of your right hand and continue tearing the other pieces. This may be done easily without its being obvious. Practice it a few times so that there is no hesitation. Drop the pieces into an ashtray and light them with a match. While they are burning, dramatically pace around the room as though in deep contemplation. At a time when your back is turned, open the corner of the paper which you have concealed in your hand and notice the message written thereon (Fig. 3). Do this quickly and without too much hesitation. Just a glance is sufficient. You do not have to read the entire message, absorb just enough information to get the gist of it. Continue pacing and concentrating. Stop in front of the dying flames, study them a moment and then reveal the message, or answer the question if one has been written. It does not have to be exact. As a matter of fact, if the reading is slightly incorrect, it is even more convincing.

156. The Devil's Handkerchief

The following effect makes use of what is called the "devil's handkerchief." This is a magician's utility item which is used to make small articles vanish. Make it up as follows. Obtain two square pieces of colored cloth. These squares of cloth should be of fairly heavy material, and should be the size of a man's handkerchief, or a bit larger. Place one on top the other and sew them together along the edges, leaving one half of one side open. When completed it should look like a single handkerchief (Fig. 1).

EFFECT: The performer removes his own wrist watch, causes it to vanish, and then mysteriously makes it reappear on his wrist.

PREPARATION: Obtain two toy wrist watches from one of the five and dime stores. These must look alike and also must look like genuine wrist watches from a short distance. Flexible wrist bands are preferred. Place one watch on your left arm, just below the elbow. Place the other one on the wrist of the same arm. Have a "devil's handkerchief" ready.

PRESENTATION: Tell the following story. "I was walking along a dimly lit street the other night, when suddenly a masked man darted out of a hallway, and pointing a gun at me, whispered, 'This is a stick up.' After searching me, he became very chagrined that I had no money on me. Suddenly he noticed my wrist watch." (Show the watch on your wrist to

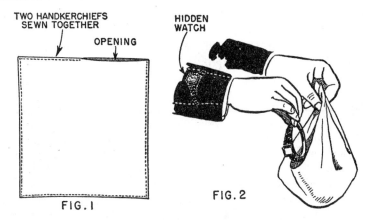

TWO HANDKERCHIEFS
SEWN TOGETHER

OPENING

FIG. I

HIDDEN
WATCH

FIG. 2

the audience.) "Pulling up my sleeve, he removed my watch, and making a bag out of his handkerchief, he dropped the watch in it."

As you say this, pull up your sleeve so that its edge is just below the hidden second watch, which of course is unseen by the audience. Remove the watch from the wrist. Pick up the "devil's handkerchief" by the four corners, forming a bag. Drop the watch into the handkerchief, actually into the secret pocket (Fig. 2). Then pull down your sleeve, but at the same time, the fingers grasp the hidden watch and pull it to the wrist with the sleeve. This action should be done naturally so that there is no hint of a suspicious movement. Then say, "As the thief was about to take off, I told him that it would do him no good, since, being a magician, I could easily foil him. He laughed derisively and ran away. When he got to his hideout, he eagerly opened the handkerchief to examine his loot, and was extremely surprised to find that the watch had vanished." At this time, open the "devil's handkerchief," shake it to show that it is empty and that the watch has vanished.

"The moral of this story is to show that you should always believe a magician, because not only did I cause the watch to vanish from the handkerchief, but I also caused it to reappear where it belongs, on my wrist." Now show the watch, back on the wrist.

157. *Scarne's Bean Trick*

EFFECT: The performer shows four small beans in the palm of his left hand. He picks them up, one at a time, with his right hand, and apparently places one in each ear and one in his nostril. He places the last one in his mouth. He opens his mouth over the table and out drop the four beans.

PRESENTATION: Drop four small beans into the palm of the left hand. Openly show them there. Cup the left hand slightly, and with the right hand pretend to remove one bean, but actually take two (Fig. 1). Immediately close your left hand. Hold up your right hand and show one bean, hiding the other between the fingers. Tell the spectators that it is necessary to lubricate the bean slightly. Bring your right hand up to your mouth, as if to wet the bean with saliva, and as you do this, drop one bean into the mouth, while wetting the other (Fig. 2). This should be done smoothly, and should look only as if you just wet the bean with your lips and tongue. Holding the closed left fist with the fingers upward, drop this bean into the palm near the tips of the fingers, and show it in this position (Fig. 3). Make a motion, with the right hand, as if to remove the bean with the fingers, instead, open the fist of the left hand

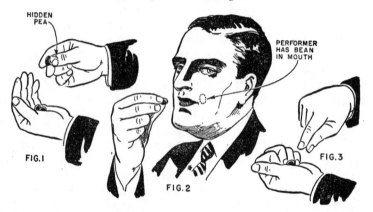

HIDDEN PEA

PERFORMER HAS BEAN IN MOUTH

FIG. 1   FIG. 2   FIG. 3

slightly, and allow the bean to drop into the palm. Immediately bring the right hand (presumably holding the bean) to the right ear and go through the motions of inserting the bean into the ear. Practice this move a bit, so that your timing is perfect and it looks as if you really are following through with this action.

Open your left fist and show the three beans. Now repeat the above actions, starting with the removal of a bean (actually two) and ending by placing the "bean" into your left ear. Open your left fist again and show two beans. At this time you have two beans secreted in your mouth. Repeat the routine again, picking up the two beans as one and ending up by placing the "bean" in your nostril. When you open your left fist this time, there is only one bean. Pick this bean up and actually place it in your mouth. Hesitate a few moments and then, bending your head forward, open your mouth and allow the four beans to drop out slowly.

If done smoothly and with proper timing, this routine becomes a real mystifier and is excellent entertainment. Incidentally, the beans may be marked in any way you wish.

158. *The Turnabout Bill*

EFFECT: The performer holds a bill with its picture face toward the audience. By a series of simple folds and unfolds, without in any way turning the bill over, the picture mysteriously appears upside down.

PRESENTATION: Hold a dollar bill with its picture face toward the audience, the portrait of George Washington upright (Fig. 1). Fold the upper half of the bill forward and down (Fig. 2). Now fold the right half of the bill forward and to the left (Fig. 3). The bill is now folded into a packet of quarters. Fold the right half of the packet forward and to the left, forming a packet of eighths (Fig. 4). The folds with the four corners are now toward you. Turn these to the right as if you were turning a page backward, unfolding the bill back into quarters (Fig. 5). Now unfold the

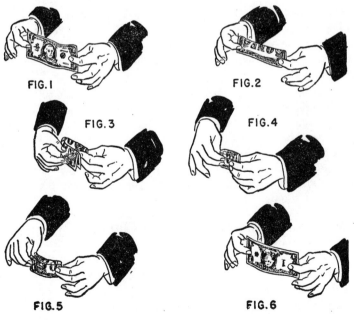

FIG.1

FIG.2

FIG.3

FIG.4

FIG.5

FIG.6

half of the bill toward you, to the right, again as if turning the page of a book, but this time to the left. Unfold the half of the bill toward the audience, bringing it up and revealing that the picture of George Washington has mysteriously turned upside down (Fig. 6).

159. *Color Separation*

EFFECT: Four packages of small pieces of tissue paper are thoroughly mixed together. Each package is composed of differently colored paper. The mixture is placed in a jar. A spectator calls for a color; the performer inserts his hand into the jar and removes a handful of pieces, all of the color called for. He repeats this performance four times.

PREPARATION: Place a tray on a table. On the tray put a glass jar, large enough so that your hand can enter and move about slightly. Into four paper bags place a quantity of small pieces of different-colored tissue paper, each bag holding the same color. Cut these pieces from colored tissue paper, making them about one inch square. Have enough of these pieces so that when they are placed in the jar they will fill about two thirds of it.

Now make four small packets of these colored papers, and bind them with a thin strip of tissue paper, of the same color. Instead of the piece of tissue paper, you may use a small rubber band. Conceal two of these packets under the edge of your vest on one side, and the other two on the other side.

PRESENTATION: Hand the jar to a spectator and ask him to empty the bags into the jar. Instruct him to mix the papers thoroughly. After everyone is satisfied, ask someone to call out one of the colors and instruct the spectator who is holding the jar, to reach his hand into the jar and take out a handful of pieces of the selected color. As he is about to do this, steal the proper packet from under your vest, and say, "No, not that way." Insert your hand, with the packet concealed in it, into the jar. Work your hand through the papers, and with a movement of the fingers, break the strip of tissue around the packet, or, if it is bound by a rubber band, slip the band off. Remove your hand and slowly allow the pieces to fall to the tray.

Repeat this procedure with another spectator and another color. At the completion of this second round, ask if there is anyone at all who feels he could perform this feat. In the meantime, steal the other packets from under your vest, and hold one in each hand.

Continue with the third and fourth colors. In order to create the illusion of a great quantity of paper, as you drop the papers in the tray, work the fingers of the hand in a rubbing motion against the palm and allow the pieces to fall slowly.

160. *Magazine Mind Reading*

EFFECT: A spectator opens any magazine to any page. He picks out the first word of any line. On a piece of paper he writes the name of the magazine, the page number and the number of the line. He seals this paper into an envelope. The envelope is marked, and is then slipped under a closed door behind which the performer has been all the time. After a few moments, the performer slips the envelope back under the door. The envelope is unopened, but across its face is written the page number of a dictionary and the line at which the selected word appears. When the spectator checks he finds the word to be correct.

PREPARATION AND PRESENTATION: Have about half a dozen different magazines and a dictionary lying on a table. Lock yourself in an adjoining room, giving the excuse that you can meditate and concentrate better when you are alone. Tell a spectator to open any of the magazines to any page. Counting down from the top he is to stop at any line, and concentrate on the first word of that line. Then he is to print on a slip of paper the name of the magazine, the page number and the number of the line. He is to slip the paper into an envelope and seal it. He may sign his name in ink across the sealed flap so that he may later make sure that the envelope was not opened. He slips this under the door to you.

In the other room, unbeknownst to the audience, you have a set of duplicate magazines, a flashlight and a duplicate dictionary. Hold the envelope up and flash the light through from behind it. You may now easily read what is printed on the paper. Open the duplicate magazine, count down to the designated line, and read the first word. Look this up in the dictionary, and write the following on the face of the envelope: "If you will open the dictionary to page __, and count down __ words, you will find the word you are concentrating on." Slip the envelope back under the door. The spectators will find, to their great surprise, that everything checks. They may examine the envelope thoroughly, but will find that it has not been disturbed.

161. *Test of Strength*

The following is one of those fake "hypnotic" effects, which, when presented properly, is quite convincing.

EFFECT: The performer asks a volunteer spectator, who looks fairly husky and strong, to stand in front of him. The performer suggests to this spectator that he will not be able to lift him (the performer). The spectator tries and fails. When the performer tells him that he may now lift him (the performer), he succeeds.

PRESENTATION: In selecting the spectator to assist you, make sure that he is larger and much huskier than yourself. The experiment becomes much more convincing under these circumstances. Have him stand in

front of and facing you. Hold your elbows to your sides, your hands pointed up. Shift your elbows forward a bit. This shifts your center of gravity backward, so that it becomes quite difficult for the spectator to lift you in this position. So, when you ask the spectator to lift you by your elbows, he will not be able to do so, or at least will find it very difficult. Now shift your elbows back to your sides. Tell the spectator he may now lift you, and he does, quite easily.

A second method is to ask the spectator to place his hands around your hips. Hold his hands tightly around the wrists, and when he attempts to lift you, twist his wrists outward. This causes the lifting force to become dissipated, and the spectator finds he cannot lift you. If you hold his wrists tightly, the spectator will not notice the twisting action. In order to restore his "strength" so that he may lift you, release the twisting pressure.

Make sure that you present this experiment in such a way as to convince the spectators that it is your power of suggestion which is the activating force.

162. *Sitting Tight*

EFFECT: A volunteer subject sits in a chair. The performer merely touches him, and he is unable to stand up.

PRESENTATION: Tell the audience that you are about to demonstrate your hypnotic powers, and would like someone to volunteer to assist you in

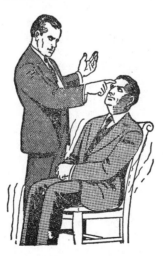

your experiment. Have your "volunteer" sit in a chair and tell him to relax completely. His feet should be flat on the floor and extended slightly forward. His hands should be in his lap in a relaxed position. His head should be tilted as far back as possible. When the person has assumed this position, tell him that at no time during the experiment is he to use his hands. Tell him that you are merely going to touch his forehead with one finger, that when you do so, try as he may, he will not be able to stand. Repeat this statement so as to give the impression that you are using hypnosis. Place your finger against the subject's forehead, and tilt his head back as far as it will go. Now tell him to try to stand. He will not be able to do so, since in this position his center of gravity has been shifted so far back that he is completely off balance. When you have completed demonstrating this, remove your finger, tell the subject to relax and bring his head forward. He will now be able to stand.

163. *Hindu Magic Papers*

EFFECT: A borrowed five-dollar bill is wrapped in several sheets of paper. When the paper is unwrapped, the five has become a one-dollar bill.

PREPARATION: Obtain one sheet of yellow tissue paper, thirteen inches by thirteen inches; two sheets of red tissue paper, twelve inches by twelve inches; two sheets of white tissue paper, ten inches by ten inches; and two sheets of blue tissue paper, eight inches by eight inches. Align the two red sheets perfectly, one on top of the other, and glue one square inch of their centers together. Place them flat on the table. On this place one white sheet, and on the white sheet place one blue sheet. Center all papers. In the center of the blue sheet, place a one-dollar bill. Fold the blue sheet over the bill so as to form a square packet, and leave it centered (Fig. 1). Over this packet fold the white sheet, again forming a square; leave this packet centered. Over the white packet fold the uppermost red sheet. Fold each side evenly so that when the packet is completed its edges are evenly aligned. This packet will naturally be centered, since it is glued to the other red sheet. Turn all the papers completely over so that the unfolded red sheet is uppermost, the packet of red, white and blue papers being hidden under it.

Place the other white sheet on this, and then the blue sheet on the white. Make a packet of these three sheets, exactly the same as the hidden packet. You now have two packets of three sheets each, glued back to back. Place these packets with the one containing the dollar bill underneath on the yellow sheet (Fig. 2). Fold the yellow sheet around

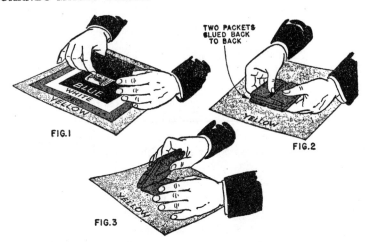

FIG.1

TWO PACKETS
GLUED BACK
TO BACK

FIG.2

FIG.3

the other papers, making another square packet. Press the folds of the papers tightly, preferably leaving them under a weight overnight. This is done so that the papers will retain their creases when unfolded and refolded. Place the papers in your coat pocket, and you are ready to perform this effect.

PRESENTATION: Remove the papers from your pocket and place them on the table. Unfold the yellow paper, then the red, then the white, and finally the blue, leaving each paper on top of those underneath it. Borrow a five-dollar bill, fold it in half and place it on the blue sheet. Fold the blue paper over the bill, then the white over the blue, making all folds on the creases. Now you must fold the red over the blue, and here is where the chicanery takes place. When you have folded three sides down, instead of folding the fourth side over the packet, fold the packet over the side (Fig. 3). This will bring the hidden packet uppermost. Fold the yellow paper over both packets again.

Make an appropriate remark and some magical passes. Unfold the packet flat on the table. Instead of the five-dollar bill, the spectators are surprised to see a one-dollar bill. Place the one-dollar bill back into the papers and repeat the process, causing the five-dollar bill to reappear. Return the five spot to the spectator, fold the papers, and place them into your pocket.

Note: Many different tricks may be performed with the Hindu magic papers, such as cashing a check, changing a coin, restoring a torn bill or card, etc.

164. *Ashes of the Phoenix*

EFFECT: A strip of red tissue paper is burned in the performer's hand. As the last inch of paper burns, he releases his hold on it. The burning paper soars high into the air, then slowly comes down in ashes. As the ashes descend to the level of the performer's hands, he reaches into them and whips out the strip of tissue paper, fully restored.

PREPARATION: Buy a package of red tissue paper at any stationery or department store (red is the only color with which this trick will work). Cut the paper into strips approximately two inches wide and twenty inches long. In cutting, *be sure* to cut the length of the strips along the grain of the paper. The trick will *not* work if the strips are cut in any other manner. Pleat one of the strips of paper, slip it into a paper clip, and with the aid of a safety pin, fasten the paper clip to your trousers just above the lower edge of the right side of your jacket. Do not permit the pin to puncture the paper. Place another paper strip in one of your pockets, and you are all set to perform.

PRESENTATION: Remove the strip of paper from your pocket. Open the paper to its full length and show it freely. Fold the strip in the center, and with your left hand hold the paper at the fold so that the free ends are horizontally in front of your hand. It is most important that the paper be held in a horizontal position to prevent the paper from burning too rapidly. Turn your left side toward your audience, so that they can see the paper, and set fire to the free ends.

As the paper burns, you will find that the ashes remain attached to the unburned portion. When only an inch of unburned paper remains, release your grip on the strip. As the last of the paper is consumed by flames, the ashes will soar high into the air as if drawn up by an unseen

hand. As you and the audience watch the ashes rise, permit your right hand to drop to your side and steal the pleated paper from the clip under your coat. As the ashes descend to your hand level, reach into them and whip out the duplicate strip of paper, holding the paper stretched between both hands. The paper is apparently reincarnated. Thanks to the type of paper and the manner in which it is cut, the ashes will float high into the air, making for perfect misdirection under cover of which you can steal the duplicate paper.

If you desire patter for this trick, the following has been found quite fitting. "You have probably heard of the Phoenix, the mythical bird who when he felt death approaching would build his own funeral pyre and cremate himself. Then from the ashes the Phoenix would rise again, reincarnated and ready for a new life. The Egyptians came to worship this bird as a god. To them it symbolized immortality and life after death. In the temple of the Phoenix the high priest performed a ceremony symbolizing the rebirth of the sacred bird. I have discovered the secret of this ritual and would like to demonstrate it to you this evening. The high priest took a piece of red paper, which symbolized the Phoenix, and set fire to it. At the proper moment, when the Phoenix's spirit was supposed to leave his body, the priest released his hold on the paper. The ashes of the Phoenix rise, symbolizing the release of the spirit, and then descend again to earth, and from the ashes steps forth a *new Phoenix, reincarnated!*"

165. *Miracle Slate*

EFFECT: The performer correctly predicts the total of four numbers selected by four different spectators.

PREPARATION: Obtain a small slate at your local five and dime or stationery store. Provide yourself with chalk, paper and a pencil. Before performing, select and memorize a four-digit number in the vicinity of 7,640.

PRESENTATION: On a piece of paper write down the number which you have memorized (in our example we will use the number 7,640), fold the paper, with the number inside, and hand it to a spectator to hold. With the chalk, draw four horizontal lines on the slate, dividing the face of the slate into five equal spaces. Present the chalk and slate to a spectator, and ask him to write down the year of his birth in the top space. After this has been done, present the slate and chalk to a second spectator; he is to write down, in the second space, the year in which some

important event in his life occurred. A third spectator is asked to write down the year in which he was married. Turn to the person who is holding the prediction, and ask him to write down any year that he wishes.

Take the slate from the fourth spectator, return to the platform, face the audience, and state that you will total the figures selected by the four spectators, and will then permit anyone in the audience to check it. Pretend to be adding the figures and placing the total in the last empty space, but in reality write down the figure which you have previously memorized (in our example, 7,640). After you have finished, look at the slate again and remark that you don't seem to be able to add correctly tonight. With a handkerchief, pretend to rub out the total, but, actually, erase the date which the fourth spectator wrote down. You now have three sets of figures, a blank space, and a total. Fill in the blank space with the proper figures, which, when added to the other three figures, will add up to your predicted total. An example is given below:

Year first person was born	1901
Year something important happened in second person's life	1942
Year third person was married	1922
Blank space where fourth date was erased	——
Total	7640

In other words, as you add up the last column you get 5, so in the blank space of that column, fill in a 5 to get 0. In the next column you get 7. Write in a 7 to get 4. Next you get 28; write in an 8 to get 36. The last column totals 6, so write in a 1 to get 7. The figures which you now have in the column total your predicted 7,640. Hand the slate to another spectator and ask him to verify the addition. Go to the first three spectators who wrote numbers, and ask them to verify their figures. As each figure is verified, erase it from the slate. Approach the fourth spectator, as if to show him the slate, then stop and say, "No, we won't show you the slate with the total until after you open my prediction and read the number which I wrote on the paper." As you say this, erase the fourth figure, leaving only the total on the slate. When the fourth spectator reads your prediction, show the total which you have on your slate to the audience.

166. *The Flying Glass*

EFFECT: A glass of water disappears from under a cloth and is found in a borrowed hat.

PREPARATION: To perform this trick it is necessary to prepare a special covering cloth. Obtain two pieces of cloth of the same design, each about eighteen inches square. Place one of these pieces of cloth flat on a table. On the center of the cloth place a cardboard disc of the same diameter as the mouth of the glass you plan to use. Place the second piece of cloth on top of the first so that all the edges match evenly. Sew the cardboard disc to the center of the two pieces of material, and then sew the matching edges of the two cloths together. You now have what appears to be a single cloth.

PRESENTATION: Borrow a hat from a member of the audience. If you are on the same level with the audience, turn up the sweat band of the hat to prevent the audience from seeing into the hat. Put the hat down on a nearby table. Show the glass and fill it with water. Holding the glass in one hand, cover it with the prepared cloth so that the cardboard disc covers the mouth of the glass. You then state that you can cause the glass to fly into the hat, either visibly or invisibly. But the visible method is not very mystifying, because all you have to do is carry the glass over to the hat and set it down. As you tell the audience this, walk over to the hat, and holding the glass through the cloth from above, lower the glass into the hat. Leave the glass in the hat, and raise your hand again, holding the cardboard in the cloth as if you still retained the glass under the

GLASS IN HAT

cloth. Inasmuch as the cloth still hangs as if the glass were concealed in it, the audience believes you have the glass in your hand.

Step as far away from the hat as possible, and with your free hand, grasp one corner of the cloth and whip it into the air. The glass of water has vanished. Walk over to the hat and remove the glass of water.

One performer I know has a confederate in the audience. After apparently removing the glass from the hat under cover of the cloth, he calls his friend forward to look into the hat and to hold it. The friend, of course, says that the hat is empty. Then, as the performer flips the cloth at the opposite end of the room, the friend, holding the hat, lets it jerk down a bit as if the glass had just arrived in the hat. This adds a lot to the trick.

The following patter will give you some idea of what to say while performing this trick. "For my next experiment—you'll notice I say experiment because the last time I attempted to do this trick the folks in the first three rows got showered with water and glass—as I said, in my next experiment I am going to attempt to cause a glass of water to fly through space and land in a hat. First, I require a hat. May I borrow yours, sir? Thank you. Just to keep the water from splashing we'll cover it with this cloth.

"I'd like you to know that I can cause this glass to travel either visibly or invisibly. Of course, if it travels visibly it isn't much of a trick. All I have to do is lower it into the hat, like this. But—I'll do it the difficult way. I'll stand way over here, and without my hands once leaving the ends of my arms, I will cause the glass to take flight. Eureka! It has gone. Unless it got caught in a strong head wind, the glass of water should be here in the hat. Yes, here it is. And that, my friends, is *Magic.*"

167. *Behind the Napkin Ball*

EFFECT: The performer tears a paper napkin to pieces and then restores it. He repeats the trick, explaining how it was accomplished. At the conclusion of the "explanation," the spectators are even more baffled.

PREPARATION: Five paper napkins are required. It is suggested that you use the small size, about eight or nine inches square. Roll one of the napkins into a ball, and roll another one over the outside of it. Roll two more napkins in the same manner. Place both sets of napkins in your right-hand jacket pocket. Take the remaining napkin, roll it into a ball, and place it in your left-hand jacket pocket. You are now ready to work the trick at any time or any place.

PRESENTATION: Remove one of the sets of napkins from your right-hand pocket and unroll it to show that it is only an ordinary paper napkin. As you unroll it you will find that the inner ball will roll unobserved into your right hand, the open napkin hiding it. Tear the napkin into several pieces, but always leave one section in the right hand so as to cover the ball. Next, roll the torn pieces inside the piece in your right hand so that the ball of torn pieces lies next to the other ball in your hand. (By holding the two balls side by side, you can freely show them as one.) As you show what appears to be one ball, roll the papers around so that the untorn napkin is nearest your fingertips. Open it in such manner as to conceal the ball of torn papers behind it. Show the napkin, apparently

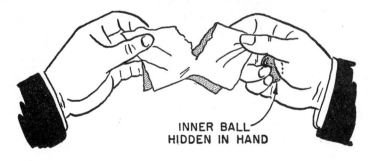

INNER BALL
HIDDEN IN HAND

restored. Roll this napkin into a ball, enclosing the torn papers inside it, and deposit in your right-hand trouser pocket.

Because the audience has been so nice to you, you volunteer to show them how the trick was done. You admit frankly that you use two napkins. To demonstrate, remove the single napkin from your left pocket, unroll it, show it to the audience and reroll it into a ball. Hold this in your right hand. Then remove the set of napkins which you still have in your right-hand jacket pocket; open the outer napkin, permitting the one inside to remain in your right hand. Press the two rolled-up napkins which you have in your right hand and show them as one. To the audience this appears to be the napkin which you just showed them and then rolled into a ball. Explain that this extra napkin is never seen by the audience because it is hidden by the open one, and demonstrate how a napkin can be hidden behind the open one. Proceed to show how the open napkin is torn and rolled up. Show how to switch this ball for another one. Open one of the other napkins and show that it is restored. Ball up this napkin, but in doing so, ball it around the pieces of the torn one. Drop this ball into your pocket. You still have a ball of paper in your hand. The audience believes it to be composed of torn papers, but it is really a complete napkin. Patter to the effect that the magician must still dispose of the ball of paper, but if he should get caught with it in his hand he'd better work some real magic. As you say this, open the napkin and show it to be whole again.

168. *The Vanishing Fountain Pen*

EFFECT: The performer passes around a fountain pen for examination, crashes the pen across his knee, and instantly the pen vanishes.

PREPARATION: Most fountain pens have a clip on the cover part. Take a length of black rubber elastic, or, if unavailable, tie several rubber bands together to form a piece about twelve inches long. On one end place a safety pin, and fasten this to the back of your vest. Fasten the other end of the elastic to the clip of the pen cap, and place the pen in your upper right-hand vest pocket.

PRESENTATION: Standing with your right side toward the audience, remove the pen from your pocket with your right hand, holding the pen so that the upper part of the cap is hidden by your hand and the rubber is hidden by your right arm. Unscrew the pen from the cap with your left hand, show the pen around, and then screw it back into the cap again. Taking the pen in both hands, raise one knee slightly. As your

ELASTIC

hands come down to crash the pen across your knee, release your grip on the pen, and it will swiftly and without being noticed be drawn under your jacket. Open both hands and show that the pen has vanished.

If you don't wear a vest, the safety pin may be fastened to the inside of your jacket between your shoulders, and the pen may be carried in your inside jacket pocket or right-hand trousers pocket.

One performer I know performs the trick in the following manner. He buys two cheap pens, and after fastening the extra cap to the elastic, places it in his vest pocket. The pen, with an unprepared cap, he places in another pocket, or has it lying on his table until he needs it. He removes the cap from the pen and passes the pen around for examination. While attention is focused on the pen, he places the regular cap in his vest pocket. When he gets the pen back, he takes the prepared cap from his vest pocket, screws it onto the pen, and concludes the trick as described above.

Another performer makes the pen vanish as described in the first method, but has a duplicate pen planted either on his own person or on some member of the audience. After making the pen vanish, he produces the duplicate and passes it for examination with the cap on it.

The following patter has been found suitable for this trick. "Have you seen the new unbreakable pens just out on the market? I bought this one today down at (local store). Here, take a look at it. Looks like an ordinary pen, but they say that it is positively unbreakable. If it breaks any time during the next million years, just send it back and they'll give you a new one. I'm going to test it by trying to break it across my knee. Hey, where did it go? It vanished. How am I going to turn it in for a new one? I knew there was a catch to that offer. I'm sorry I hocked my old pen to buy this new one."

169. *The Uncrushable Glass*

EFFECT: The performer takes a glass of water, clears the table in front of himself, and places the glass of water up under the table cloth, holding the glass by its top rim. Suddenly he crashes the glass down to the table top. The glass vanishes. Casually reaching under the table, the performer produces the missing glass of water. It has apparently passed right through the center of the table.

PREPARATION: Take a strip of fairly heavy cardboard or celluloid and cut it into a disc about the diameter of the mouth of the average glass tumbler. Keep this in your coat pocket, and you are always ready to perform this trick.

PRESENTATION: While seated at the table, secretly remove the disc from your pocket and place it on your lap. Show the glass of water, and as your hand comes down with it, apparently to slip it under the table cloth, leave the glass in your lap, between your legs. At the same time, pick up the disc on your lap and place it under the upheld table cloth. By holding the disc through the cloth at approximately the same height as if holding the glass, you give the impression that the glass of water is under the cloth. At the proper time crash the cloth down to the table top. Then, as your hand goes under the table to retrieve the glass, pick up the glass of water which is resting in your lap.

There you have the trick. Build it up and make a lot of it. It will really prove amusing..

170. *The Melting Half Dollar*

EFFECT: A borrowed half dollar is placed under a handkerchief and handed to a spectator. The spectator is instructed to hold the half dollar and handkerchief over a glass of water. At the performer's command, the spectator releases his hold on the coin, permitting it to drop audibly into the glass of water. When the handkerchief is removed from the glass, the coin is found to have vanished. The performer produces the half dollar from his pocket and returns it to its owner.

PREPARATION: Purchase a glass watch crystal or flat round glass disc about the same size as a half dollar. Place this in your left-hand jacket pocket so that you can reach it easily. Equip yourself with a water glass, partially filled, and a man's handkerchief.

PRESENTATION: Hold the watch crystal in your left hand, keeping it concealed in the palm of your hand by curling your fingers enough to hide it.

Request some member of your audience to lend you a half dollar, but before he gives it to you he is to note its date, or mark it in some manner so that he can identify it later. Take the coin with your right hand and step back to the table where the glass of water is resting. Place the coin in your left hand, holding it between thumb and fingers at the fingertips. Open the handkerchief with your right hand, and place it over your left hand. With the right hand reach through the cloth and pretend to grasp the half dollar. In reality, grasp the watch crystal with your fingers and thumb at its rim, and permit the half dollar to drop into your left palm. Hold the handkerchief and watch crystal over the glass of water as illustrated, and request one of the spectators to hold the coin in the

handkerchief in the same manner. As soon as he has a grip on the handkerchief, step back from the table and instruct him to release his grip on
the coin, permitting it to drop into the glass. As he does this, the watch
crystal hits the glass and sounds like the coin, convincing the audience
that the coin is actually in the glass. Instruct the spectator to remove the
handkerchief from the glass. As he is doing this, drop the coin into your
left jacket pocket. The glass watch crystal, resting on the bottom of the
glass of water is not visible to the audience. The coin has apparently vanished. Show that your left hand is empty, reach into your jacket pocket,
and produce the coin. Return it to its owner for identification.

171. *Coin Divination*

EFFECT: While the performer's back is turned, each of three spectators
picks up a coin, each of different value. Almost immediately the performer announces which coin is held by each spectator.

PREPARATION: Make up a small chart like the following:

MATCHES LEFT	PENNY	DIME	QUARTER
1	NO. 1	NO. 2	NO. 3
2	NO. 2	NO. 1	NO. 3
3	NO. 1	NO. 3	NO. 2
5	NO. 3	NO. 1	NO. 2
6	NO. 2	NO. 3	NO. 1
7	NO. 3	NO. 2	NO. 1

Place this chart in a pocket where it can be reached easily. Obtain
twenty-four wooden or paper matches, and place them in another pocket.
Supply yourself with a penny, dime, and quarter.

PRESENTATION: Place the twenty-four matches on the table without calling attention to how many matches you have, and call for three spectators to assist you. Numbering these spectators 1, 2, and 3, give Number 1
one match, Number 2 two matches, and the last spectator three matches.
Arrange the remaining matches on the table so that you can count them
at a glance. Place a penny, dime, and quarter on the table. Turn your

back to the table and instruct each spectator to select one of the coins and place it in his pocket. After this has been done, give them the following instructions: "Will the person who selected the penny please remove from the table as many matches as I originally gave him. Next, whoever has taken the dime please remove twice as many matches as I gave him; and the person who took the quarter, please remove four times as many matches as I gave him. Please conceal the coins and matches which you have taken." While this is going on, secure the chart and conceal it in your hand.

Now turn around for an instant to ask them if the instructions have been followed. During this instant, glance at the table and observe the number of matches remaining on the table. Turn your back again, and glance at the chart. Look down the column marked "Matches Left" until you reach the figure corresponding to the number of matches remaining on the table. Reading across the chart, the figure in each column signifies the number of the spectator who is holding a particular coin.

For example, if six matches remain on the table, the penny is held by spectator Number 2, the dime by spectator Number 3, and the quarter by spectator Number 1.

Of course, the chart is never seen by the spectators.

172. Magic Key Rings

EFFECT: A coin is borrowed from a spectator and is placed flat on the table near two key rings and two small squares of cardboard. One cardboard square is placed over one of the key rings. This ring and square are then stacked on top of the other piece of cardboard; the ring and squares of cardboard are stacked on top of the remaining key ring, and the entire stack is placed over the borrowed coin. The performer removes the top square of cardboard, then the first ring, and then the other square of cardboard—and reveals that the coin which had been in the center of the remaining ring has vanished. Restacking the rings and squares, the performer causes the ring to reappear on the table.

PREPARATION: Obtain two key rings, a piece of cardboard, and two sheets of eight and one-half inch by eleven inch white paper. From the piece of cardboard, cut two squares whose sides are a little shorter than the diameter of the rings. To determine if the cardboard is the proper size, place one of the squares on one of the key rings. The rim of the ring should protrude from all sides of the square, but you should be unable to see anything inside the ring.

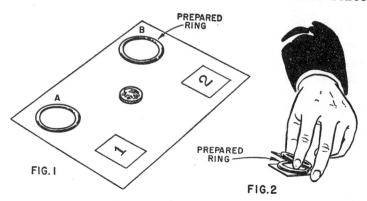

FIG. I

FIG. 2

Apply mucilage to one surface of the rim of one of the key rings, and glue one of the sheets of paper to the ring. After the mucilage has dried, cut away the excess paper, leaving a small circle glued to the underside of the ring. This circle should not extend beyond the perimeter of the ring.

When ready to perform the effect, place the other sheet of paper flat on the table with the rings and squares lying on the sheet of paper. In this way, the paper glued to the one ring will not be visible.

PRESENTATION: Borrow a coin from one of the spectators and place it on the center of the sheet of paper. Fig. 1 shows how the coin, rings, and squares are placed on the paper. With your left hand, pick up square number 1, holding it with your thumb on one edge and your first two fingers on the opposite edge, holding the cardboard from above. Place square 1 over ring A and pick up both in the manner described above. Place them on top of square 2 and, adding this square to the stack, place them all on top of ring B (the prepared ring). Lift up the entire stack and place it on top of the coin. With your right hand, remove square 1, placing it in the lower right-hand corner of the sheet of paper. Remove the ring from the stack and place it on top of square 1. With the left hand, remove square 2 and place it in the lower left-hand corner of the sheet of paper. The coin is now hidden under the circle of paper glued to ring B. To the audience it appears that the coin has vanished.

To cause the coin to reappear again, pick up square 1, with ring A on top of it, with your right hand. Place these on top of the prepared ring. Raise the prepared ring slightly off the paper, and with the left hand slide square 2 under the prepared ring, but over the coin. With the left hand, raise the entire stack and show that the coin has reappeared.

Now for an original move that again permits you to show the rings and the squares. You are holding the squares and rings in your left hand. With your left forefinger, raise the front edge of square 1 (top square) slightly. The second finger retains a grip on the rear corner of square 2 while the thumb remains in its original position (Fig. 2). With a slight throwing motion to your right, permit the prepared ring to slide from between the squares and onto the paper. Hold your hand close to the paper during this action. Drop square 2 next to the prepared ring. Drop the remaining ring next to square 2, and the remaining square next to this ring. This move again places all equipment in full view of the audience without revealing the secret.

173. *Roping a Handkerchief*

EFFECT: The performer holds a piece of rope, about five feet long, with his foot on one end, the other end held between his teeth. Holding a large handkerchief by diagonally opposite corners, he ties it around the rope twice. Yet, when he pulls the two tied ends of the handkerchief toward the audience, it penetrates the rope, leaving a knot still tied in the handkerchief.

PRESENTATION: Hold a five-foot length of clothesline vertically by placing your foot on the lower end, holding the other end in your teeth (Fig. 1). Remove a large pocket handkerchief from your pocket (for a pretty effect, use a large silk scarf available at women's shops and five and ten cent stores) and hold the cloth by diagonally opposite corners (Fig. 2). End A is held between the first and second fingers of your left hand; the third and fourth fingers are curled around the handkerchief. End B is held in the right hand between the first and second fingers. The palms of both hands face upward. The handkerchief is held in this manner between the rope and your body.

Carry end B around in front of the rope and place it in your left hand, holding it between your left thumb and the base of the first finger, and between your left second and third fingers (Fig. 3). With the thumb and first finger of your right hand, reach through the loop from above and grasp corner A (Fig. 4). As you pull end A through the loop, turn your left hand so the fingertips point downward, the second finger of your left hand forming a smaller loop in the cloth (Fig. 5). Do not permit the audience to see that this finger has fouled the knot. Pull the knot rather tightly around the rope as you slip your left second finger out of the handkerchief. Hold end B in your left hand and end A in your right. To

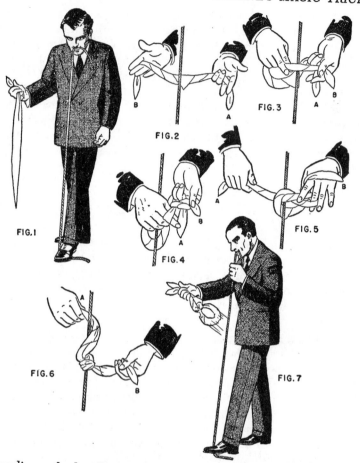

FIG.1

FIG.2

FIG.3

FIG.4

FIG.5

FIG.6

FIG.7

the audience the handkerchief appears to be securely tied around the rope. In reality, the knot is now a slip knot.

Carry end A in front of and above end B, completely around the rope in a counter clockwise direction (Fig. 6). Tie ends A and B together in front of the rope. Your left hand grasps the rope near your mouth, while your right hand grasps the tied ends of the handkerchief. Now pull the handkerchief away from the rope. The handkerchief will apparently penetrate the rope, the ends remaining tied together (Fig. 7).

Note: The above trick can be performed on a spectator's wrist or on the back of a chair, by executing the same moves as above. Naturally, they must be executed at a different angle.

174. *The Astonishing Match*

EFFECT: A wooden match mysteriously rises out of a match box. The match is lit and the fire extinguished. The burnt match is then wrapped in a handkerchief and is made to vanish. The match reappears in the performer's pocket. The performer takes the burned match, and striking it against the match box, causes the match to burn again.

PREPARATION: Take a penny match box and punch a hole in the top cover near one end (Fig. 1). A paper punch is ideal for making the hole. Place a few matches in the box, and slip another match through the hole in the cover and down into the drawer, so that just the head of the match sticks out of the top of the box (Fig. 2). Place this box in one of your pockets. Next, take several matches and dip their heads in black ink. After the ink has dried, place the matches in another pocket. Finally, take another match, light it, and quickly blow out the flame. Slip this burned match into the seam of a pocket handkerchief. This can be done by cutting a little slit in the seam at one corner. Force the match into the seam, place the handkerchief in your pocket, and you are ready to perform.

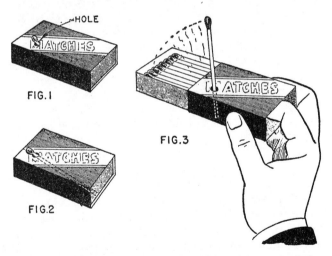

PRESENTATION: Remove the match box from your pocket, and show it on all sides, concealing the protruding match head with your thumb. Hold the box in your right hand, slightly above the eye level of the audience. Hold the box with the thumb and second finger at its edges, the index finger pushing the drawer slowly forward. This causes the match to rise out of the hole, but to the audience it looks as if it is rising from the opening drawer (Fig. 3). Remove the match from the box, light it, then blow out the flame, replacing the box in your pocket. Next, remove the prepared handkerchief from your pocket and pretend to wrap the burned match in the center of it. Actually, you keep the match stick in your hand and bring the handkerchief corner, in which you have secreted the other match, into the center of the cloth. You can now permit anyone at all to hold the match through the folds of cloth. Grasp one of the free corners of the handkerchief, and at the count of three, shake the handkerchief, causing the match to "vanish."

Next, drop the hand, which is holding the burned match, into the pocket in which the ink-dipped matches are resting. Switch the burned match for one of the others, and produce the inked match. This match appears to be the one which you had just burned.

Show this match, and remove the match box from your pocket. Rub the match head along the striking surface of the match box, causing the match to burst into flame once again. Apparently a burnt match has been relit.

You might like to model your patter on the following: "I'd like to show you my latest invention—one which should revolutionize the match industry. You see, with my invention you merely push the match box open, and a match rises to meet you. But, you might say that this is not matchless, so I will make this a matchless trick by striking the poor thing, and then wrapping it in my pocket handkerchief. Will you please hold the match, sir? Are you sure you have it? That's fine. At the count of three, you let go. One-two-*three.* And the match is gone, so, as you can see, this is a matchless trick. But, we are friends, so I'll show you where it went. And now, to cast a little light on the mystery—a little light with a burned-out match."

175. *Three Shell Game*

EFFECT: The performer places a small pea on the table, covers it with one of three walnut shells, and then moves the shells around a little. A spectator is then asked to point to the shell under which he thinks the pea is hidden. Regardless of which shell is selected, the pea is found under one of the other shells. This can be repeated many times without the spectator's ever selecting the correct shell.

PREPARATION: Go to your local grocery store and purchase a few English walnuts. Separate the shells, taking care not to crack them, and clean the insides of the half-shells carefully. From this group select three half-shells of medium size and not too deep. These half-shells should also have

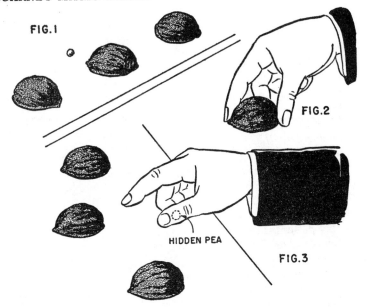

FIG.1

FIG.2

HIDDEN PEA

FIG.3

the largest openings on the rear of their rims to permit the easy removal and entry of the pea. It is advisable to fill part of the inside of the half-shells with putty or plumbers' cement. This extra weight prevents the half-shells from sliding too easily when you don't wish them to. (During the remainder of this description the half-shells will be referred to as shells.) After the putty has dried, use a piece of emery cloth to smooth the edges of the putty.

The "pea" that you will use is a small piece of sponge rubber cut from a rubber sponge or rubber knee pad available at most five and ten cent stores. This piece of rubber should be very small. Experiment to obtain the proper size by placing it under the shell. It must not be so large as to lift the shell when you slide the shell across the table top.

Several sheets of newspaper or a piece of cloth spread on the table make a suitable surface on which to push the shells and the pea.

PRESENTATION: Place the three shells on the spread newspapers or cloth table cover, and place the pea in front of the center shell (Fig. 1). Cover the pea with this shell. With your right hand, grasp the shell with your forefinger on the front end of the shell, and the thumb and second finger at the rear (Fig. 2). The tips of the fingers holding the shell must be touching the table top lightly. Move the shell forward five to eight inches, holding the shell as instructed. You will notice that as the shell is pushed forward the pea slides out from under the rear of the shell and comes between your thumb tip and forefinger. Press these fingers together and hold the pea (Fig. 3). The pea is now in your hand, and if you keep your hand close to the table, the pea will be hidden from the spectators' view.

Grasp one of the other shells with your right hand in the same manner, then move it back to its original position. Do this several times with each shell, bringing them all back to their original positions, as at the start of the trick. As you draw one of the shells back, introduce the pea into it, being sure you do not hide it in the shell from which you had secretly removed it. This is done merely by releasing your grip on the pea as you slide the shell toward your body. In other words, it is the reverse of stealing the pea from under the shell. To remove the pea secretly, push the shell forward. To hide it secretly in another shell, pull back. Practice these two movements until they can be performed without detection.

In actual performance, invite a spectator to keep his eye on the shell hiding the pea. Secretly remove the pea from the shell and introduce it into another. He will, of course, select the wrong shell as the one housing the pea. Another method is to keep the pea concealed in your hand after removing it from under the shell until after the spectator has selected a shell as the one he believes hides the pea. After showing that he is wrong, merely move one of the other shells back and introduce the pea under it. Show it to be there by raising the shell. Using this method it is even possible to permit the spectator to select two shells without discovering the pea under either of them. In any event, the spectator is always wrong.

Note: If you have difficulty removing the pea secretly from under the shell, a slight downward pressure on the front of the shell with your forefinger will help. By the same token, a slight upward pressure on the rear of the shell while drawing it back will aid you to introduce the pea secretly into the shell.

176. *Blowing a Knot Out of a Handkerchief*

EFFECT: The performer ties a knot in the center of a large handkerchief. He blows on the knot, and it disappears.

PRESENTATION: Show a large pocket handkerchief and hold the cloth by diagonally opposite corners. The end in your left hand is held between the first and second fingers; the third and fourth fingers are curled around the handkerchief. Your right hand holds the other end between the first and second fingers. About three inches of each end should extend beyond the hands. The palms of both hands face upward (Fig. 1).

FIG.1   FIG.2   FIG.3

FIG.4   FIG.5   FIG.6

Place the right-hand end in your left hand, holding it between your left thumb and the base of the first finger, and between your left second and third fingers (Fig. 2). With the thumb and first finger of your right hand, reach through the loop from above and grasp the lower corner (Fig. 3). Pull the end through the loop, at the same time turning your left hand so the finger tips point downward, the second finger of your left hand forming a smaller loop in the cloth (Fig. 4). Do not permit the audience to see that this finger has fouled the knot. Make the knot rather tight as you slip your left second finger out of it.

With your left hand, hold the handkerchief, as shown in Fig. 5. With your right hand press downward on the knot, causing it to become loosened. Continue to hold the supposed knot with your right hand and throw the uppermost corner of the handkerchief over your right index finger. Blow on the knot, and release the pressure of the right hand on the knot (Fig. 6). To the audience, it appears that you have blown the knot out of the handkerchief.

177. *Human Magnetism*

EFFECT: The performer places his hand flat on the table top, palm down. He then takes a group of calling cards and inserts them, one at a time, under the palm of his hand from all angles. The performer then raises his hand slowly, the cards clinging to his hand in a most mysterious manner. At a command, the cards leave the performer's hand and cascade to the table.

PREPARATION: It is necessary that you wear a ring to perform this trick. Paint a toothpick white, and after the paint has dried, insert the toothpick under your ring so that it runs the length of your finger (Fig. 1). If possible, use a strip of clear celluloid cut to the shape of a toothpick.

Obtain approximately twenty calling cards, or cut twenty pieces of cardboard measuring about two and one-fourth inches by three and one-half inches. Carry these cards with you.

PRESENTATION: Place the cards on the table, and place your hand on which you are wearing the ring flat on the table, palm down. When you place the first two cards under your hand, place them between the toothpick and your hand, at each side of the ring (Fig. 2). The other cards are placed between the first two calling cards and your hand. Insert each calling card from a different angle so as to provide supporting surface large enough to hold all the cards.

With the calling cards held in this manner, you can lift them off the table with no apparent means of support. By pressing your ring finger lightly against the toothpick, and by rotating the palm of your hand toward your body so that the toothpick won't be seen, you can turn the

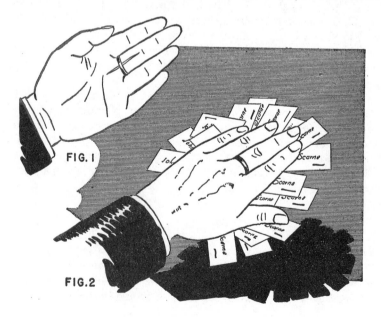

FIG. 1

FIG. 2

cards completely over without dropping them. By painting the toothpick white you cut the possibility of its being seen.

At the conclusion of the trick, when you want the cards to leave your hand and cascade to the table, merely bend your fingers in against the toothpick, causing it to break. The falling cards will conceal the pieces of toothpick.

Patter for this trick might be: "We have all heard about magnetism, that everyone's body contains a certain amount of electricity. This experiment will prove what a wonderful force human electricity or magnetism can be when one knows how to control it by thought and action. For example, I merely rub my feet on the carpet like this, touch my fingers to a piece of metal, and I draw a spark which charges my body with electrical forces that make it possible for me to take these calling cards and place them under the palm of my hand like this, and lift them right off the table without any support. As you see, the cards cling to my hand in a most magical manner. But this is not magic—it is magnetism at work. By snapping my fingers I break the electrical circuit, and the cards leave my hand."

178. The Mystic Fortune-Telling Cards

Although fortune telling is not strictly within the magical field, it is so greatly favored by some spectators, especially women, that it does not hurt the general entertainment value of a program to include it in one's repertoire. The following routine is based on a bit of mathematical trickery, but is quite entertaining and will even convince a few gullible ones of your prowess as a fortune teller and mind reader.

EFFECT: A card, upon which are listed most of the possible questions that are generally asked of a fortune teller, is handed to a spectator. He mentally selects one of the questions which he wishes answered. Several other cards are handed to him, each card containing some of the questions found on the master list. He discards all the cards except those upon which his question is recorded. The performer studies the master list for a moment and then answers the spectator's question, although this question is not mentioned at any time.

PREPARATION: Using six blank four-inch by six-inch index cards, make up the following question cards. All cards are of the same size, therefore use single space on the master chart and double space on the other five. On the master card, type the thirty questions, as shown. Type five more charts, also as shown. (Bear in mind that these charts must be the same

size. Limited space prevents us from showing these cards full size.)
Each of the five supplementary cards is numbered at the top. The arrangement of the questions and the number on top of each of the five
cards make the trick almost self-working.

QUESTIONS

1. Will there be another war?
2. Will I win the lawsuit?
3. When will I get married?
4. Will I get out of this mess?
5. Will I get the money?
6. Should I tell all?
7. Am I a sucker?
8. Should I borrow the money?
9. Will I take a trip?
10. Is she (he) true to me?
11. Will my health improve?
12. Will I be successful?
13. What is my greatest fault?
14. Should I believe all I hear?
15. When will I get a job?
16. Will I keep the date?
17. When will I retire?
18. Should I go on a diet?
19. Should I sell the property?
20. Should I make a change?
21. Will I take an ocean voyage?
22. How many children will I have?
23. Should I sign the papers?
24. Should I take out insurance?
25. Will the operation be a success?
26. Can I afford a vacation?
27. Will I be wealthy?
28. Will I buy a new car?
29. Should I offer to help?
30. Have I any enemies?

2

Will there be another war?
When will I get married?
Will I get the money?
Am I a sucker?
Will I take the trip?
Will my health improve?
What is my greatest fault?
When will I get a job?
When will I retire?

Should I sell the property?
Will I take an ocean voyage?
Should I sign the papers?
Will the operation be a success?
Will I be wealthy?
Should I offer to help?

3

Will I win the lawsuit?
When will I get married?
Should I tell all?
Am I a sucker?
Is she (he) true to me?
Will my health improve?
Should I believe all I hear?
When will I get a job?
Should I go on a diet?
Should I sell the property?
How many children will I have?
Should I sign the papers?
Can I afford a vacation?
Will I be wealthy?
Have I any enemies?

4

Will I get out of this mess?
Will I get the money?
Should I tell all?
Am I a sucker?
Will I be successful?
What is my greatest fault?
Should I believe all I hear?
When will I get a job?
Should I make a change?
Will I take an ocean voyage?
How many children will I have?
Should I sign the papers?
Will I buy a new car?
Should I offer to help?
Have I any enemies?

5	6
Should I borrow the money?	Will I keep the date?
Will I take the trip?	When will I retire?
Is she (he) true to me?	Should I go on a diet?
Will my health improve?	Should I sell the property?
Will I be successful?	Should I make a change?
What is my greatest fault?	Will I take an ocean voyage?
Should I believe all I hear?	How many children will I have?
When will I get a job?	Should I sign the papers?
Should I take out insurance?	Should I take out insurance?
Will the operation be a success?	Will the operation be a success?
Can I afford a vacation?	Can I afford a vacation?
Will I be wealthy?	Will I be wealthy?
Will I buy a new car?	Will I buy a new car?
Should I offer to help?	Should I offer to help?
Have I any enemies?	Have I any enemies?

PRESENTATION: Before beginning this trick, say: "From ancient times to the present day, fortune telling has been a thriving business. In the old days, the priests and soothsayers held the people completely under their control with their powers, the generally superstitious nature of the minds of the people making this possible. Anything the soothsayers said was accepted without question. In modern times, of course, things have changed. There is much less superstition and fear of the unknown, but among many people there still exists a belief in the ability of some individuals to read minds and foretell the future. I am going to attempt an experiment along these lines. You may use your own judgment as to the authenticity of the demonstration. Will the spectator who wishes his fortune told please assist me?"

After a spectator volunteers, give him the master list and instruct him to select mentally one of the questions. After he has done this, retrieve the master list and hand him one of the other five cards. Ask him to look at the questions on this card. Should his question be on this card, he should retain it and concentrate on it once again; if not, he is to return the card to you. Pass the other four cards to him, singly, with the same instructions.

Here is where the key number at the top of each card comes into action. Card Number 1 has a value of one, card Number 2 is valued at two, the value of card Number 3 is four, card Number 4 is valued at eight, and card Number 5 counts sixteen. You will note that the value of each card is twice that of the preceding card. You should experience no difficulty in remembering these values. When the spectator returns the cards upon which his question does not appear, note their number designations, so that you will be able to determine which cards he is holding. For example, if he returns cards 1, 3, and 5, you know that he is still holding cards 2 and 4. Add the values of the cards which he still retains; in our example, card 2 with a value of two and card 4 with a value of eight gives you a total of ten. The spectator has selected question Number 10. Looking at the master list, you determine what the question is.

After you have located this question, do not read it, but proceed to answer it, either seriously or humorously, permitting your answer to signify that you know what question he has in mind. The author suggests a humorous answer, since it is more entertaining. With good presentation and a bit of ingenuity, you may convince the audience, or at least most of it, of your ability to tell fortunes, and also to read minds.

179. *Hypnotic Rigidity*

Perhaps the best known of all hypnotic experiments is that of muscular rigidity. For years this test has been accepted without question as proof that the subject is in a hypnotic trance. Now you can duplicate this experiment, and with the proper presentation cause it to appear to be a genuine demonstration of hypnotism.

EFFECT: A male spectator is put into a "hypnotic trance" and becomes as rigid as a board. He is then placed horizontally, face up, supported only by chairs at his head and feet. The performer may stand or sit on the spectator's unsupported middle without the spectator's body sagging or collapsing.

PREPARATION: Two chairs are required to support the subject while he is rigid. A heavy cloth, approximately two feet square, or a small board, will be useful in permitting the performer to stand upon the subject without soiling or damaging his suit. A third chair is used by the performer to facilitate stepping up and on or off the subject's body.

Although at times a volunteer spectator can be used in this trick, the author suggests that you practice with a friend, and later use him as the stooge or confederate who volunteers from the audience to assist you.

PRESENTATION: Call for three volunteer spectators, and while they are coming forward, state that you never use confederates in any of the experiments which you perform. Only you and your confederate know that this is a slight warping of the truth. He is among the first to volunteer, and takes his place with the other two volunteers on the platform.

Look at the three volunteers for a minute or so as if trying to deter-

mine which one will make the best subject. Ask your confederate to step forward. Standing in front of him, gaze into his eyes, and in a firm voice, loud enough for the audience to hear, command him to relax, and hold his hands at his sides. You then pretend to hypnotize him, saying something like, "Your eyes are becoming heavy. You would like to sleep. Your eyes are closing. They are becoming heavy. Sleep, Sleep." Repeat this several times. As you say these words, your confederate slowly closes his eyes. When his eyes are completely closed, step behind him, at the same time saying, "You are in a deep sleep. You will not awaken until I tell you to." As soon as you are behind him, place your fingertips on his shoulders momentarily to assure him that you are in position. You next suggest to him that he is becoming rigid, more rigid. The confederate stiffens visibly, and then begins to fall backward. As he falls, catch him under the shoulders and ask one of the other volunteers to grasp his feet. Now place him, face up, on two chairs, so that his head and shoulders rest on one chair, and his feet on the other. His middle is left unsupported.

You may now sit or stand on him without causing him to lose this rigidity, provided you do not place your weight directly on the center of his body. Place the cloth on him at the position where you plan to stand, and gradually raise yourself onto his body. Remember, he can retain his rigidity as long as you do not step upon the center of his body. You may stand off center, or straddle his middle, without causing him to collapse. When standing on the rigid body, hold the hand of one of the volunteers for support. Use the third chair, as mentioned above, to help step up or down. Step down, and with the aid of one of the volunteers stand your confederate on his feet. To bring him out of the "trance," support him from behind with one hand as you tell him that when you snap your fingers he is to awaken and will not remember anything that has happened to him while he was in the trance. Snap your fingers loudly. Your confederate awakens. Thank him and the other volunteers and permit them to return to their seats, unless you want to keep one of them on stage to assist you in your next trick. In any event, do no more with your confederate.

This demonstration may be very convincing, according to your presentation. The use of the extra volunteers lends support to the statement that you do not use confederates. By telling the confederate that he will be unable to remember anything that occurred while he was in the trance, you provide him with a perfect out should any member of the audience ask him what it felt like to be hypnotized. It is especially important that the confederate does not overplay his part. If possible, witness several authentic hypnotism demonstrations, and observe the actions of both the hypnotist and his subjects, and model your own behavior after theirs.

Should anyone challenge you at the completion of the experiment, by stating that he is capable of maintaining his rigidity under the same conditions, even though not hypnotized, accept the challenge. Just sit or stand on the center of his unsupported body, and he will cave in. Before doing this, it is advisable that you have the heckler swear before the audience that he will in no way hold you responsible for personal injury should he be unable to remain rigid, for it is very possible to become injured as he collapses with you on top of him.

180. *The Self-Restoring Ribbon*

EFFECT: Two ribbons are tied securely around a pencil. The ribbons are then cut in half and burned by the performer. When the two halves of the ribbons are removed from the pencil, it is found that the pieces have joined together to form one continuous piece of ribbon.

PRESENTATION: Show a ribbon approximately thirty inches long, and cut it so as to form two pieces of equal length. Ask a spectator to hold an ordinary wooden pencil in a horizontal position, grasping it at the eraser end. Place the two ribbons over the pencil, as shown in Fig. 1. Ordinarily, in tying the ribbons around the pencil, you would grasp one end of ribbon A and one end of ribbon B in one hand, and the other two ends in the other hand. *Instead,* grasp both ends of ribbon A in one hand, and both ends of ribbon B in the other. Tie them around the pencil, to form an ordinary knot, as shown in Fig. 2.

Cut the ribbons at one side, near the pencil. (In Fig. 3 you see both ends of ribbon A being cut.) With one hand, cover the ribbons where they go around the pencil, and pull the ribbons clear of the pencil. Hold the ribbons so that your thumb covers the point where the two ribbons meet. To the audience it appears that you are holding two pieces of ribbon of equal length. In reality, you have one long and one short piece of ribbon (Fig. 4).

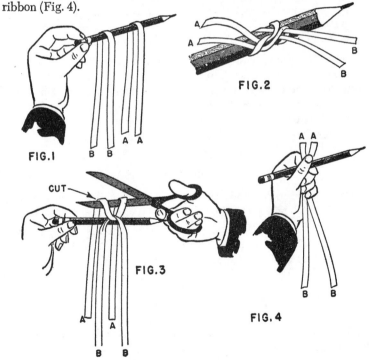

FIG.2

FIG.I

CUT

FIG.3

FIG.4

Set fire to the ends of ribbon A, and after permitting them to burn for a time, blow the fire out. Then, as a sure fire extinguisher, tap the sparks with a pocket handkerchief. While tapping, grasp the ends of ribbon A through the handkerchief and carry them away inside the folds of cloth, which you deposit in your pocket. Next, grasp one end of ribbon B with your free hand and draw it up so that it rises vertically out of the hand holding the ribbon. Stretching the ribbon taut, pull it straight up out of the lower hand, showing the ribbon to be completely restored. Give the ribbon to a spectator for a souvenir, and, incidentally, for his examination.

In performing this effect a good policy is to have the spectator who is holding the pencil join in the patter. Other spectators will be more inclined to believe that what you are saying is true if one of their members verifies it. Patter might go something like this.

"Here is a rather odd stunt with a piece of ribbon and a pencil. If I cut the ribbon in the center like this, how many pieces do I have? Two is correct. Now if you will hold the pencil, we can tie the ribbons around it like this. If I cut the ribbons on this side of the pencil, like this, and let the cut ends fall to the floor, like this, how many pieces of ribbon are still tied to the pencil? You say two, and you're right. Two ribbons. I'll remove them from the pencil and endeavor to weld them together with heat. See, the burning ends are starting to join already. I just want to burn the ribbon, not my hand, so I'd better extinguish the fire. Still some sparks. Don't want to burn the place down, you know. There. I put them out with my handkerchief. Now, here's where the magic comes in. See, there's the ribbon joined in one piece again, just like at the start. Would anyone care for a souvenir? All right, then. The ribbon is yours."

181. Serial Reading

EFFECT: The performer reads the date and serial number of a borrowed dollar bill, which had been rolled into a ball without being unfolded.

PREPARATION: This trick depends on the fact that the average person does not realize that the majority of dollar bills in circulation today are dated as a part of the series of 1935 (all bills bearing two circles, one containing the great seal of the United States, the other the pyramid with an eye at its apex, are a part of this series). In fact, many people do not even realize that there is a date on bills.

Note and memorize the serial number on a dollar bill. Crumple it into a ball, and place it in your left-hand trouser pocket. Place a folded dollar bill in the same pocket. This is all the preparation required.

PRESENTATION: Remove the folded bill from your pocket and explain that most people are not aware of the fact that all bills have series dates printed on them. Point to the lower right-hand corner of the bill and pretend to read the date as 1932. This is a bit of misdirection which lays the foundation for making your audience believe that different bills carry different series dates. Now replace the bill in your left-hand trouser pocket, and remove the crumpled bill, hiding it from view by curling your fingers around it.

Ask some member of the audience to remove a dollar bill, not too old or too new, from his pocket and ask him to memorize the date of the bill. He is then instructed to crumple the bill into a ball. Take the bill from him and place it in your left hand, pressing it against the bill you have hidden there. In this way you can show the two bills as one, and indicate that your hands are otherwise empty. Put the bundle of bills to your forehead, and pretend to concentrate. Then call out that the date of the bill is 1935. Ask the owner of the bill if you are correct. Naturally, you are.

Then explain that occasionally some members of the audience suspect that you receive the bill from a confederate in the audience. To dispel any such thoughts, you offer to let another member of the audience verify the date. Here is where the dirty work comes in. Hand the person *your* bill, keeping the borrowed bill concealed in your hand. As the spectator opens the bill to verify the date, your hand containing the borrowed bill drops to your pocket for a handkerchief. Wipe your brow with the handkerchief and return it to your pocket, leaving the borrowed bill in the pocket with it.

The spectator is apparently holding the borrowed bill, but in reality he is holding the bill whose serial number you memorized. You are now ready to perform the final miracle. Ask the man who is holding the bill to concentrate on its serial number. You then call off the number, digit by digit, including the letters preceding and following the number. The bill is then returned to the person from whom you borrowed the original bill.

Note the strong points of this trick. You give the date of the bill before there is any chance for an exchange of bills. You then prove that there is no exchange by permitting a second spectator to verify the number. While the bill is in his hands you then tell the serial number of the bill without ever having seen its face. This reading of the serial number will even fool anyone present who may know about the date business. Nor do you have to worry about the owner of the bill looking at the serial number before he hands you the bill, for you have him concentrating on the date of the bill.

If you experience difficulty memorizing the number on the bill, you can have it written on a calling card, and as you name the numbers pretend to write them on the card. Another idea is to write the numbers lightly on the wooden frame of a slate with pencil. As you call the numbers write them on the slate with chalk so the audience can see them.

182. *Matchless Matches*

Here are three quickie tricks with matches that take only a few seconds to perform. They are useful when matches are handy, and if properly presented, produce quite a bit of comment among your audience. Such routining of tricks employing one piece of equipment is always good magic.

EFFECT: A lighted wooden match is produced from the performer's pocket. He holds the match upright, high above his head, between the thumb and forefinger of his right hand. When the performer blows down into his left sleeve, the match in his right hand goes out. He then produces a second lighted match from his pocket and permits it to burn for a while. Pulling an invisible hair from his head, he ties it around the match and pulls the head of the match off.

PREPARATION: Place a large piece of sandpaper and several wooden matches in your right trouser pocket.

PRESENTATION: Reach into your trouser pocket and grasp a wooden match, holding it between the thumb and forefinger of your right hand. Strike the match on the sandpaper and remove it from your pocket (Fig. 1). This usually gets a laugh from your audience. Holding the match between your thumb and forefinger, permit the second finger of your left hand to rest against the tip of the match (Fig. 2). Hold the

FIG.1   FIG.2

match high above your head, and raise your left hand so that the left sleeve is near your mouth. Blow into your left sleeve. As you do so, snap the second finger of your right hand against the match stick. The fire will go out. The snap will not be detected simply because the audience is watching your left sleeve. Discard the match.

Produce another lighted match from your pocket. Hold this one in front of you, in the same manner as described, ready to snap it out. Permit this match to burn down about one-third of its length. Pull an imaginary hair from your head, and pretend to wrap it around the burned match head. Pull at the "hair," and as you do, snap your second finger against the match tip. The sudden blow will dislodge the burnt match head and cause it to fall to the floor, thanks to the fact that the head of the match has carbonized and is very weak.

183. *Air Knots*

EFFECT: Two handkerchiefs, securely tied together by the performer and examined by the spectators, are thrown into the air. When they fall, they are found to be untied.

PRESENTATION: Borrow two handkerchiefs. If not available, use your own. Hold one handkerchief in each hand between the thumb and forefinger, permitting about three inches of the corner of each handkerchief to extend beyond the point at which you are holding them (Fig. 1). Tie these two corners securely, preferably in a square knot, although this is not essential. A square knot is suggested because the knot is well known, and its strength is unquestioned. Pass the handkerchiefs for examination. After they are returned to you, hold one of them in your left hand between the thumb and forefinger, grasping it just below the knot. With the right hand, grasp the corner of the same handkerchief, just above the knot. Pull both hands apart firmly. To the spectators it appears that you are tightening the knot. In reality you are fouling the knot, causing the handkerchief which you are holding to form a straight line about which the other handkerchief is now tied in a sort of slip knot. (This is

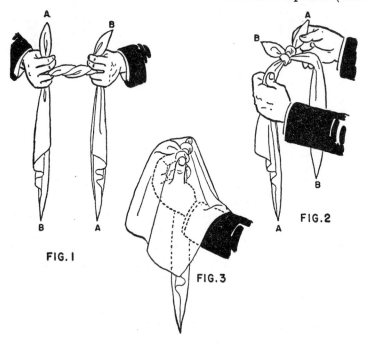

FIG. I

FIG. 2

FIG. 3

shown in Fig. 2, where the handkerchief and corner to be pulled are both marked A.) It may be necessary to jerk this handkerchief rather hard to cause it to form a straight line.

Release your right hand grip, and drape the handkerchief which is hanging from the knot (handkerchief B in Fig. 2) over the front of your left hand. Grasp the handkerchief below the knot with the left thumb and forefinger, and keep applying pressure against the knot with your left hand until the handkerchief has cleared the knot (Fig. 3). Do not permit this handkerchief to be drawn out of the left hand. Instead, hold it in your left hand by pressing the third and fourth fingers against the handkerchief, thus holding it against the palm of your left hand. As soon as the handkerchief has cleared the knot, drape it over the front of your left hand, and roll both handkerchiefs into a loose ball, being certain not to reveal the fact that they are no longer tied together. Throw the handkerchiefs high into the air, and they will fall separated. To perform this trick properly, considerable practice is required.

184. *Pulse Control*

One of the most startling and really puzzling effects is that of stopping the pulse at will. People are generally very much impressed by this feat. This stunt is a sure reputation builder.

EFFECT: The performer, using sheer will power, slows the beat of his pulse until it finally stops. Then he slowly reactivates it and brings it back to normal. He also succeeds in stopping a spectator's pulse.

PREPARATION: Secure a small ball, or tie a handkerchief into a number of knots until it assumes the shape of a ball. Place the ball or handkerchief under your naked armpit. You are now ready for the experiment.

PRESENTATION: Say to your audience: "In the course of studying magic and mentalism, I have developed my will power to such an extent that I am able to control my bodily functions by will and thought alone. I would like to demonstrate this. Will someone please step forward and feel my pulse." When the spectator has located, and begins to feel your pulse beat, ask him to raise his other hand and to drop it when the beat can no longer be felt. While he is holding your pulse, slowly press your arm in toward your body. The ball in your armpit will apply a steady pressure against the artery supplying the pulse. The spectator will feel the pulse slowly stopping. When the pressure on your arm has reached a certain level the pulse beat will not be detectible, and the spectator will drop his hand signifying to the rest of the audience that the beat has ceased. Then, slowly release the pressure against the ball, and your pulse will return to normal. Raise your arm and allow the ball to drop to your waist inside your shirt. You are now free to permit the spectator to examine your arm to prove that you have nothing hidden there.

After this initial experiment has been performed, announce: "I have just demonstrated on myself the extent to which I have developed my will power. I should now like to perform a similar experiment on another individual. In this experiment I shall use the power of suggestion to cause another person to stop his pulse." Ask for a volunteer and place him in front of, and to the left of, you. With your left hand, grasp his left arm near the armpit, holding your thumb on top and the fingers under his arm. Hold his arm up with your right hand under his elbow. Ask another spectator to step forward and feel the subject's pulse on his left wrist. Tell the subject to relax, and to concentrate on his pulse. By slowly applying pressure with your left hand, you can cause his pulse to slow down and finally to stop. By applying the pressure slowly, as you tell the subject to relax you can stop his pulse without his realizing you are pressing on his artery. To bring the pulse back to normal gradually release the pressure on his left arm. During this time you can enhance the effect by stroking his arm with your right hand as if stimulating circulation.

If you are unprepared to stop your pulse completely, as described above, you may still demonstrate your ability to control your pulse, as follows. Have two spectators step forward, and have each one feel one of your wrists for your pulse. As you patter, slow up your breathing, finally stopping it completely. This action will slow the pulse sufficiently to be noticed by the spectators holding your wrists. When you become uncomfortable, begin breathing again, slowly at first and then speeding it up. This will speed up the pulse again. It is advisable to practice this several times so that you are able to talk without breathing. When you become adept at this, the audience will never suspect the subterfuge employed.

185. *Blindfold Cigarette Test*

EFFECT: The performer hands three different brands of cigarettes to three spectators, a different brand to each person. He is then blindfolded. Each spectator lights his cigarette, and one at a time wafts some smoke toward the performer's nose. By the odor of the smoke, the blindfolded performer correctly identifies the brand of each cigarette.

PRESENTATION: This effect is based on the fact that a person blindfolded with a handkerchief can still see downward to the floor. The bridge of the nose causes the handkerchief to be elevated slightly under each eye, permitting the blindfolded person a limited degree of vision.

While performing this effect you might say, "I am about to attempt an experiment to prove how well developed my senses are. In this experiment I shall subject my sense of smell to a test that has never been equaled. To each of three people I shall give a cigarette, each person receiving a different brand. As a matter of fact, rather than use my own cigarettes and give anyone cause to believe that I have altered the tobacco content of them in any manner, I would like to borrow three cigarettes from you people in the audience. Will everyone please take out your package of cigarettes and select for yourselves the three brands to be used in this demonstration."

After the selection has been made, take the three cigarettes and hand one to each of three spectators. As you are doing this, notice the color and shape of the spectator's shoes and cuffs. Coupling this information with the brand of cigarette given each spectator, it is an easy matter to identify the brand when you see the person's shoes or cuffs after you are blindfolded. After the audience is satisfied that you can't see through the blindfold, request one of the spectators to stand about a foot away from you, and gently blow some of his cigarette smoke toward you. By looking down your nose you will once again be able to see his shoes and cuffs, and can identify the brand of cigarette he is smoking. Name the brand. Repeat with the other two spectators. This experiment will give you the reputation of having powers much beyond those of normal human beings.

Note: You can simplify the memorizing of the cigarette brand by using one or two women for the test. The difference in women's footwear is much greater than in men's, making identification that much easier.

186. *Mnemonics*

Mnemonics is a word meaning a means of aiding the memory. It is the basis of most memory courses, and is an excellent prop to the memory. It may be applied easily to your magical entertainment, and with proper use may bring you the reputation of being a memory wizard. The basic requirement is the following table of letters and their numerical equivalents. The third column contains a brief explanation of why these letters have been selected to represent each number. This explanation should help you remember which numbers and letters are paired. You will notice that only consonants have any numerical value, vowels being ignored.

1	l	one vertical stroke
2	n	two vertical strokes
3	m	three vertical strokes
4	r	predominant sound in word fouR
5	f, v	predominant sounds in word FiVe
6	b, p	resemble number
7	t, d, k	resemble number
8	h, th, sh, ch	letter h sounds like number 8
9	g, j	letters sound similar, and 9 resembles g
0	s, z	predominant sound in zero

After you have memorized this table you will find it an easy task to translate words into numbers and numbers into words. For example, the word FORTUNE, stripped of vowels becomes F R T N. By substituting numbers for these sounds, FORTUNE becomes 5472. To translate this 5472 into a word, we find that the letters FRTN are the predominant sounds in the word. A brief experiment in vowel placement gives us the word FORTUNE again. A truly mystifying effect can be obtained by using mnemonics with a person's name.

EFFECT: You are introduced to a stranger. You tell him that you are going to assign a number to him, and that he should write down the number some place and carry it with him at all times. You then tell him that the next time you meet, whether it be the next day, the next week, month, year, or many years later, you will repeat his number for him upon request.

EXPLANATION: Knowing his name, you translate it into a number. For example, his name is Jack Brown. Translating this into a number, you have 97642. This is the number you assign him. No matter when you meet him again, as long as you hear his name (if you have forgotten it) you can repeat his number for him.

This is a very impressive demonstration of memory, and will keep the folks in the hometown talking about you for many years to come. Should you be called back to a place in which you have already given a performance, the members of the organization hiring you will be mystified by this feat of memory, and in many cases it will pay off in repeat performances.

A great many mental and magical effects may be devised by using this system. Use your ingenuity to produce an effect performed by no one but yourself.

Note: Two magicians I know, working as a two-man magic team, produced a variation on the above effect worthy of note. Because of the difference in the length of different names, they devised a method of giving everyone a five-digit number, and incidentally of assigning a number to a husband and wife without duplicating any part of the number. Their method was to use only a man's last name and a woman's first name.

We will assume that Jack Brown and Mary Brown are husband and wife. Taking the name BROWN for the man, they were able to translate this into the number 642. To obtain two more digits, they added the last two digits of the number, 4 and 2, to obtain the fourth digit, 6. The number became 6426. Once again, adding the last two digits, they got the fifth number, 8. The number became finally 64268. This was Jack BROWN's number. By the same method, his wife Mary received the number 43707.

Where the name could be translated to form more than three numbers, they still only took three from the name. Where only two numbers could be obtained from the name, as in the case of Mary, these two numbers were added to form the third digit, and the process continued from there. In those few cases where only one digit could be obtained from the name, as in the case of Joy, where only the number 9 is found in the name, the digit was repeated (99) before using the addition to form the number 99875.

Should the total of the two digits exceed 10, the first digit of the total is dropped, and only the last digit is considered. Thus, 9 plus 9 equals 8. Should the name begin with the letter S or Z, as in Smith or Zelda, ignore the letter so that no number will begin with a zero.

230 of 272 reason

187. *Match Antics*

Here are two effects with book matches that can be routined and presented together.

EFFECT No. 1: The performer balances a pack of matches on end. The spectator is unable to acomplish this feat.

PREPARATION: Have two full books of matches in your pocket. Both packets are closed, but one match remains outside the cover of one of the packets (Fig. 1).

PRESENTATION: Remove the two packs of matches from your pocket, and casually throw one to a spectator, retaining for yourself the book having the one match outside the cover. Hold this book of matches so that the spectator cannot see the match outside the packet (Fig. 2). Placing the match book on the table with the curved end downward, spread the match out slightly to form a prop and release your hold on the match book. Propped by the match, the pack of matches will stand on end, apparently balanced in that position (Fig. 3). Ask the spectator to balance his packet of matches on end. Naturally, he will be unable to do so, the center of gravity of the match book being too high to permit the packet to remain in this position. Saying, "In case you think this book of matches I have is prepared in some manner, I'll prove to you that it isn't," open the packet, permitting the protruding match to spring back into place. Casually show that your hands are empty, and throw the match book to the spectator. He will probably examine the packet and attempt to balance it. Of course, he will still be unsuccessful.

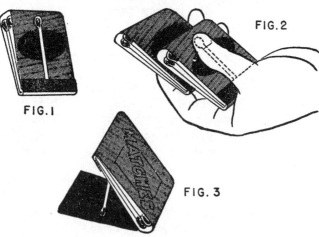

FIG. 2

FIG. I

FIG. 3

EFFECT No. 2: Three full match books, preferably borrowed, are handed to a spectator. While the performer's back is turned, a spectator opens one of the match packets and removes one match. Closing the packet, he returns all three books to the performer. Without opening any of the packets, the performer weighs them in his hand, one at a time. After weighing each one, he returns one to the spectator. This is the packet from which one match was just removed.

PREPARATION: Use the two packets of matches used in the previous effect, plus another full packet which you may borrow or supply yourself. It helps to have different designs on the covers of each so that the spectator can easily identify that packet from which he removed the one match.

PRESENTATION: While the spectators are examining the two books of matches used in the previous effect, obtain the third packet. Open all three packets, one at a time, and then close them again. As you close each one, press the cover down firmly with your thumb so that the covers are tightly wedged into place. Hand all three books of matches to a spectator, turn your back, and instruct him to select one of the books of matches and remove a match from that packet. He is then told to close the cover of the packet, and to hand all three packets of matches to you. When he closes the packet he will not wedge the cover as firmly as you did. Pattering to the effect that you can tell from which book the match was taken merely by weighing them in your hand, apply a slight sliding pressure on the cover with your thumb. You can immediately determine which cover is loose, and thus tell from which packet the match was taken.

188. *Liquid Suspension*

EFFECT: A soda bottle is filled with water. When the bottle is inverted, water pours out. The bottle is turned upright again, refilled with water, and inverted again. At a command from the magician, the water does not pour out. Toothpicks are inserted into the opening of the inverted bottle to show that it is not blocked in any way. Only when the performer wills it, does the water begin to pour.

PREPARATION: From a piece of thin, transparent, colorless celluloid cut a circle the exact size and shape of the mouth of a soda bottle. With a pin, punch several small holes in the celluloid, just large enough for a toothpick to pass through. Place this piece of celluloid in your right-hand jacket pocket. Supply yourself with several toothpicks, a soda bottle, and a pitcher of water.

PRESENTATION: Pass the bottle for examination, if you wish. Fill the bottle with water from the pitcher, invert the bottle over the pitcher and per-While you are doing this, unobtrusive-mit some of the water to pour out.

ly obtain the celluloid disc with your right hand. Refill the bottle with water. Place your hand over the mouth of the bottle so that the disc covers the opening of the bottle. Invert the bottle with your hand still over the mouth. Command the water to remain in the bottle, and remove your hand from the bottle's mouth. External air pressure and surface tension of the liquid will prevent the disc from falling off, and will keep the water from flowing out through the pin holes. To prove that nothing is blocking the opening, take several toothpicks and insert them, one at a time, through the holes in the disc. The toothpicks will shoot up through the water to the surface where they will float. When you have convinced the audience that all is fair, turn the bottle upright, and at the same time steal the cap with your right hand. The bottle of water may once again be examined freely.

Note: Some performers punch a hole large enough for a pencil to pass through in the center of the disc, and fasten two short pieces of scotch tape to the disc so that some of the tape protrudes at opposite ends. The disc is then placed against the bottle so that the tape adheres to the side of the bottle. In addition to passing toothpicks through the opening, they also pass a pencil through the hole and into the bottle. The tape is needed to hold the disc to the bottle because the large hole does not leave a large enough surface for the external air pressure to hold the disc in place. In this case, the bottle is not presented to the audience for examination, it being too difficult to remove the cap cleanly from the bottle.

Other performers prefer to use a piece of wire mesh rather than a cel-luloid disc. To prepare this piece of equipment, cut a disc from a piece of wire screening. Border the edge by bending the excess screening in toward the disc while shaping the disc to fit the neck of the bottle. The border is necessary to prevent water from leaking out between the screen and the bottle. This disc is then inserted inside the neck of the bottle. Water can be poured from the bottle by tilting the bottle slightly. When the bottle is held vertically no water will flow out. Toothpicks can still be inserted through the screening. When wire mesh is used the bottle cannot be examined at any time.

Instead of using water, some performers take a full bottle of soda, open the bottle, and pour some salt into the liquid to remove the carbona-tion. After the reaction has ceased, they recap the bottle and present the effect, as described, after opening the bottle on stage. Under no circum-stances should you use a carbonated beverage for this effect. The gas given off by the liquid might create sufficient pressure to blow the disc off the bottle, or if the disc is fastened to the bottle, the gas can force the liquid through the holes.

189. *Scarne's Changing Cigar*

EFFECT: The performer shows a certain brand of cigar and rolls it inside a handkerchief. When the handkerchief is unrolled the cigar is found to have changed to the brand selected by a spectator. (Created by the author.)

PREPARATION: Secure two cigars of similar size and shape but of different brands. Be sure that the cigar band on one of them is under the cello-phane wrapper. Certain sizes of Dutch Masters and El Productos meet all these requirements. We will assume that these are the particular cigars you are using in performing this effect. Remove the cigar band from the El Producto and place it over the cellophane wrapping of the Dutch Master, so as to conceal the Dutch Master cigar band which is under the cellophane (Fig. 1). If the outside cigar band fits too tightly, separate the glued ends and reglue them closer to their tips. Use only a spot of glue, and be sure not to get any glue on the cellophane. Place this cigar in your jacket breast pocket.

Obtain a sheet of eight and one-half inch by eleven inch paper. Tear the sheet in half, placing one half in a convenient pocket. Tear the other half into eight equal pieces. Discard one of these small pieces. On the seven remaining slips of paper write the names of different brands of cigars, one brand on each slip. Do not write the names of the cigars you are using in the trick—in our example, El Producto and Dutch Master.

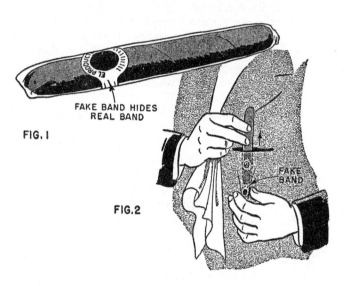

FAKE BAND HIDES
REAL BAND

FIG. 1

FAKE
BAND

FIG. 2

If you are not familiar with seven brands of cigars, here are a few that you might use: White Owl, Phillies, Blackstone, Harvester, Webster, Cinco, Romeo & Juliet, Corona, Optimo, Admiration, La Magnita, and La Primadora. Fold each slip with the writing inside, and place all seven of them in your right-hand jacket pocket.

Arm yourself with a pencil and a handkerchief and you are ready to perform this trick.

PRESENTATION: Remove the prepared cigar (the Dutch Master with the El Producto band on the outside) from your breast pocket, show it to your audience, and state, "A friend of mine became a father today, and he's been passing out free cigars to everyone he meets. I thought I was in luck when he gave me this El Producto"—show the El Producto band on the cigar—"but unfortunately I don't care for El Productos at all, so I might as well use it in a trick. Now just watch what happens to this El Producto."

Place the cigar in your breast pocket, with the end closest to the cigar band pointing downward. Remove the handkerchief from your pocket, saying, "First we'll wrap the El Producto in a handkerchief." Open the

handkerchief and freely show both sides. Holding the handkerchief in
your left hand, grasp the exposed end of the cigar with your right hand.
At the same time your left hand takes hold of the cigar through the cloth
of your breast pocket just above the cigar band. As you pull the cigar out
of your pocket with your right hand, you will find that your left hand
causes the cigar band to slide off the cigar and remain in your pocket
(Fig. 2). As soon as the cigar is out of your pocket wrap it inside the
handkerchief, so that no one will see the Dutch Master cigar band under
the cellophane wrapper. Place the wrapped cigar on a table, or hand it
to a spectator, with the words, "Will you please hold this El Producto for
a few moments."

Pretending to search for a piece of paper, find, as if by accident, the
half sheet of paper you had placed in your pocket. Look at the paper for
a moment as if seeing whether or not it is important to you. Saying, "This
will do," tear the paper into eight equal pieces as you did in your preparation.

Stating that you are going to write the name of a different brand of
cigar on each slip, pick up one slip of paper, cup your left hand in front
of it and write "Dutch Master" on it. Fold the paper as you did those in
the preparation, and place it on the table. Pick up a second piece of paper
and pretend to think of another brand of cigar, and then again write
"Dutch Master" on the paper. Fold this slip and place it on the table. Repeat this process with each of the other six papers. A bit of acting to con-
vey the impression that you are actually thinking of another brand of
cigar is good misdirection. It also helps if you say "White Owl [or some
other brand which you have already written on the slips in your pocket]
is a good one," as you pretend to write that brand on a slip of paper.

You now have eight slips of paper on the table, each having "Dutch
Master" written on it. The audience believes each slip of paper contains
the name of a different brand of cigar. Request one of the spectators to
select a slip from the pile on the table, and to hold the paper in his hand.
After he has selected one of the slips, pick up the remaining papers and
place them in the small change pocket in your right-hand coat pocket.
Immediately grasp the seven pieces of folded paper which you had
previously placed in your right jacket pocket during your preparation,
remove them from your pocket, and throw them into an ash tray, saying,
"What do I want with these papers?" You have thus switched the papers
bearing the name "Dutch Master" for seven papers, each bearing the
name of a different cigar.

Request the spectator who selected one of the slips of paper to unfold the slip and read what is written on it. Naturally, it reads "Dutch Master." Have someone unfold the handkerchief and see what brand of cigar is wrapped in it. The audience will be surprised to find that the El Producto has changed to a Dutch Master. The slips in the ash tray can now be examined by the spectators, and each will have written on it the name of a different brand.

190. X-Ray Ropes

EFFECT: The performer freely shows two ropes about ten feet long. He then asks for two spectators to assist him in the trick. Upon receiving volunteers, he requests one of them to remove his jacket. The ropes are then passed through the jacket sleeves so that the ends of each rope protrude from both sleeves. The spectator dons his jacket again. The performer then ties a knot in one of the ropes. Requesting the other spectator to hold the ends of the ropes on one side of the first spectator, the performer grasps the other two ends of rope. At a command the ropes are pulled tightly; both ropes apparently pass through the spectator's body and are held outstretched between the performer and the other spectator.

PREPARATION: The only preparation required is to tie a piece of white thread once around the center of both ropes (Fig. 1). Next, fold the ropes so that both ends of the same rope are together (Fig. 2), the ropes being held together by the thread. Place this rope on the table.

PRESENTATION: Pick up the ropes in your left hand, so that the thread holding the ropes together is concealed by your hand. You can pull lightly on the ropes to show that they are whole. Ask two spectators to assist you. Request one of the volunteers to remove his jacket. Thread the ends of the rope through the jacket sleeves, permitting two ends to protrude from each sleeve. Do not permit both ropes to hang out equally from both sleeves. Instead, thread the ropes through the sleeves so that the thread is off center, and is concealed in one of the sleeves (Fig. 3). Assist the spectator in donning his jacket again, making certain that the audience is aware that the ropes are behind his body. After the jacket has been placed on the spectator, pull lightly on the short ends of the rope in order to even off the ends protruding from the sleeves. This brings the thread to the center of his back.

Now instruct the spectator to bring both hands in front of his body. Grasp one end of rope from each sleeve, and tie a single knot in front of his body. Here is where the chicanery comes in. In tying the knot, take one end of rope A and one end of rope B. Tie the knot, and place

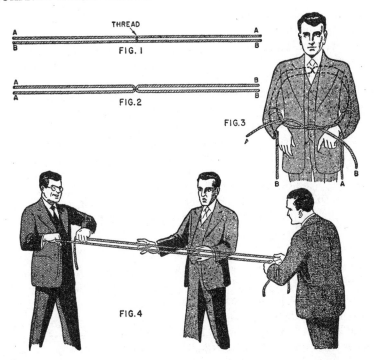

FIG. 1

THREAD

FIG. 2

FIG. 3

FIG. 4

end A on the side where the free end of rope A is hanging (Fig. 3). Ask the other spectator to take one pair of rope ends, handing him one end of rope A and one of rope B. Retain the other ends. Both of you then step back, one on each side of the first spectator. At a command, both of you pull tightly on the ropes. This will cause the thread to break and the ropes to be pulled out of the jacket sleeves, the ropes appearing to have passed through the spectator's body (Fig. 4).

Here is a pocket-size version of this trick.

EFFECT: The performer shows a string of beads strung on a double strand of string, that is, on two strings instead of the usual one. One end of string from each side of the beads is brought around the beads and tied to form a knot. When these ends and the free ends of string are pulled, the beads fall off the strings, although the strings are not in any way damaged.

PREPARATION: Instead of rope, use two pieces of thin, but strong, string, about twenty inches long. Tie the thread around the strings, as in the first effect. Bend the cords, and thread eight or ten large wooden beads

onto the strings, so that the beads conceal the point where the thread is
tied about the strings.

PRESENTATION: Hold the string of beads by each end, showing that you
have two strings through the beads. Explain that you have done this for
reinforcement, and to make the trick doubly difficult. Drop two ends of
string, one on each side, and hold the beads by the remaining ends. To
the audience it appears that you are holding both ends of one string,
thus supporting the beads. Bring these ends around the beads and tie a
single knot. The single knot causes the ends to cross (as in the first effect).
Holding one of the tied ends in each hand, grasp the free ends of the
string, each hand grasping the end nearest to it. Pull the cords suddenly.
This will break the thread, allowing the beads to fall off the strings. The
strings will remain intact and drawn taut between your hands. Apparently you have performed the feat of passing a solid through solid.

191. *Squash*

EFFECT: The performer shows a small glass, partially filled with liquid,
and places it on the palm of one hand. With the other hand, he squashes
the glass, causing it and its contents to vanish.

PREPARATION: Obtain a piece of elastic cord about twenty inches long,
and affix a small safety pin to each end. To one of these pins affix a small
rubber ball (Fig. 1). The ball should be of such size that when forced
into the mouth of a whiskey glass it will remain there firmly, and will
act as a cork in preventing the liquid from spilling out of the glass
(Fig. 2). Fasten the other safety pin to the back of your shirt or vest, high
between the shoulder blades, so that when the ball hangs free it is con-

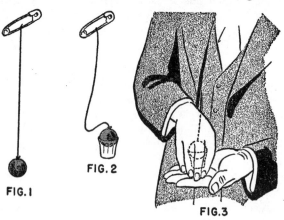

FIG. 1

FIG. 2

FIG. 3

cealed by your jacket, and hangs three to four inches above the lower edge of the jacket. Experiment with the placement of the pin on your back until you reach the point where the ball can be reached easily with your right hand. When ready to perform, fill a small glass, about halfway, with colored liquid. Place the glass on your table.

PRESENTATION: Hold up your left hand horizontally, palm up. With your right hand, pick up the glass and stand it on the palm of your left hand. While pattering and drawing attention to the glass, turn the right side of your body slightly away from your audience, and, reaching back, obtain the ball with your right hand, keeping the ball concealed. Lower the glass in front of your body until it reaches a point slightly below the hips, and bend the upper part of your body forward, keeping the glass near your body. Bring your right hand to the glass, and force the ball into its mouth (Fig. 3), cupping the hands so as to conceal the ball in the glass. Suddenly squeeze your hands together, at the same time permitting the glass to be drawn back and under your jacket by the elastic band. Practice this move, concentrating on angles of visibility and timing until you have no trouble concealing the movement. Separate your hands, and show that the glass has vanished.

192. *Smoke without Fire*

EFFECT: The performer shows two empty clay pipes. Placing the pipes bowl to bowl, he produces smoke from them. Even after he breaks the pipes into small pieces, he still produces smoke from them.

PREPARATION: Saturate a wad of cotton with liquid ammonia, and stuff it into the bowl of one clay pipe, being sure that none of the liquid runs down the stem. Into the bowl of the other pipe stuff a wad of cotton which has been saturated with spirits of salt, once again taking care not to permit any of the chemical to run down the stem. Both chemicals may be obtained at any drugstore. The clay, being porous, will absorb some of these chemicals. After a time remove the cotton from the pipes, and permit them to dry. Always keep these pipes separated until ready to perform.

PRESENTATION: Place the ammonia-soaked pipe in your mouth, as if for smoking, after first showing that the bowl is empty. Pick up the second pipe, invert it, and place it, stem forward, with the mouth of its bowl covering the mouth of the bowl of the first pipe. If you blow through the stem of the pipe in your mouth, a smokelike substance will emerge from the stem of the second pipe (Fig. 1). This smoke is ammonium chloride,

FIG. I   FIG. 2   FIG. 3

a white powder, produced by the reaction of the chemicals. When ammonium chloride is produced by sublimation (that is, produced as a solid directly from two gases without first passing through the liquid stage), very fine flakes of the powder are formed. This powder is light enough, and is produced in sufficient volume, to appear to be smoke.

Pattering to the effect that some skeptics may believe that something in the pipe stems is producing the smoke, break off about two-thirds of the stems of both pipes. Discard the stems, and repeat the smoke production (Fig. 2). In order to convince the skeptics further, crush each pipe under foot, mix the pieces, and scoop them up in your hands. Keep the pieces enclosed in the palms of your hands (Fig. 3), and blow through your hands. A great deal of smoke will be generated.

193. *The Floating Table*

EFFECT: Several people, including the performer, sit around a table as if for a spirit séance. Everyone places his hands on top of the table. In a few moments the table rises from the floor and "floats" in mid-air.

PREPARATION: Obtain a full length, unsharpened pencil, or an inch-wide flat stick about eight inches long. Place it lengthwise on the palm side of your right hand, the upper end about one inch from the base of the palm. With two- or three-inch-wide adhesive tape, bind the lower end of the pencil or stick tightly to your arm. Pass the tape around your arm several times so that the pencil or stick is firmly secured. With your jacket on, this arrangement cannot be seen. If possible, prepare a confederate in the same manner. The effect can be obtained alone, but with a confederate the results will be much more convincing.

PRESENTATION: Speak to the audience about "spiritualism," and the belief that so-called "mediums" have the power of invoking the aid of spirits to produce phenomena contrary to the laws of nature. Tell them how you, as a magician, have developed your magical powers to the extent that you are able to duplicate these feats. Invite them to join you in a séance. Invite as many spectators as there is room for to sit around a bridge table, or any other lightweight table. Sit at the table with them. If you are using a confederate, he should sit opposite you. As in an actual séance, ask everyone to place his hands flat on the table, palms down. As you place your hands in this position, allow the free end of the pencil or stick to go under the table. Do this naturally, and without hesitation. Then pencil or stick will not be seen, your hand and sleeve concealing it from view. Your confederate does the same with his pencil. Now ask for complete silence, so that everyone can concentrate his attention on causing the table to rise. By exerting a slow, steady, upward force with the right hand, you and your confederate can cause the table to rise from the floor and float in mid-air (see illustration). Inasmuch as your hands are flat on the table it is obvious that you "cannot" possibly be lifting the table.

It is possible to perform this effect without any equipment on your body. In this method, ask everyone to place his right hand flat on the table, near the edge. In order to steady the spiritual forces, tell them to grasp their right wrists tightly with their left hands. In grasping the wrist, the left hand should approach from below the right hand so that the fingers curl up over the wrist. In order to cause the table to rise, you and your confederate extend your left forefingers under cover of the right hand, so that the finger reaches under the edge of the table. An upward pressure will now lift the table. Because everyone's attention is on the table, no one will notice that one finger on your left hand is not visible.

194. Reproducing Sponges

EFFECT: A small sponge is shown, and may be examined. It is placed in a spectator's hand, and even though the spectator closes his hand tightly, upon opening his hand he finds that the one sponge has become two. He closes his hand over these two sponges, and then finds three when he again opens his hand.

PREPARATION: From a fine rubber bath sponge, obtainable at your local drugstore, cut three pieces of equal size. Trim the corners of these pieces, and round them to form balls one to one and one half inches in diameter. Place these balls in your right jacket pocket until you are ready to perform the trick.

PRESENTATION: Invite a spectator to assist you. Reach into your jacket pocket with your right hand and take out a sponge. Actually, you remove two sponge balls, concealing one behind your second, third, and fourth fingers by curling your fingers toward the palm of the hand. The other ball is shown freely between your thumb and forefinger (Fig. 1). Drop this sponge on the table and ask the spectator to examine it.

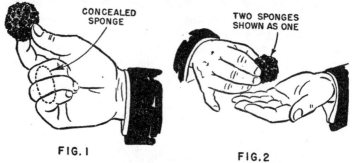

CONCEALED SPONGE

TWO SPONGES SHOWN AS ONE

FIG. 1   FIG. 2

After he has been satisfied that all is fair with the sponge ball, say, "Of course, you know that sponges are living things, and that all living things are capable of reproducing themselves. The same is true of this sponge. All that is required is a satisfactory environment in which it can grow. As it happens, the palm of your hand closely approximates the conditions required for a sponge to reproduce itself. If you will please hold out one hand, holding it palm upward, I will demonstrate."

Pick up the sponge from the table with your right hand. With a slight rolling motion of the fingers, bring the two sponges together, holding them between your fingers. As you do this, squeeze the sponges together so that they appear to be one sponge ball (Fig. 2). With a bit of practice you can do this smoothly and without hesitation. Place these sponges in the palm of the spectator's hand, and close his fingers, forming a fist of his hand. Ask him how many sponges he is holding. He will, of course, signify that he has one. Tell him to open his hand. He will be surprised to find he has two sponges; in fact, he will be so surprised that neither he nor any member of the audience will notice that your right hand has dropped into your jacket pocket. Instructing the spectator to drop the sponges on the table, remove your hand from your pocket, concealing the third sponge in your hand, as you did before.

Pick up one of the sponges and place it in the spectator's hand. Pick up the other sponge, and place it, together with the concealed sponge, in his hand, and close his fingers over them. When he opens his hand he will find that he now has three sponges.

195. Handkerchief Penetration

EFFECT: A spectator ties two handkerchiefs together at their centers. The performer causes the handkerchiefs to separate, the knots remaining in the handkerchiefs. Apparently the handkerchiefs have penetrated one another.

PREPARATION: There is no preparation other than obtaining two men's handkerchiefs, which may be borrowed from the audience. It is advisable to use one handkerchief that has a colored border or some other means of distinguishing it from the other. For a pretty effect, substitute square silk scarfs, about eighteen by eighteen, available at five and ten cent stores and women's stores.

PRESENTATION: Unfold the handkerchiefs, and taking one at a time, hold them by diagonally opposite corners, stretching and twisting the cloth while with a throwing motion you wind up each handkerchief to form a ropelike length. Hold your left hand in front of your body, fingers curled slightly, with the hand parallel to the front of the body. Place one of the curled handkerchiefs in your left hand so that the ends of the handkerchief drape down on both sides of your hand, one end draping over the forefinger, the other end over the little finger, the handkerchief lying in the palm of the hand and held loosely by your curled fingers. (For clarification, ends of this handkerchief are marked 1A and 2A in Fig. 1.) Place the other rolled handkerchief across the first at a right angle, placing your left thumb above the point where the handkerchiefs cross, to prevent

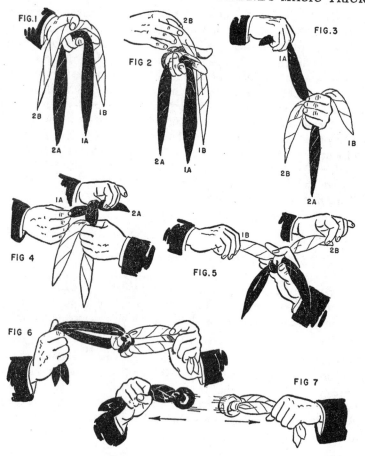

them from slipping. (Ends of this handkerchef are marked 1B and 2B in Fig. 1.)

Grasp the end of the top handkerchief and wrap it around the lower handkerchief by carrying the end 2B over the other handkerchief and back to its original position. Place your left thumb above this twist to prevent it from slipping. The top handkerchief is now securely wrapped around the lower one (Fig. 2).

Grasp that end of the other handkerchief which is marked 1A with your right hand, and wrap it around the bottom of the handkerchiefs encircling end 2B and bring it back to its original position (Fig. 3). This twist should cover the first one. Place your left thumb over the twist to prevent it from slipping. Both handkerchiefs now appear to be securely wrapped around one another.

Request a spectator to tie the ends of one handkerchief, and to pull the knot fairly tight (Fig. 4). Apparently you are asking the spectator to imprison the handkerchiefs firmly. Actually, the knot keeps them from falling apart, for, despite the wrapping, the handkerchiefs are not wrapped around one another. Be sure to remove your left thumb from the handkerchief before it is caught in the knot.

Turn your left hand over, and request the spectator to tie the ends of the other handkerchief together in a similar manner (Fig. 5). Calling attention to the fact that both handkerchiefs have been wrapped around one another and tied by a spectator, grasp the ends of one handkerchief in one hand, and the ends of the other in the other hand (Fig. 6), and pull your hands apart. The handkerchiefs will separate, with the knots still tied in them (Fig. 7). Apparently one has passed through the other.

Here is some suggested patter for this trick: "Our scientists have told us that solids are not really so solid after all. According to them, all solids are composed of atoms, which I'm sure you've all heard about, but the surprising part of their announcement is that there are spaces between these atoms. Well, I figured that if there are spaces between atoms, I should be able to pull a solid through another solid. But then the scientists told me that would be impossible, because the atoms are moving so fast that there are always a couple in the spaces. I still believed I could pass a solid through a solid, so I began to experiment. Tonight, ladies and gentlemen, I should like to demonstrate my latest discovery.

"By an adaptation of the ultra-dimensional theory of hyperbolic equations based upon the elliptic paraboloid, I discovered a formula for passing solid through solid. Of course, I am still in the experimental stage, but I can now cause two handkerchiefs to penetrate one another. First, two handkerchiefs must be twisted along their x-axes according to the equation x equals cosine y. Next, crossing these handkerchiefs at their midpoints, we wrap them around one another, following the formula x equals secant y tangent z. To firmly press the spaces between atoms together, I would like someone to tie tightly the ends of this handkerchief. Thank you. And now would you please tie the ends of the other handkerchief. Thank you again. Now, despite the fact that these handkerchiefs have been securely wrapped and tied about one another, they can be separated at the exact moment when their molecular vibrations are in phase, like this. As you see, solid has passed through solid, leaving the knots tied in the handkerchief."

196. Scarne's Non-Burning Bill

EFFECT: The performer borrows a one-dollar bill from a member of the audience, asking the owner to note the serial number of the bill before giving it up. The bill is folded and placed in an envelope, which may also be borrowed. A lighted match is held behind the envelope, permitting the audience to see the outline of the bill still inside. The envelope is then burned. Reaching into the ashes, the performer retrieves the bill, unharmed, and returns it to its owner for identification. (Created by the author.)

PREPARATION: Obtain a stage bill (if unavailable, a piece of green paper cut to the size of a dollar bill can be substituted), and fold the bill in half, across its width, green side outward. Fold the bill twice again in the same direction, and then finally fold the bill so the top edge matches the bottom edge (Fig. 1). Place this bill in your right jacket pocket. In the same pocket place several wooden matches. Equip yourself with an ordinary letter envelope and a saucer or small flat metal tray. Place these items on the table.

PRESENTATION: Unobtrusively reach for and hold the folded fake bill in your right hand, concealing it behind the first and second fingers. The fold of the bill should be along the line where the fingers join the palm of your hand, the open end of the bill pointing toward your fingertips. By slightly curling the fingers in toward your right palm, you can grip the bill tightly while concealing it from the audience (Fig. 2, performer's view).

Request the loan of a bill of any denomination from some member of the audience (we will assume that a one-dollar bill is offered to you), and ask the owner of the bill to note the serial number of the bill, or to mark it in some manner so that he can identify it later. Take the bill in your left hand, then place it in your right hand, green side toward the audience. The fake bill is concealed behind it (Fig. 3). Transfer the borrowed bill to your left hand, grasping it with the fingers facing the audience, the thumb holding the folded fake bill from the rear. By pulling the thumb in slightly toward the palm of your hand, you pull the folded fake bill to the left so that it overlaps the exposed bill by about a half inch, this being concealed by your fingers. (Fig. 4 shows the performer's view of this). The upper edge of the folded fake bill should be on the center line of the borrowed bill.

With your right hand, grasp the top of the borrowed bill, and bend it toward your body, folding the bill in half (Fig. 5). Continue to fold

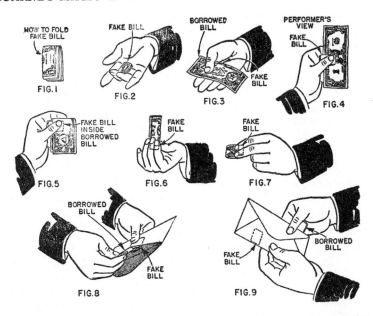

the bill by twisting it around, until it is one-eighth its regular size (Fig. 6). While you are doing this, be careful that you do not open the fingers of your left hand and expose the hidden fake bill. The left thumb covers the bottom of the borrowed bill and the protruding part of the hidden fake bill, so that your hand can be turned to show the audience all sides of the borrowed bill. This is very deceptive, as the audience is certain that nothing is concealed in your left hand. With your right hand, fold the top edge of the borrowed bill toward the palm of your left hand, bringing the top edge even with the bottom edge of the same bill (Fig. 7). Take the two bills in your right hand, so that the protruding part of the fake bill is facing skyward.

Pick up the envelope with your left hand, open it, and holding the envelope with the flap side toward the audience, insert both bills into the envelope with your right hand, until the protruding part of the fake bill touches the inside bottom of the envelope. Then, with your left hand, grasp the protruding part of the fake bill through the paper. The right hand, still holding the borrowed bill, pulls it slightly upward until the bills are separated from each other. While your right hand is still in the envelope, conceal the borrowed bill in your right hand by curling your fingers around it (Fig. 8).

Remove your right hand from the envelope, with the back of the hand facing the audience. Your right hand takes the envelope by its side, hiding the borrowed bill from view. Casually show the bill inside the envelope again. To the audience this appears to be the borrowed bill, but actually it is the fake bill.

Moisten the gummed portion of the envelope flap and seal it. Slide the envelope out of your right hand with your left hand, leaving the borrowed bill in your right hand (Fig. 9).

Drop your right hand into your jacket pocket and remove one of the matches, leaving the borrowed bill in your pocket. Strike the match, and hold it behind the envelope so that the light passing through the paper will reveal the dark outline of the bill inside the envelope. The audience is now fully convinced that the bill is actually in the envelope. Hold the lighted match to one corner of the envelope. After the paper has burned for a few seconds, place the envelope on the saucer or tray and permit it to burn completely. While all attention is on the burning paper, place your right hand naturally into your jacket pocket and pull out the bill, as you did at the beginning of the trick. Remove your hand from the pocket, keeping the bill concealed. After the envelope has completely burned, reach into the ashes with your right hand, and stir them around a bit. Show the bill at your fingertips as if you had produced it from the ashes. Open the bill to show that it is unharmed, and return it to its owner for identification.

197. Scarne's Telepathic Sugar Cubes

EFFECT: A spectator mentally selects two designs from four that are drawn on two cubes of sugar. The performer concentrates a moment and tells the spectator what designs he is thinking of. (Created by the author).

PRESENTATION: While you are seated at a dinner table, take two cubes of sugar from the sugar bowl. Remove the paper wrappings, and draw the following markings with a pencil. On one of the wide surfaces of the cube, draw a cross (X). On the opposite side of the sugar cube draw a circle (O). Now, on the second cube of sugar, draw a square (□) on one side and a triangle (△) on the opposite side (Figs. 1, 2, 3, and 4). Remark to your audience that with these sugar cubes marked thus, you are about to try an experiment in telepathy. Turn your back, and instruct the spectator sitting opposite you to do as follows: stack the two cubes together (one on top of the other), in the meantime making a mental note

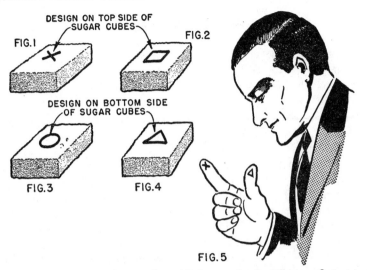

DESIGN ON TOP SIDE OF SUGAR CUBES

FIG.1 FIG.2

DESIGN ON BOTTOM SIDE OF SUGAR CUBES

FIG.3 FIG.4

FIG.5

of the designs that are face to face. With your back still turned, instruct the spectator to hold the sugar cubes under the table in the same stacked position. You now moisten the tip of your right thumb and forefinger with your lips.

Turn back to face the audience. Reach under the table with your right hand. Ask the spectator to permit you to take the sugar cubes for a moment. While you are holding the sugar cubes, press heavily with the thumb and forefinger; this action creates a pencil imprint on these fingers of the designs on the outside surfaces of the sugar cubes. Immediately return the sugar cubes to the spectator by dropping them into his hand. Now look the spectator straight in the eyes and state that he is not concentrating. Ask him to concentrate on the two designs he noted mentally at the start of the experiment. While these instructions are being given to the spectator, withdraw your right hand from under the table and get a glimpse of the imprints on your thumb and forefinger (Fig. 5). As mentioned above, these two designs imprinted there were made from the two outer surfaces of the sugar cubes. The spectator is concentrating on the two designs on the inner surfaces of the sugar cubes. Therefore, the designs on your fingertips are not the ones the spectator is thinking of. Since you know the four designs, you call out the two that are not imprinted on your fingertips. And these prove to be the designs the spectator is concentrating on. You then rub your right thumb and forefinger together and the imprints will disappear, leaving no trace as to how the trick was done.

198. *Color-Changing Cube*

EFFECT: A colored cube is shown, first on one side and then on the underside. The top side is shown again. A spectator places a finger on the underside. When he removes his finger from this spot, the color has changed.

PREPARATION: Secure, from any novelty or magic shop, a six-sided cube which measures one cubic inch or less and has a different color on each side. If this cannot be secured in your locality, you can make the necessary cube by employing a little carpentry. After making the cube, sandpaper all sides so they are all even and slick. With either crayons or paint, color each one of the sides differently. For example, let us assume that one surface of the cube is black, the opposite or underside is white; red on one side and blue on the opposite side; green on one side and yellow on the opposite side. If you are making your own cube and do not have the crayons or the six colors of paint available, you may instead print the name of each color on the side where it belongs.

PRESENTATION: Hold the cube between the thumb and forefinger of the right hand, the red-colored side showing (Fig. 1). Turn your hand over

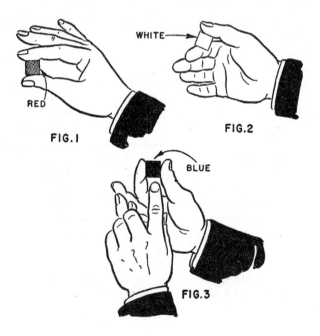

FIG. 1

FIG. 2

FIG. 3

so that the palm faces skyward, but at the same time, the forefinger and the thumb give the cube a turn to the right (Fig. 2). This puts the white-colored side (originally against the forefinger) at the bottom. Reverse the motion, and show the red-colored side again. Have a spectator place a finger on the underside or bottom of the cube. Then slowly turn the cube over. Have the spectator remove his finger, and behold!—the white side has changed to blue (Fig. 3). The cube can be held with any color uppermost—the effect is the same.

199. Ring Around the Pencil

EFFECT: A borrowed ring is made to vanish. A pencil is then pushed through the sides of a paper bag. At a magic command, the ring suddenly appears on the pencil under seemingly impossible conditions.

PREPARATION: In this effect a specially prepared handkerchief is used. This can be made by covering an inexpensive ring with a small square of the same material of which the handkerchief is made, and sewing the edges of this square to one corner of the handkerchief. Have this hand-

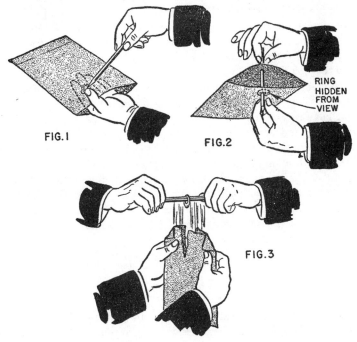

FIG. 1

FIG. 2

RING HIDDEN FROM VIEW

FIG. 3

kerchief in your pocket when ready to perform the effect. Also, supply yourself with a long sturdy pencil and a small paper bag, which should be placed, opened, on the table.

PRESENTATION: Borrow a ring from a spectator. Remove your handkerchief, and holding it by its center, place the ring under it. Actually, as you move your hand with the ring under the handkerchief, grasp the prepared corner between the second and third fingers of the same hand. Grasp the sewn-in ring through the center of the handkerchief with your other hand, and remove your hand from under the handkerchief with the ring concealed in it. Hand the handkerchief to a spectator, and have him hold the ring through the folds of the cloth from above, permitting the rest of the cloth to hang down.

With the same hand in which the borrowed ring is concealed, pick up the paper bag by its open end, fingers inside the bag and thumb outside. The ring is hidden between the fingers and the inner surface of the bag. Pick up the pencil with the other hand, and penetrate the paper near the thumb with the pencil, pushing it through the ring, and then penetrating the other side of the bag (Fig. 1). You can now show that the bag is empty by backing away from your audience slightly and turning the open end of the bag toward them in such a manner that the pencil will be in a vertical position. When the pencil is in this position, the ring will, naturally, slide to the lower side of the bag. By tilting the open end of the bag upward slightly, the ring will be hidden from view (Fig. 2). Close the bag by twisting the ends together.

Have a second spectator hold the pencil at both ends, holding it in front of his body, with the bag hanging down between his hands. He should have a firm grip on the pencil. Approach the spectator who is holding the handkerchief, and grasping one corner of the cloth, say the magic word and pull the handkerchief from his hand. Shake the cloth and show both sides, proving that the ring has vanished.

Approach the spectator who is holding the pencil and the bag. Grasp the lower part of the bag and give it a sudden downward thrust, tearing the paper away from the pencil. The ring is then seen dangling on the pencil between the spectator's hands (Fig. 3). Return the ring to its owner.

200. The Magic Bag

EFFECT: An egg is produced from an empty cloth bag. The egg is replaced in the bag, and vanishes. It is once again produced from the bag.

PREPARATION: For this effect a special bag is used. It may be prepared as follows: Obtain a piece of heavy woolen colored cloth, about twenty-two inches long, and eight inches wide. Lay the cloth flat on the table. Fold about six inches of the top end flat over the cloth and sew the side edges, forming a pocket (Fig. 1). Now fold the strip of cloth in half, aligning the free end with the first fold, enclosing the pocket. Sew the sides together so as to form a bag. When completed, it should look like an ordinary cloth bag, except that it has an upside down inside (Fig. 2). It is a good idea to sew a cloth border around the edges of the bag to keep the cloth from unraveling. Do not sew a border on the open end of the pocket. When the bag is turned inside out the open end of the pocket should barely be visible, so that when the bag is in motion the pocket cannot be seen. Turn the bag right side out, and place a hard-boiled egg within the hidden pocket, near the top of the bag. Place the bag on a table until ready to perform the trick.

PRESENTATION: Pick the bag up with your right hand, enclosing the egg through the edge of the bag, and say, "Here I have an empty bag." (Fig. 3 shows how the egg is held in the pocket.) Prove that the bag is empty

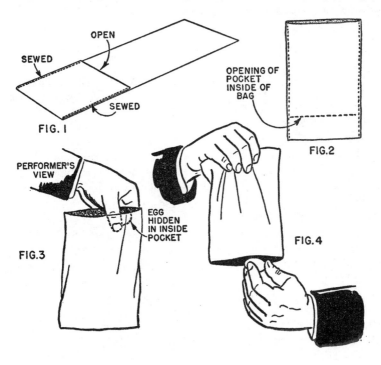

OPEN

SEWED

SEWED

FIG. I

OPENING OF POCKET INSIDE OF BAG

FIG.2

PERFORMER'S VIEW

EGG HIDDEN IN INSIDE POCKET

FIG.3

FIG.4

by turning it inside out, keeping a firm grip on the egg. Keep the bag in motion so that the edge of the pocket cannot be seen while the bag is inside out. Restore the bag to its natural form, and have a spectator reach into it to verify that the bag is really empty. After he has done this, walk away from him, saying, "I think this gentleman has laid an egg." As you say this, release your grip on the egg, and permit it to fall to the bottom of the bag. Walk to another spectator and ask him to insert his hand into the bag to remove whatever he finds inside. His removing the egg should produce a laugh from the audience.

Now hold the egg in one hand, and place the bag upside down over it (Fig. 4). Turn the bag right side up and let the egg fall to the bottom of the bag. Permit a spectator to feel the egg through the bag. Holding the egg with one hand, turn the bag upside down again, guiding the egg into the secret pocket. Grasp the top of the bag, and again enclose the egg in the grip. Turn the bag right side up again, and transfer the bag from hand to hand, casually showing that both hands are empty. Do not make the action too deliberate. Make a magic pass and show that the egg has again disappeared, turning the bag inside out to prove it. With another magic pass, cause it to reappear.

201. *Scarne's Names from Nowhere*

EFFECT: The performer tears a sheet of paper into eight pieces and places four of these pieces in a spectator's hand. The spectator is instructed to close his hand over these papers. The performer asks four spectators their first names and writes a name on each of the four remaining pieces of paper.

The performer burns these papers (with the names) in an ash tray. After they are burned, the spectator is requested to examine the four pieces of paper he is holding. Upon examination, the four spectators' names are found written on these four pieces of paper.

PREPARATION: Fold a sheet of paper, approximately eight inches by four inches, in half, making a packet four inches by four inches. Fold into quarters and then into eighths. Make a crease out of the folds of the paper by applying pressure on them. The paper is now folded into eight two-inch squares. The creases are made as a guide when tearing the sheet into two-inch squares during the performance of the trick.

Place the folded sheet of paper in your pocket for use later on. The other requirements are an ash tray, a packet of matches and a pencil. The trick is best performed while seated at a table.

PRESENTATION: You are seated at a table with several spectators. (Make sure that an ash tray is available.) You must learn the first names of four of these spectators. These people may be friends, or you can learn their first names by a little detective work.

Armed with this information, you create an opportunity to leave the table. Secretly remove the folded sheet of paper from your pocket. Unfold the sheet and with a pencil write a spectator's first name on each of the four left-handed folded squares. For example, let us assume that the spectators' names are John, Arthur, Mary and Jane (Fig. 1). Refold the paper with the writing inside. Place the paper back in your pocket. After

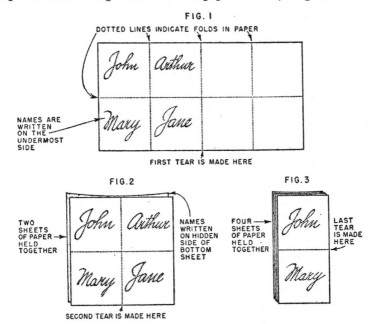

returning to the table, inquire if anyone present has a blank piece of paper, but before you give anyone a chance to oblige, reach into your pocket and come out with your prepared sheet. Act a little surprised at finding this sheet of paper—a little acting helps at this time.

To impress the spectators that the paper has no writing on it, do the following:

Unfold the sheet downward, so that the writing cannot be seen. A little practice will give you the right angle.

With the writing on the undermost side, tear the paper in the center (Fig. 1).

Place the sheet in your right hand under the sheet in your left hand. The writing is now covered by the bottom sheet of paper. Tear these two sheets in half by the fold in the paper (Fig. 2).

Place the papers in your right hand on top of the papers in your left hand. Square them up and tear them through the center fold (Fig. 3).

Place the papers in your right hand on top of the papers in your left hand. You now have eight pieces of paper, each approximately two inches square.

Every other piece of paper has a name written on its undermost side. You pretend not to know how many pieces of paper you hold. Therefore, you indulge in a little counting. The counting is done in the following manner: you put the papers down in two piles on the table—one to the right and one to the left, and so on. This division has separated the papers into a pile of four blank papers and a pile of four papers with the names on them. If you have followed directions, the left-hand pile will be the four papers with names written on their undermost sides. Pick up these papers and place them in the hand of a spectator (with the writing hidden from view, of course) and instruct him to close his hand over the papers.

Now ask the four spectators (whose names are written on the other papers) to call out their first names. Each name is written on one of these four sheets. In our example the names are John, Arthur, Mary and Jane. Drop these four pieces of paper into the ash tray, apply a lighted match, and burn them completely.

After the papers have turned to ashes, mumble a few magical words, like "Hocus Pocus." Have the spectator open his hand and examine the papers. He will be surprised to find the names written on the papers.

Note: When writing the names secretly on the large sheet of paper, use a soft pencil so that the writing cannot be seen through the paper. If you desire, you may use one name four times or you can use the letter X.

A CATALOG OF SELECTED
DOVER BOOKS
IN ALL FIELDS OF INTEREST

A CATALOG OF SELECTED DOVER
BOOKS IN ALL FIELDS OF INTEREST

CONCERNING THE SPIRITUAL IN ART, Wassily Kandinsky. Pioneering work by father of abstract art. Thoughts on color theory, nature of art. Analysis of earlier masters. 12 illustrations. 80pp. of text. 5⅜ x 8½. 23411-8

ANIMALS: 1,419 Copyright-Free Illustrations of Mammals, Birds, Fish, Insects, etc., Jim Harter (ed.). Clear wood engravings present, in extremely lifelike poses, over 1,000 species of animals. One of the most extensive pictorial sourcebooks of its kind. Captions. Index. 284pp. 9 x 12. 23766-4

CELTIC ART: The Methods of Construction, George Bain. Simple geometric techniques for making Celtic interlacements, spirals, Kells-type initials, animals, humans, etc. Over 500 illustrations. 160pp. 9 x 12. (Available in U.S. only.) 22923-8

AN ATLAS OF ANATOMY FOR ARTISTS, Fritz Schider. Most thorough reference work on art anatomy in the world. Hundreds of illustrations, including selections from works by Vesalius, Leonardo, Goya, Ingres, Michelangelo, others. 593 illustrations. 192pp. 7⅛ x 10¼. 20241-0

CELTIC HAND STROKE-BY-STROKE (Irish Half-Uncial from "The Book of Kells"): An Arthur Baker Calligraphy Manual, Arthur Baker. Complete guide to creating each letter of the alphabet in distinctive Celtic manner. Covers hand position, strokes, pens, inks, paper, more. Illustrated. 48pp. 8¼ x 11. 24336-2

EASY ORIGAMI, John Montroll. Charming collection of 32 projects (hat, cup, pelican, piano, swan, many more) specially designed for the novice origami hobbyist. Clearly illustrated easy-to-follow instructions insure that even beginning papercrafters will achieve successful results. 48pp. 8¼ x 11. 27298-2

THE COMPLETE BOOK OF BIRDHOUSE CONSTRUCTION FOR WOOD-WORKERS, Scott D. Campbell. Detailed instructions, illustrations, tables. Also data on bird habitat and instinct patterns. Bibliography. 3 tables. 63 illustrations in 15 figures. 48pp. 5¼ x 8½. 24407-5

BLOOMINGDALE'S ILLUSTRATED 1886 CATALOG: Fashions, Dry Goods and Housewares, Bloomingdale Brothers. Famed merchants' extremely rare catalog depicting about 1,700 products: clothing, housewares, firearms, dry goods, jewelry, more. Invaluable for dating, identifying vintage items. Also, copyright-free graphics for artists, designers. Co-published with Henry Ford Museum & Greenfield Village. 160pp. 8¼ x 11. 25780-0

HISTORIC COSTUME IN PICTURES, Braun & Schneider. Over 1,450 costumed figures in clearly detailed engravings–from dawn of civilization to end of 19th century. Captions. Many folk costumes. 256pp. 8⅜ x 11¾. 23150-X

STICKLEY CRAFTSMAN FURNITURE CATALOGS, Gustav Stickley and L. & J. G. Stickley. Beautiful, functional furniture in two authentic catalogs from 1910. 594 illustrations, including 277 photos, show settles, rockers, armchairs, reclining chairs, bookcases, desks, tables. 183pp. 6½ x 9¼.   23838-5

AMERICAN LOCOMOTIVES IN HISTORIC PHOTOGRAPHS: 1858 to 1949, Ron Ziel (ed.). A rare collection of 126 meticulously detailed official photographs, called "builder portraits," of American locomotives that majestically chronicle the rise of steam locomotive power in America. Introduction. Detailed captions. xi+ 129pp. 9 x 12.   27393-8

AMERICA'S LIGHTHOUSES: An Illustrated History, Francis Ross Holland, Jr. Delightfully written, profusely illustrated fact-filled survey of over 200 American light-houses since 1716. History, anecdotes, technological advances, more. 240pp. 8 x 10¾.
                                                                        25576-X

TOWARDS A NEW ARCHITECTURE, Le Corbusier. Pioneering manifesto by founder of "International School." Technical and aesthetic theories, views of industry, economics, relation of form to function, "mass-production split" and much more. Profusely illustrated. 320pp. 6⅛ x 9¼. (Available in U.S. only.)   25023-7

HOW THE OTHER HALF LIVES, Jacob Riis. Famous journalistic record, exposing poverty and degradation of New York slums around 1900, by major social reformer. 100 striking and influential photographs. 233pp. 10 x 7⅞.   22012-5

FRUIT KEY AND TWIG KEY TO TREES AND SHRUBS, William M. Harlow. One of the handiest and most widely used identification aids. Fruit key covers 120 deciduous and evergreen species; twig key 160 deciduous species. Easily used. Over 300 photographs. 126pp. 5⅜ x 8½.   20511-8

COMMON BIRD SONGS, Dr. Donald J. Borror. Songs of 60 most common U.S. birds: robins, sparrows, cardinals, bluejays, finches, more—arranged in order of increasing complexity. Up to 9 variations of songs of each species.
                                                        Cassette and manual 99911-4

ORCHIDS AS HOUSE PLANTS, Rebecca Tyson Northen. Grow cattleyas and many other kinds of orchids—in a window, in a case, or under artificial light. 63 illustrations. 148pp. 5⅜ x 8½.   23261-1

MONSTER MAZES, Dave Phillips. Masterful mazes at four levels of difficulty. Avoid deadly perils and evil creatures to find magical treasures. Solutions for all 32 exciting illustrated puzzles. 48pp. 8¼ x 11.   26005-4

MOZART'S DON GIOVANNI (DOVER OPERA LIBRETTO SERIES), Wolfgang Amadeus Mozart. Introduced and translated by Ellen H. Bleiler. Standard Italian libretto, with complete English translation. Convenient and thoroughly portable—an ideal companion for reading along with a recording or the performance itself. Introduction. List of characters. Plot summary. 121pp. 5¼ x 8½.   24944-1

TECHNICAL MANUAL AND DICTIONARY OF CLASSICAL BALLET, Gail Grant. Defines, explains, comments on steps, movements, poses and concepts. 15-page pictorial section. Basic book for student, viewer. 127pp. 5⅜ x 8½.   21843-0

THE CLARINET AND CLARINET PLAYING, David Pino. Lively, comprehensive work features suggestions about technique, musicianship, and musical interpretation, as well as guidelines for teaching, making your own reeds, and preparing for public performance. Includes an intriguing look at clarinet history. "A godsend," *The Clarinet,* Journal of the International Clarinet Society. Appendixes. 7 illus. 320pp. 5⅜ x 8½. 40270-3

HOLLYWOOD GLAMOR PORTRAITS, John Kobal (ed.). 145 photos from 1926-49. Harlow, Gable, Bogart, Bacall; 94 stars in all. Full background on photographers, technical aspects. 160pp. 8⅜ x 11¼. 23352-9

THE ANNOTATED CASEY AT THE BAT: A Collection of Ballads about the Mighty Casey/Third, Revised Edition, Martin Gardner (ed.). Amusing sequels and parodies of one of America's best-loved poems: Casey's Revenge, Why Casey Whiffed, Casey's Sister at the Bat, others. 256pp. 5⅜ x 8½. 28598-7

THE RAVEN AND OTHER FAVORITE POEMS, Edgar Allan Poe. Over 40 of the author's most memorable poems: "The Bells," "Ulalume," "Israfel," "To Helen," "The Conqueror Worm," "Eldorado," "Annabel Lee," many more. Alphabetic lists of titles and first lines. 64pp. 5$^{3}/_{16}$ x 8¼. 26685-0

PERSONAL MEMOIRS OF U. S. GRANT, Ulysses Simpson Grant. Intelligent, deeply moving firsthand account of Civil War campaigns, considered by many the finest military memoirs ever written. Includes letters, historic photographs, maps and more. 528pp. 6⅛ x 9¼. 28587-1

ANCIENT EGYPTIAN MATERIALS AND INDUSTRIES, A. Lucas and J. Harris. Fascinating, comprehensive, thoroughly documented text describes this ancient civilization's vast resources and the processes that incorporated them in daily life, including the use of animal products, building materials, cosmetics, perfumes and incense, fibers, glazed ware, glass and its manufacture, materials used in the mummification process, and much more. 544pp. 6⅛ x 9¼. (Available in U.S. only.) 40446-3

RUSSIAN STORIES/RUSSKIE RASSKAZY: A Dual-Language Book, edited by Gleb Struve. Twelve tales by such masters as Chekhov, Tolstoy, Dostoevsky, Pushkin, others. Excellent word-for-word English translations on facing pages, plus teaching and study aids, Russian/English vocabulary, biographical/critical introductions, more. 416pp. 5⅜ x 8½. 26244-8

PHILADELPHIA THEN AND NOW: 60 Sites Photographed in the Past and Present, Kenneth Finkel and Susan Oyama. Rare photographs of City Hall, Logan Square, Independence Hall, Betsy Ross House, other landmarks juxtaposed with contemporary views. Captures changing face of historic city. Introduction. Captions. 128pp. 8¼ x 11. 25790-8

AIA ARCHITECTURAL GUIDE TO NASSAU AND SUFFOLK COUNTIES, LONG ISLAND, The American Institute of Architects, Long Island Chapter, and the Society for the Preservation of Long Island Antiquities. Comprehensive, well-researched and generously illustrated volume brings to life over three centuries of Long Island's great architectural heritage. More than 240 photographs with authoritative, extensively detailed captions. 176pp. 8¼ x 11. 26946-9

NORTH AMERICAN INDIAN LIFE: Customs and Traditions of 23 Tribes, Elsie Clews Parsons (ed.). 27 fictionalized essays by noted anthropologists examine religion, customs, government, additional facets of life among the Winnebago, Crow, Zuni, Eskimo, other tribes. 480pp. 6⅛ x 9¼. 27377-6

FRANK LLOYD WRIGHT'S DANA HOUSE, Donald Hoffmann. Pictorial essay of residential masterpiece with over 160 interior and exterior photos, plans, elevations, sketches and studies. 128pp. 9¼ x 10¾.   29120-0

THE MALE AND FEMALE FIGURE IN MOTION: 60 Classic Photographic Sequences, Eadweard Muybridge. 60 true-action photographs of men and women walking, running, climbing, bending, turning, etc., reproduced from rare 19th-century masterpiece. vi + 121pp. 9 x 12.   24745-7

1001 QUESTIONS ANSWERED ABOUT THE SEASHORE, N. J. Berrill and Jacquelyn Berrill. Queries answered about dolphins, sea snails, sponges, starfish, fishes, shore birds, many others. Covers appearance, breeding, growth, feeding, much more. 305pp. 5¼ x 8¼.   23366-9

ATTRACTING BIRDS TO YOUR YARD, William J. Weber. Easy-to-follow guide offers advice on how to attract the greatest diversity of birds: birdhouses, feeders, water and waterers, much more. 96pp. 5³⁄₁₆ x 8¼.   28927-3

MEDICINAL AND OTHER USES OF NORTH AMERICAN PLANTS: A Historical Survey with Special Reference to the Eastern Indian Tribes, Charlotte Erichsen-Brown. Chronological historical citations document 500 years of usage of plants, trees, shrubs native to eastern Canada, northeastern U.S. Also complete identifying information. 343 illustrations. 544pp. 6½ x 9¼.   25951-X

STORYBOOK MAZES, Dave Phillips. 23 stories and mazes on two-page spreads: Wizard of Oz, Treasure Island, Robin Hood, etc. Solutions. 64pp. 8¼ x 11. 23628-5

AMERICAN NEGRO SONGS: 230 Folk Songs and Spirituals, Religious and Secular, John W. Work. This authoritative study traces the African influences of songs sung and played by black Americans at work, in church, and as entertainment. The author discusses the lyric significance of such songs as "Swing Low, Sweet Chariot," "John Henry," and others and offers the words and music for 230 songs. Bibliography. Index of Song Titles. 272pp. 6½ x 9¼.   40271-1

MOVIE-STAR PORTRAITS OF THE FORTIES, John Kobal (ed.). 163 glamor, studio photos of 106 stars of the 1940s: Rita Hayworth, Ava Gardner, Marlon Brando, Clark Gable, many more. 176pp. 8⅜ x 11¼.   23546-7

BENCHLEY LOST AND FOUND, Robert Benchley. Finest humor from early 30s, about pet peeves, child psychologists, post office and others. Mostly unavailable elsewhere. 73 illustrations by Peter Arno and others. 183pp. 5⅜ x 8½.   22410-4

YEKL and THE IMPORTED BRIDEGROOM AND OTHER STORIES OF YIDDISH NEW YORK, Abraham Cahan. Film Hester Street based on *Yekl* (1896). Novel, other stories among first about Jewish immigrants on N.Y.'s East Side. 240pp. 5⅜ x 8½.   22427-9

SELECTED POEMS, Walt Whitman. Generous sampling from *Leaves of Grass*. Twenty-four poems include "I Hear America Singing," "Song of the Open Road," "I Sing the Body Electric," "When Lilacs Last in the Dooryard Bloom'd," "O Captain! My Captain!"—all reprinted from an authoritative edition. Lists of titles and first lines. 128pp. 5³⁄₁₆ x 8¼.   26878-0

THE BEST TALES OF HOFFMANN, E. T. A. Hoffmann. 10 of Hoffmann's most important stories: "Nutcracker and the King of Mice," "The Golden Flowerpot," etc. 458pp. 5⅜ x 8½. 21793-0

FROM FETISH TO GOD IN ANCIENT EGYPT, E. A. Wallis Budge. Rich detailed survey of Egyptian conception of "God" and gods, magic, cult of animals, Osiris, more. Also, superb English translations of hymns and legends. 240 illustrations. 545pp. 5⅜ x 8½. 25803-3

FRENCH STORIES/CONTES FRANÇAIS: A Dual-Language Book, Wallace Fowlie. Ten stories by French masters, Voltaire to Camus: "Micromegas" by Voltaire; "The Atheist's Mass" by Balzac; "Minuet" by de Maupassant; "The Guest" by Camus, six more. Excellent English translations on facing pages. Also French-English vocabulary list, exercises, more. 352pp. 5⅜ x 8½. 26443-2

CHICAGO AT THE TURN OF THE CENTURY IN PHOTOGRAPHS: 122 Historic Views from the Collections of the Chicago Historical Society, Larry A. Viskochil. Rare large-format prints offer detailed views of City Hall, State Street, the Loop, Hull House, Union Station, many other landmarks, circa 1904-1913. Introduction. Captions. Maps. 144pp. 9⅜ x 12¼. 24656-6

OLD BROOKLYN IN EARLY PHOTOGRAPHS, 1865-1929, William Lee Younger. Luna Park, Gravesend race track, construction of Grand Army Plaza, moving of Hotel Brighton, etc. 157 previously unpublished photographs. 165pp. 8⅞ x 11¾. 23587-4

THE MYTHS OF THE NORTH AMERICAN INDIANS, Lewis Spence. Rich anthology of the myths and legends of the Algonquins, Iroquois, Pawnees and Sioux, prefaced by an extensive historical and ethnological commentary. 36 illustrations. 480pp. 5⅜ x 8½. 25967-6

AN ENCYCLOPEDIA OF BATTLES: Accounts of Over 1,560 Battles from 1479 B.C. to the Present, David Eggenberger. Essential details of every major battle in recorded history from the first battle of Megiddo in 1479 B.C. to Grenada in 1984. List of Battle Maps. New Appendix covering the years 1967-1984. Index. 99 illustrations. 544pp. 6½ x 9¼. 24913-1

SAILING ALONE AROUND THE WORLD, Captain Joshua Slocum. First man to sail around the world, alone, in small boat. One of great feats of seamanship told in delightful manner. 67 illustrations. 294pp. 5⅜ x 8½. 20326-3

ANARCHISM AND OTHER ESSAYS, Emma Goldman. Powerful, penetrating, prophetic essays on direct action, role of minorities, prison reform, puritan hypocrisy, violence, etc. 271pp. 5⅜ x 8½. 22484-8

MYTHS OF THE HINDUS AND BUDDHISTS, Ananda K. Coomaraswamy and Sister Nivedita. Great stories of the epics; deeds of Krishna, Shiva, taken from puranas, Vedas, folk tales; etc. 32 illustrations. 400pp. 5⅜ x 8½. 21759-0

THE TRAUMA OF BIRTH, Otto Rank. Rank's controversial thesis that anxiety neurosis is caused by profound psychological trauma which occurs at birth. 256pp. 5⅜ x 8½. 27974-X

A THEOLOGICO-POLITICAL TREATISE, Benedict Spinoza. Also contains unfinished Political Treatise. Great classic on religious liberty, theory of government on common consent. R. Elwes translation. Total of 421pp. 5⅜ x 8½. 20249-6

PERSPECTIVE FOR ARTISTS, Rex Vicat Cole. Depth, perspective of sky and sea, shadows, much more, not usually covered. 391 diagrams, 81 reproductions of drawings and paintings. 279pp. 5⅜ x 8½. 22487-2

DRAWING THE LIVING FIGURE, Joseph Sheppard. Innovative approach to artistic anatomy focuses on specifics of surface anatomy, rather than muscles and bones. Over 170 drawings of live models in front, back and side views, and in widely varying poses. Accompanying diagrams. 177 illustrations. Introduction. Index. 144pp. 8⅜ x11¼. 26723-7

GOTHIC AND OLD ENGLISH ALPHABETS: 100 Complete Fonts, Dan X. Solo. Add power, elegance to posters, signs, other graphics with 100 stunning copyright-free alphabets: Blackstone, Dolbey, Germania, 97 more–including many lower-case, numerals, punctuation marks. 104pp. 8⅛ x 11. 24695-7

HOW TO DO BEADWORK, Mary White. Fundamental book on craft from simple projects to five-bead chains and woven works. 106 illustrations. 142pp. 5⅜ x 8. 20697-1

THE BOOK OF WOOD CARVING, Charles Marshall Sayers. Finest book for beginners discusses fundamentals and offers 34 designs. "Absolutely first rate . . . well thought out and well executed."–E. J. Tangerman. 118pp. 7¾ x 10⅝. 23654-4

ILLUSTRATED CATALOG OF CIVIL WAR MILITARY GOODS: Union Army Weapons, Insignia, Uniform Accessories, and Other Equipment, Schuyler, Hartley, and Graham. Rare, profusely illustrated 1846 catalog includes Union Army uniform and dress regulations, arms and ammunition, coats, insignia, flags, swords, rifles, etc. 226 illustrations. 160pp. 9 x 12. 24939-5

WOMEN'S FASHIONS OF THE EARLY 1900s: An Unabridged Republication of "New York Fashions, 1909," National Cloak & Suit Co. Rare catalog of mail-order fashions documents women's and children's clothing styles shortly after the turn of the century. Captions offer full descriptions, prices. Invaluable resource for fashion, costume historians. Approximately 725 illustrations. 128pp. 8⅜ x 11¼. 27276-1

THE 1912 AND 1915 GUSTAV STICKLEY FURNITURE CATALOGS, Gustav Stickley. With over 200 detailed illustrations and descriptions, these two catalogs are essential reading and reference materials and identification guides for Stickley furniture. Captions cite materials, dimensions and prices. 112pp. 6½ x 9¼. 26676-1

EARLY AMERICAN LOCOMOTIVES, John H. White, Jr. Finest locomotive engravings from early 19th century: historical (1804–74), main-line (after 1870), special, foreign, etc. 147 plates. 142pp. 11⅜ x 8¼. 22772-3

THE TALL SHIPS OF TODAY IN PHOTOGRAPHS, Frank O. Braynard. Lavishly illustrated tribute to nearly 100 majestic contemporary sailing vessels: Amerigo Vespucci, Clearwater, Constitution, Eagle, Mayflower, Sea Cloud, Victory, many more. Authoritative captions provide statistics, background on each ship. 190 black-and-white photographs and illustrations. Introduction. 128pp. 8⅞ x 11¾. 27163-3

LITTLE BOOK OF EARLY AMERICAN CRAFTS AND TRADES, Peter Stockham (ed.). 1807 children's book explains crafts and trades: baker, hatter, cooper, potter, and many others. 23 copperplate illustrations. 140pp. 4⅝ x 6. 23336-7

VICTORIAN FASHIONS AND COSTUMES FROM HARPER'S BAZAR, 1867–1898, Stella Blum (ed.). Day costumes, evening wear, sports clothes, shoes, hats, other accessories in over 1,000 detailed engravings. 320pp. 9⅜ x 12¼. 22990-4

GUSTAV STICKLEY, THE CRAFTSMAN, Mary Ann Smith. Superb study surveys broad scope of Stickley's achievement, especially in architecture. Design philosophy, rise and fall of the Craftsman empire, descriptions and floor plans for many Craftsman houses, more. 86 black-and-white halftones. 31 line illustrations. Introduction 208pp. 6½ x 9¼. 27210-9

THE LONG ISLAND RAIL ROAD IN EARLY PHOTOGRAPHS, Ron Ziel. Over 220 rare photos, informative text document origin (1844) and development of rail service on Long Island. Vintage views of early trains, locomotives, stations, passengers, crews, much more. Captions. 8⅞ x 11¾. 26301-0

VOYAGE OF THE LIBERDADE, Joshua Slocum. Great 19th-century mariner's thrilling, first-hand account of the wreck of his ship off South America, the 35-foot boat he built from the wreckage, and its remarkable voyage home. 128pp. 5⅜ x 8½. 40022-0

TEN BOOKS ON ARCHITECTURE, Vitruvius. The most important book ever written on architecture. Early Roman aesthetics, technology, classical orders, site selection, all other aspects. Morgan translation. 331pp. 5⅜ x 8½. 20645-9

THE HUMAN FIGURE IN MOTION, Eadweard Muybridge. More than 4,500 stopped-action photos, in action series, showing undraped men, women, children jumping, lying down, throwing, sitting, wrestling, carrying, etc. 390pp. 7⅞ x 10⅝. 20204-6 Clothbd.

TREES OF THE EASTERN AND CENTRAL UNITED STATES AND CANADA, William M. Harlow. Best one-volume guide to 140 trees. Full descriptions, woodlore, range, etc. Over 600 illustrations. Handy size. 288pp. 4½ x 6⅜. 20395-6

SONGS OF WESTERN BIRDS, Dr. Donald J. Borror. Complete song and call repertoire of 60 western species, including flycatchers, juncoes, cactus wrens, many more–includes fully illustrated booklet. Cassette and manual 99913-0

GROWING AND USING HERBS AND SPICES, Milo Miloradovich. Versatile handbook provides all the information needed for cultivation and use of all the herbs and spices available in North America. 4 illustrations. Index. Glossary. 236pp. 5⅜ x 8½. 25058-X

BIG BOOK OF MAZES AND LABYRINTHS, Walter Shepherd. 50 mazes and labyrinths in all–classical, solid, ripple, and more–in one great volume. Perfect inexpensive puzzler for clever youngsters. Full solutions. 112pp. 8⅛ x 11. 22951-3

PIANO TUNING, J. Cree Fischer. Clearest, best book for beginner, amateur. Simple repairs, raising dropped notes, tuning by easy method of flattened fifths. No previous skills needed. 4 illustrations. 201pp. 5⅜ x 8½. 23267-0

HINTS TO SINGERS, Lillian Nordica. Selecting the right teacher, developing confidence, overcoming stage fright, and many other important skills receive thoughtful discussion in this indispensible guide, written by a world-famous diva of four decades' experience. 96pp. 5⅜ x 8½. 40094-8

THE COMPLETE NONSENSE OF EDWARD LEAR, Edward Lear. All nonsense limericks, zany alphabets, Owl and Pussycat, songs, nonsense botany, etc., illustrated by Lear. Total of 320pp. 5⅜ x 8½. (Available in U.S. only.) 20167-8

VICTORIAN PARLOUR POETRY: An Annotated Anthology, Michael R. Turner. 117 gems by Longfellow, Tennyson, Browning, many lesser-known poets. "The Village Blacksmith," "Curfew Must Not Ring Tonight," "Only a Baby Small," dozens more, often difficult to find elsewhere. Index of poets, titles, first lines. xxiii + 325pp. 5⅝ x 8¼. 27044-0

DUBLINERS, James Joyce. Fifteen stories offer vivid, tightly focused observations of the lives of Dublin's poorer classes. At least one, "The Dead," is considered a masterpiece. Reprinted complete and unabridged from standard edition. 160pp. 5$\frac{3}{16}$ x 8¼. 26870-5

GREAT WEIRD TALES: 14 Stories by Lovecraft, Blackwood, Machen and Others, S. T. Joshi (ed.). 14 spellbinding tales, including "The Sin Eater," by Fiona McLeod, "The Eye Above the Mantel," by Frank Belknap Long, as well as renowned works by R. H. Barlow, Lord Dunsany, Arthur Machen, W. C. Morrow and eight other masters of the genre. 256pp. 5⅜ x 8½. (Available in U.S. only.) 40436-6

THE BOOK OF THE SACRED MAGIC OF ABRAMELIN THE MAGE, translated by S. MacGregor Mathers. Medieval manuscript of ceremonial magic. Basic document in Aleister Crowley, Golden Dawn groups. 268pp. 5⅜ x 8½. 23211-5

NEW RUSSIAN-ENGLISH AND ENGLISH-RUSSIAN DICTIONARY, M. A. O'Brien. This is a remarkably handy Russian dictionary, containing a surprising amount of information, including over 70,000 entries. 366pp. 4½ x 6⅛. 20208-9

HISTORIC HOMES OF THE AMERICAN PRESIDENTS, Second, Revised Edition, Irvin Haas. A traveler's guide to American Presidential homes, most open to the public, depicting and describing homes occupied by every American President from George Washington to George Bush. With visiting hours, admission charges, travel routes. 175 photographs. Index. 160pp. 8¼ x 11. 26751-2

NEW YORK IN THE FORTIES, Andreas Feininger. 162 brilliant photographs by the well-known photographer, formerly with *Life* magazine. Commuters, shoppers, Times Square at night, much else from city at its peak. Captions by John von Hartz. 181pp. 9¼ x 10¾. 23585-8

INDIAN SIGN LANGUAGE, William Tomkins. Over 525 signs developed by Sioux and other tribes. Written instructions and diagrams. Also 290 pictographs. 111pp. 6⅛ x 9¼. 22029-X

ANATOMY: A Complete Guide for Artists, Joseph Sheppard. A master of figure drawing shows artists how to render human anatomy convincingly. Over 460 illustrations. 224pp. 8⅜ x 11¼. 27279-6

MEDIEVAL CALLIGRAPHY: Its History and Technique, Marc Drogin. Spirited history, comprehensive instruction manual covers 13 styles (ca. 4th century through 15th). Excellent photographs; directions for duplicating medieval techniques with modern tools. 224pp. 8⅜ x 11¼. 26142-5

DRIED FLOWERS: How to Prepare Them, Sarah Whitlock and Martha Rankin. Complete instructions on how to use silica gel, meal and borax, perlite aggregate, sand and borax, glycerine and water to create attractive permanent flower arrangements. 12 illustrations. 32pp. 5⅜ x 8½. 21802-3

EASY-TO-MAKE BIRD FEEDERS FOR WOODWORKERS, Scott D. Campbell. Detailed, simple-to-use guide for designing, constructing, caring for and using feeders. Text, illustrations for 12 classic and contemporary designs. 96pp. 5⅜ x 8½. 25847-5

SCOTTISH WONDER TALES FROM MYTH AND LEGEND, Donald A. Mackenzie. 16 lively tales tell of giants rumbling down mountainsides, of a magic wand that turns stone pillars into warriors, of gods and goddesses, evil hags, powerful forces and more. 240pp. 5⅜ x 8½. 29677-6

THE HISTORY OF UNDERCLOTHES, C. Willett Cunnington and Phyllis Cunnington. Fascinating, well-documented survey covering six centuries of English undergarments, enhanced with over 100 illustrations: 12th-century laced-up bodice, footed long drawers (1795), 19th-century bustles, 19th-century corsets for men, Victorian "bust improvers," much more. 272pp. 5⅜ x 8¼. 27124-2

ARTS AND CRAFTS FURNITURE: The Complete Brooks Catalog of 1912, Brooks Manufacturing Co. Photos and detailed descriptions of more than 150 now very collectible furniture designs from the Arts and Crafts movement depict davenports, settees, buffets, desks, tables, chairs, bedsteads, dressers and more, all built of solid, quarter-sawed oak. Invaluable for students and enthusiasts of antiques, Americana and the decorative arts. 80pp. 6½ x 9¼. 27471-3

WILBUR AND ORVILLE: A Biography of the Wright Brothers, Fred Howard. Definitive, crisply written study tells the full story of the brothers' lives and work. A vividly written biography, unparalleled in scope and color, that also captures the spirit of an extraordinary era. 560pp. 6⅛ x 9¼. 40297-5

THE ARTS OF THE SAILOR: Knotting, Splicing and Ropework, Hervey Garrett Smith. Indispensable shipboard reference covers tools, basic knots and useful hitches; handsewing and canvas work, more. Over 100 illustrations. Delightful reading for sea lovers. 256pp. 5⅜ x 8½. 26440-8

FRANK LLOYD WRIGHT'S FALLINGWATER: The House and Its History, Second, Revised Edition, Donald Hoffmann. A total revision—both in text and illustrations—of the standard document on Fallingwater, the boldest, most personal architectural statement of Wright's mature years, updated with valuable new material from the recently opened Frank Lloyd Wright Archives. "Fascinating"—The New York Times. 116 illustrations. 128pp. 9¼ x 10¾. 27430-6

CATALOG OF DOVER BOOKS

PHOTOGRAPHIC SKETCHBOOK OF THE CIVIL WAR, Alexander Gardner. 100 photos taken on field during the Civil War. Famous shots of Manassas Harper's Ferry, Lincoln, Richmond, slave pens, etc. 244pp. 10⅝ x 8¼. 22731-6

FIVE ACRES AND INDEPENDENCE, Maurice G. Kains. Great back-to-the-land classic explains basics of self-sufficient farming. The one book to get. 95 illustrations. 397pp. 5⅜ x 8½. 20974-1

SONGS OF EASTERN BIRDS, Dr. Donald J. Borror. Songs and calls of 60 species most common to eastern U.S.: warblers, woodpeckers, flycatchers, thrushes, larks, many more in high-quality recording. Cassette and manual 99912-2

A MODERN HERBAL, Margaret Grieve. Much the fullest, most exact, most useful compilation of herbal material. Gigantic alphabetical encyclopedia, from aconite to zedoary, gives botanical information, medical properties, folklore, economic uses, much else. Indispensable to serious reader. 161 illustrations. 888pp. 6½ x 9¼. 2-vol. set. (Available in U.S. only.) Vol. I: 22798-7
Vol. II: 22799-5

HIDDEN TREASURE MAZE BOOK, Dave Phillips. Solve 34 challenging mazes accompanied by heroic tales of adventure. Evil dragons, people-eating plants, blood-thirsty giants, many more dangerous adversaries lurk at every twist and turn. 34 mazes, stories, solutions. 48pp. 8¼ x 11. 24566-7

LETTERS OF W. A. MOZART, Wolfgang A. Mozart. Remarkable letters show bawdy wit, humor, imagination, musical insights, contemporary musical world; includes some letters from Leopold Mozart. 276pp. 5⅜ x 8½. 22859-2

BASIC PRINCIPLES OF CLASSICAL BALLET, Agrippina Vaganova. Great Russian theoretician, teacher explains methods for teaching classical ballet. 118 illustrations. 175pp. 5⅜ x 8½. 22036-2

THE JUMPING FROG, Mark Twain. Revenge edition. The original story of The Celebrated Jumping Frog of Calaveras County, a hapless French translation, and Twain's hilarious "retranslation" from the French. 12 illustrations. 66pp. 5⅜ x 8½. 22686-7

BEST REMEMBERED POEMS, Martin Gardner (ed.). The 126 poems in this superb collection of 19th- and 20th-century British and American verse range from Shelley's "To a Skylark" to the impassioned "Renascence" of Edna St. Vincent Millay and to Edward Lear's whimsical "The Owl and the Pussycat." 224pp. 5⅜ x 8½. 27165-X

COMPLETE SONNETS, William Shakespeare. Over 150 exquisite poems deal with love, friendship, the tyranny of time, beauty's evanescence, death and other themes in language of remarkable power, precision and beauty. Glossary of archaic terms. 80pp. 5³⁄₁₆ x 8¼. 26686-9

THE BATTLES THAT CHANGED HISTORY, Fletcher Pratt. Eminent historian profiles 16 crucial conflicts, ancient to modern, that changed the course of civilization. 352pp. 5⅜ x 8½. 41129-X

THE WIT AND HUMOR OF OSCAR WILDE, Alvin Redman (ed.). More than 1,000 ripostes, paradoxes, wisecracks: Work is the curse of the drinking classes; I can resist everything except temptation; etc. 258pp. 5⅜ x 8½. 20602-5

SHAKESPEARE LEXICON AND QUOTATION DICTIONARY, Alexander Schmidt. Full definitions, locations, shades of meaning in every word in plays and poems. More than 50,000 exact quotations. 1,485pp. 6½ x 9¼. 2-vol. set.
Vol. 1: 22726-X
Vol. 2: 22727-8

SELECTED POEMS, Emily Dickinson. Over 100 best-known, best-loved poems by one of America's foremost poets, reprinted from authoritative early editions. No comparable edition at this price. Index of first lines. 64pp. 5$\frac{3}{16}$ x 8¼. 26466-1

THE INSIDIOUS DR. FU-MANCHU, Sax Rohmer. The first of the popular mystery series introduces a pair of English detectives to their archnemesis, the diabolical Dr. Fu-Manchu. Flavorful atmosphere, fast-paced action, and colorful characters enliven this classic of the genre. 208pp. 5$\frac{3}{16}$ x 8¼. 29898-1

THE MALLEUS MALEFICARUM OF KRAMER AND SPRENGER, translated by Montague Summers. Full text of most important witchhunter's "bible," used by both Catholics and Protestants. 278pp. 6⅝ x 10. 22802-9

SPANISH STORIES/CUENTOS ESPAÑOLES: A Dual-Language Book, Angel Flores (ed.). Unique format offers 13 great stories in Spanish by Cervantes, Borges, others. Faithful English translations on facing pages. 352pp. 5⅜ x 8½. 25399-6

GARDEN CITY, LONG ISLAND, IN EARLY PHOTOGRAPHS, 1869–1919, Mildred H. Smith. Handsome treasury of 118 vintage pictures, accompanied by carefully researched captions, document the Garden City Hotel fire (1899), the Vanderbilt Cup Race (1908), the first airmail flight departing from the Nassau Boulevard Aerodrome (1911), and much more. 96pp. 8⅞ x 11¾. 40669-5

OLD QUEENS, N.Y., IN EARLY PHOTOGRAPHS, Vincent F. Seyfried and William Asadorian. Over 160 rare photographs of Maspeth, Jamaica, Jackson Heights, and other areas. Vintage views of DeWitt Clinton mansion, 1939 World's Fair and more. Captions. 192pp. 8⅞ x 11. 26358-4

CAPTURED BY THE INDIANS: 15 Firsthand Accounts, 1750-1870, Frederick Drimmer. Astounding true historical accounts of grisly torture, bloody conflicts, relentless pursuits, miraculous escapes and more, by people who lived to tell the tale. 384pp. 5⅜ x 8½. 24901-8

THE WORLD'S GREAT SPEECHES (Fourth Enlarged Edition), Lewis Copeland, Lawrence W. Lamm, and Stephen J. McKenna. Nearly 300 speeches provide public speakers with a wealth of updated quotes and inspiration–from Pericles' funeral oration and William Jennings Bryan's "Cross of Gold Speech" to Malcolm X's powerful words on the Black Revolution and Earl of Spenser's tribute to his sister, Diana, Princess of Wales. 944pp. 5⅜ x 8⅜. 40903-1

THE BOOK OF THE SWORD, Sir Richard F. Burton. Great Victorian scholar/adventurer's eloquent, erudite history of the "queen of weapons"–from prehistory to early Roman Empire. Evolution and development of early swords, variations (sabre, broadsword, cutlass, scimitar, etc.), much more. 336pp. 6⅛ x 9¼. 25434-8

CATALOG OF DOVER BOOKS

AUTOBIOGRAPHY: The Story of My Experiments with Truth, Mohandas K. Gandhi. Boyhood, legal studies, purification, the growth of the Satyagraha (nonviolent protest) movement. Critical, inspiring work of the man responsible for the freedom of India. 480pp. 5⅜ x 8½. (Available in U.S. only.) 24593-4

CELTIC MYTHS AND LEGENDS, T. W. Rolleston. Masterful retelling of Irish and Welsh stories and tales. Cuchulain, King Arthur, Deirdre, the Grail, many more. First paperback edition. 58 full-page illustrations. 512pp. 5⅜ x 8½. 26507-2

THE PRINCIPLES OF PSYCHOLOGY, William James. Famous long course complete, unabridged. Stream of thought, time perception, memory, experimental methods; great work decades ahead of its time. 94 figures. 1,391pp. 5⅜ x 8½. 2-vol. set.
Vol. I: 20381-6   Vol. II: 20382-4

THE WORLD AS WILL AND REPRESENTATION, Arthur Schopenhauer. Definitive English translation of Schopenhauer's life work, correcting more than 1,000 errors, omissions in earlier translations. Translated by E. F. J. Payne. Total of 1,269pp. 5⅜ x 8½. 2-vol. set.
Vol. 1: 21761-2   Vol. 2: 21762-0

MAGIC AND MYSTERY IN TIBET, Madame Alexandra David-Neel. Experiences among lamas, magicians, sages, sorcerers, Bonpa wizards. A true psychic discovery. 32 illustrations. 321pp. 5⅜ x 8½. (Available in U.S. only.) 22682-4

THE EGYPTIAN BOOK OF THE DEAD, E. A. Wallis Budge. Complete reproduction of Ani's papyrus, finest ever found. Full hieroglyphic text, interlinear transliteration, word-for-word translation, smooth translation. 533pp. 6½ x 9¼. 21866-X

MATHEMATICS FOR THE NONMATHEMATICIAN, Morris Kline. Detailed, college-level treatment of mathematics in cultural and historical context, with numerous exercises. Recommended Reading Lists. Tables. Numerous figures. 641pp. 5⅜ x 8½. 24823-2

PROBABILISTIC METHODS IN THE THEORY OF STRUCTURES, Isaac Elishakoff. Well-written introduction covers the elements of the theory of probability from two or more random variables, the reliability of such multivariable structures, the theory of random function, Monte Carlo methods of treating problems incapable of exact solution, and more. Examples. 502pp. 5⅜ x 8½. 40691-1

THE RIME OF THE ANCIENT MARINER, Gustave Doré, S. T. Coleridge. Doré's finest work; 34 plates capture moods, subtleties of poem. Flawless full-size reproductions printed on facing pages with authoritative text of poem. "Beautiful. Simply beautiful."–Publisher's Weekly. 77pp. 9¼ x 12. 22305-1

NORTH AMERICAN INDIAN DESIGNS FOR ARTISTS AND CRAFTSPEOPLE, Eva Wilson. Over 360 authentic copyright-free designs adapted from Navajo blankets, Hopi pottery, Sioux buffalo hides, more. Geometrics, symbolic figures, plant and animal motifs, etc. 128pp. 8⅜ x 11. (Not for sale in the United Kingdom.) 25341-4

SCULPTURE: Principles and Practice, Louis Slobodkin. Step-by-step approach to clay, plaster, metals, stone; classical and modern. 253 drawings, photos. 255pp. 8⅛ x 11. 22960-2

THE INFLUENCE OF SEA POWER UPON HISTORY, 1660–1783, A. T. Mahan. Influential classic of naval history and tactics still used as text in war colleges. First paperback edition. 4 maps. 24 battle plans. 640pp. 5⅜ x 8½. 25509-3

CATALOG OF DOVER BOOKS

THE STORY OF THE TITANIC AS TOLD BY ITS SURVIVORS, Jack Winocour (ed.). What it was really like. Panic, despair, shocking inefficiency, and a little heroism. More thrilling than any fictional account. 26 illustrations. 320pp. 5⅜ x 8½.
20610-6

FAIRY AND FOLK TALES OF THE IRISH PEASANTRY, William Butler Yeats (ed.). Treasury of 64 tales from the twilight world of Celtic myth and legend: "The Soul Cages," "The Kildare Pooka," "King O'Toole and his Goose," many more. Introduction and Notes by W. B. Yeats. 352pp. 5⅜ x 8½.
26941-8

BUDDHIST MAHAYANA TEXTS, E. B. Cowell and others (eds.). Superb, accurate translations of basic documents in Mahayana Buddhism, highly important in history of religions. The Buddha-karita of Asvaghosha, Larger Sukhavativyuha, more. 448pp. 5⅜ x 8½.
25552-2

ONE TWO THREE . . . INFINITY: Facts and Speculations of Science, George Gamow. Great physicist's fascinating, readable overview of contemporary science: number theory, relativity, fourth dimension, entropy, genes, atomic structure, much more. 128 illustrations. Index. 352pp. 5⅜ x 8½.
25664-2

EXPERIMENTATION AND MEASUREMENT, W. J. Youden. Introductory manual explains laws of measurement in simple terms and offers tips for achieving accuracy and minimizing errors. Mathematics of measurement, use of instruments, experimenting with machines. 1994 edition. Foreword. Preface. Introduction. Epilogue. Selected Readings. Glossary. Index. Tables and figures. 128pp. 5⅜ x 8½.   40451-X

DALÍ ON MODERN ART: The Cuckolds of Antiquated Modern Art, Salvador Dalí. Influential painter skewers modern art and its practitioners. Outrageous evaluations of Picasso, Cézanne, Turner, more. 15 renderings of paintings discussed. 44 calligraphic decorations by Dalí. 96pp. 5⅜ x 8½. (Available in U.S. only.)   29220-7

ANTIQUE PLAYING CARDS: A Pictorial History, Henry René D'Allemagne. Over 900 elaborate, decorative images from rare playing cards (14th–20th centuries): Bacchus, death, dancing dogs, hunting scenes, royal coats of arms, players cheating, much more. 96pp. 9¼ x 12¼.
29265-7

MAKING FURNITURE MASTERPIECES: 30 Projects with Measured Drawings, Franklin H. Gottshall. Step-by-step instructions, illustrations for constructing handsome, useful pieces, among them a Sheraton desk, Chippendale chair, Spanish desk, Queen Anne table and a William and Mary dressing mirror. 224pp. 8⅛ x 11¼.
29338-6

THE FOSSIL BOOK: A Record of Prehistoric Life, Patricia V. Rich et al. Profusely illustrated definitive guide covers everything from single-celled organisms and dinosaurs to birds and mammals and the interplay between climate and man. Over 1,500 illustrations. 760pp. 7½ x 10⅛.
29371-8

Paperbound unless otherwise indicated. Available at your book dealer, online at **www.doverpublications.com**, or by writing to Dept. GI, Dover Publications, Inc., 31 East 2nd Street, Mineola, NY 11501. For current price information or for free catalogues (please indicate field of interest), write to Dover Publications or log on to **www.doverpublications.com** and see every Dover book in print. Dover publishes more than 500 books each year on science, elementary and advanced mathematics, biology, music, art, literary history, social sciences, and other areas.